and moving when confined to the darkest an[...] life. Kelly's ability to jump hurdles is certair[...] has crafted this into an art form in the wo[...] powerfully reclaims her agency and her awareness of the mu[...]p[...] [...] herself and her choices. An awareness that sees the truth of shame for what it is: the neglected property of the abuser, for whom trust is nothing more than a currency. I highly recommend this book to people of all walks of life, from survivors to professionals, and all those with curious minds and open hearts.

- DILIP BALU - CLINICAL SOCIAL WORKER, SUPERVISOR & TRAINER

"Act for Kids supports Kelly Humphries in her journey to heal from her experiences and in her desire to help others."

- ACT FOR KIDS - AUSTRALIA

Kelly Humphries' book '*Unscathed Beauty*' is a raw, gritty and honest exploration of life following sexual assault. With great courage, she shares poignant insights into her own story and, in doing so, reminds all adults of their responsibility to keep children safe. Kelly shares her deepest secrets, ones that were for a long time held within the recesses of pain and shame. She also pays tribute to the many adults in her life who have supported her journey through to adulthood, those whose belief in her never faltered and triumphed over all else. Ultimately, she writes of the hope and light that can follow such personal despair.

- DR LINDA EVANS – PRINCIPAL, FAIRHOLME COLLEGE TOOWOOMBA

UNSCATHED
Beauty™

From the library of

Yasmin Muhammad Jones

Written and set in Australia

Editing: Wendy Millgate, Wendy & Words (www.wendyandwords.com)
Karen Crombie, Exact Editing (www.facebook.com/ExactEditing)
Cover Design: Sarah Sculley (www.sculleydesign.com)
Typesetting: Sarah Sculley
Published by: Frayed Edge Publishing
ISBN: 978-0-6482434-0-3

Categories:

Disclaimer:
The author has tried to recreate events, locales and conversations from her memories of them. In order to maintain their anonymity, in some instances the author has changed the names of individuals and places. The author may have changed some identifying characteristics and details such as physical properties, occupations and places of residence.

Although the author and publisher have made every effort to ensure that the information in this book was correct at press time, the author and publisher do not assume and hereby disclaim any liability to any party for any loss, damage or disruption caused by errors or omissions, whether such errors or omissions result from negligence, accident or any other cause.

Trigger Warning:
This book contains sexual references and sexual abuse scenes. If you have been a victim of abuse, or been associated with abuse situations, you may find some scenes are emotional triggers. Please refer to the back of this book for resources where you can find help, or seek advice from your professional health-care provider. You may also contact the author for moral support. Contact details are also at the back of this publication.

If you are in immediate danger, please call 000 in Australia.
To report sexual abuse to police, please attend a Police Station or call 131444 for Policelink.
(Within Australia)

A catalogue record for this
book is available from the
NATIONAL LIBRARY OF AUSTRALIA
National Library of Australia

Dedication

For those lost souls whose cries echo through the night,
For those who wonder if there is hope in sight.
For those who feel broken beyond repair
Or so completely alone that no one cares.
For the ones that have spoken and now stand tall,
I stand with you and answer the call.
For those who feel there is no end in sight,
There is hope, there is life and together we can fight.

For my family, my friends and my faith - Jesus.
You never gave up on me; you are worth it all.

Foreword

Sonya Ryan

Founder & CEO, The Carly Ryan Foundation

This is a book of hope and love ... the journey of a young girl who chose light over darkness. It is the transformation of a child victim who became a survivor with a willingness to help others, despite her own suffering. She would not only endure, she would thrive.

Kelly has tremendous courage, resilience and an increased capacity and compassion for others. She has confronted her own fear and pain to write a book that will provide connection and a link to your own inner light; to remind victims of child abuse that you are all valuable and loved, and that you are far more than the abuse that happened to you.

It is my belief that energy patterns formed in positive action can generate an ever- expanding spiral of influence that spreads across the globe. Each wave of that spiral interacts with those of others, creating new and unimagined consequences. By sharing her story, Kelly gives hope to those who have suffered child abuse, enlightens those untouched by it and provides hope for other victims. It also serves as a reminder that our society must do more to end violence against children.

Unscathed Beauty is a spiritually uplifting book, which is beautifully written, deeply profound, and a reminder to all of us of the universe influencing the importance of our choices, and the supreme value of staying open and loving on every level, at all times.

The strength of the heart triumphs over suffering in *Unscathed Beauty*. In Kelly's own words, 'My darkest fight has become my brightest light.'

A Word from the Author

My greatest fear is that I have left it too long to share this message with those who most need to hear it; the time *for me* to speak up was yesterday. I feel a sense of urgency now to raise my voice and roar like a lion - fear has kept me hidden for too long. But I am not afraid anymore. I hope this book will impact people's lives and help them realise that despite their circumstances, demographic or background, they can rise above any challenges and still shine an incredible light. If I can achieve this, I will know I have done something worthwhile and turned my mess into something powerful.

While I know my story of childhood sexual abuse is echoed in the lives of thousands of people across the world, most of their stories, hopes and dreams will go unheard. It doesn't have to be that way. I write with faith that sharing my story will open pathways of hope and light in many dark lives, as others are inspired, and given permission to tell their stories, expose their perpetrators and begin or further their healing journey. My ultimate prayer is that chains will be broken, abuse cycles shattered and lives healed. It is why my mother also shares her perspective in this book, which further shines a light on the impact of abuse on families and offers a greater perspective in a most unique way.

I am passionate, not only about my personal growth so I can be at my best, but also seeing transformation within others and providing revelation, understanding, conviction, and the chance to be brave, show courage and grow beyond what they had ever imagined. My hope is that from this journey, sharing my vulnerabilities and fears, others will then have the strength to face adversity and overcome their inner battles. I learned to survive, and I am still learning. I believe I have a solid foundation and a deep understanding of what childhood trauma looks like, in one's past, present and future. I have chosen to face my fears and challenged myself on every level to bring these pages to light, taking you into my darkness to show you how I found my light. After all, from my darkest fight now shines my brightest light.

How did I get to this point? As an athlete for over twenty-five years, a serving and sworn member of the Police Service for over ten years, and an overcomer of sexual abuse at the hands of a paedophile within my close family circle, I hold a unique and holistic perspective. The perspective I have gained through my work has unlocked a passion to tell my story, break down barriers to reporting childhood abuse, and help people overcome their circumstances to make choices and move forward boldly. My message is one of love, hope, empowerment and support, not only for victims of child abuse of any kind, but anyone who chooses to connect with me.

I have crossed paths with thousands of individuals and seen the cycles of abuse and pain, which continues to devastate people from all walks of life, and all community groups. It tears apart families and destroys the very soul that sustains hopes and dreams. A good part of this is due to cycles of self-destruction learned from patterns of survival, a sad result of child trauma. Our choices as adults are ultimately our own, but there are times when people, especially children, become victims of circumstance and the cycles that perpetuate them. This includes, but is certainly not limited to; domestic violence, poverty, sexual abuse, drug abuse and physical abuse, to name just a few.

From my darkest fight now shines my brightest light.

From my experience with childhood sexual abuse, I learned behaviours that held me captive for many years. But I can confidently say I am now a survivor who feels a sense of responsibility to make a change, to rise above and bring about change. I am on a mission to do something about what's happening in our homes and families. I cannot tell you what that looks like for each individual. I know it starts with telling my story… Unscathed Beauty.

My healing process continues, and sometimes, old pain resurfaces. There were moments, not so long ago, when all I had left were my screams. Most of the time they were silent screams from a place deep in my mind, splintering into salty tears that felt like they burned my already open wounds. I had to remind myself why I was writing this, why I was taking myself down this path. I knew why... I just lost sight of it every now and then while I faced one fear after another to get to this point. When I did cry, it was to release the pressure inside. At times I struggled with the words writing this memoir, hurting with the recollection of those moments, those feelings and asking myself the questions I never dared to ask before. I fortunately had the tools, my family, friends and partner, along with my faith and an amazing editor who helped me move through this writing journey.

From a first draft that took all of three weeks to write, I have been unravelled, dishevelled and completely levelled through this process. I have had to put the pages down and wait for time to heal and for understanding to reach me, so I could recommence writing. Soon the tears slowed... and the sun came out again... and the rain felt like sun showers, and my tears became something else. They became passion and love. Desire and hope... What I have gratefully learned through writing this book has allowed a depth of healing I could not have imagined possible, had I not been willing to face my fears. It has certainly challenged every fibre of my being as the layers have come peeling off, sometimes in sheets. I have felt alone and yet conversely more supported than ever, as I learned to be transparent and open about my experiences. It is why I have also included a bonus section on *Working with Police and the Courts* at the back of this book and avenues for practical support on my website.

Everyone has their own story, told through their eyes and experience. This is my story. I have tried to recreate events, locales and conversations from my recollections. In the interests of anonymity in some instances, I have changed the names of individuals and places, but essentially it is very much how I remember it. I have been as faithful to my memory as I can.

While I feel my story is not the worst of its kind (as a police officer

I've been privy to some atrocious scenarios, and some have inspired hope in me as I have seen people come from a much darker place than mine and learn to live again). Sexual abuse does not define you. It can happen to anyone, no matter where you live, what you do, the colour of your skin or how much money you have. No matter the duration, the regularity, or what type of abuse is occurring, it all has devastating effects on the victim. Some of us may have more tools in our coping cabinet than others, yet regardless, the violation and the hurt is not ever OK, but you do learn and you do heal. That is what makes us survivors.

It is my hope to break the cycles of silence and the patterns of denial and shame in individuals' lives; to bring about freedom and help people understand this abhorrent and sometimes highly complex issue of sexual abuse. So I had to tell my story. I believe there is something in this account of my journey that will encourage and uplift those who choose to open its pages. The 'hard times' in our lives do not have to dictate who or what we will become. Adversity does not assume its own failure and is not pre-determined. Essentially, it is our own choices that will determine our ability to overcome, our strength and our persistence. I believe life is about how you run the race, despite the hurdles on the track.

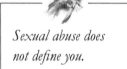

Sexual abuse does not define you.

Why 'Unscathed Beauty'?

Why the title, *Unscathed Beauty*? Because my darkest fight has become my passion and subsequently my brightest light. Through my journey, I have come to realise that there are some things about the human condition that no one can take away from you. It is about spirit, our core, and the innermost 'thing' that makes us who we are. It is the heartbeat of your soul, and like your physical heart, it is what sustains you when all else fails; it's your own unique thing. YOU own that. I own that.

The world can throw situations and circumstances at us that sometimes we have a choice in and sometimes we don't. What matters is the kind of person you are despite these circumstances and who you become when adversity rears its head. That is your Unscathed Beauty.

The things that I hold close to me are the things that echo and speak love to me. They are the smell of fresh rain on the damp earth or Mum's amazing cooking. The wonderful smell of smoke when lighting the old wood stove and the sound of the crackling campfire. There is nothing more beautiful than fresh clean sheets and the feel and smell of Mum's fabric softener or wood smoke in my pillow. It's the crinkle in Mum's and Dad's eyes when they smile, the passion in my heart and resolve not to give up, not to conform to the ways of the world, but to be who I am made to be, however long or hard that journey may become. It's rising above my worst fears and circumstances and somehow finding the courage and strength to go forward. I am very passionate, as you may have noticed. I try to become a better and stronger person in spite of what has happened, and seek to understand my mistakes and childhood abuse. In doing this I turn them into lessons I can share with others, even though they can sometimes take an eternity to learn for myself. It's acknowledging that I'm not alone, even though it has taken my whole lifetime so far to finally really understand this, and it's the love and warmth of those closest to my heart that will sustain the long nights and hard days. That love is irreplaceable and smiles in the darkness when you can finally lift your head, and is something that will never dim. That love is unconditional.

Letting people in has been difficult for me because I tried so hard to protect everyone around me. It has also broken me more times than I can count. I sometimes think it is a bit like digging for diamonds in a coal mine. There has been a lot of hard work required to get to the sparkly thing, and sometimes it seems all a bit much. Let's face it, everyone expresses love in different ways, and it has taken me some time to allow that love to come in, to understand how different people show love and how, in this, we can experience real freedom. It's understanding that when we know how that love is shown, we can accept that perhaps we are loved after all - we just weren't getting the message. Few people communicate properly, but as one of my mentors, leadership expert John Maxwell, says, 'Everybody communicates but few connect.' Don't be afraid to let go of your pride and pain to connect with those closest to you. Find out how to show them a love they will understand, and share with them what you need so you can heal and grow.

I know first-hand how hard it can be when you feel broken and ashamed, but really, when you can push past that, healing can be found with the people closest to you.

No one can turn off your inner light; nothing can darken your inner spirit that is yours and yours alone - your Unscathed Beauty. The essence of who we truly are is a treasured and beautiful thing that we must fight for. I fought so hard sometimes to keep my inner light and passion alive. You can too, but never give up on yourself. Why? Because you never really know what's going to happen; the thing you are looking for may be just around the corner.

I give my story to you, honestly, without expectation or judgement, and I hope that you read it in the same way. I hide nothing; I hid for long enough. My experience is that when we hide our hurts, they fester and lead to all sorts of problems.

This memoir covers the beginning of my journey - sharing my hurt and pain and undeniably my joy and strength. It is real and raw. Not pretentious - it's as if we were sitting down for a coffee, having a chat and a heartfelt conversation.

When all else is stripped away and faded, I can still love, and I am worthy to be loved. I am beautiful, no matter what anyone else's actions caused me to feel. I am certainly not a shameful secret, and I am cleansed and whole. I am blessed and by fighting for me, for myself, the beauty of my soul, like yours, will forever remain unscathed.

Contents

Journey

We are all on a journey,
This much is true.
Fighting, believing, hoping, weeping, crying, laughing, screaming, living,
dying, euphoria, victory, existing,
waiting, waiting and waiting.
Dreaming.
Life.
Learning. Unlearning.
Love.
A journey;
To self, to you, to truth.

[Kelly Humphries © 1999 – 18 years old]

Prologue

I felt the nakedness of being alone, my soul stripped bare. I was 17. I looked deep into the infinite blackness around me - a straitjacket of fear and guilt swallowed me whole. I felt tiny. Insignificant. I was numb, lying on the floor, searching into the darkness for something - anything - my heart racing, my head a prison for my self-sabotaging and sickening thoughts. I wanted to run. No one could hear me. Then again, I would never speak, not even a whisper from my lips ... How could I? Everyone would suffer.

The tightness in my throat felt almost like I was being strangled, as if the talons of the devil himself had a hold of my windpipe. Rivulets of sweat slid down my body, not in droplets but like a waterfall. I felt as though I had been forced to swallow a tennis ball and it had wedged itself in the pit of my stomach. I gagged.

I shook with fear and a deep sadness that encompassed my whole being, creating such turmoil inside me that my breath came out in short bursts and blackness prickled the back of my eyes. I clutched my knees to my chest and curled up in a foetal position. My little heart broke. I sobbed, I begged and screamed into my pillow, pleading for someone, something, maybe God - if He could hear me - to take the pain away.

As I lay curled up, my thoughts cycled for hours. I was angry. I was broken. I punched into the pillow like I was fighting for my life. I poured my heart out on that tear-stained pillow, which never lied to me. My pillow that never hurt me and was always there. It was safe, and it kept my secrets.

I longed in silence for this deep anguish to leave me, for someone to come and rescue me. Over and over I prayed to Jesus to forgive me for what I had done wrong. I felt everything was my fault. I wished I could be made into a fearless bird and soar far away from the darkness in my mind, or perhaps I could leave and go to another place where I wasn't scared anymore. No one cared anyway, right?

I cried countless tears and sent silent prayers echoing around the universe to a God I did not yet truly know. Maybe He didn't care either? I felt sick with shame, and while I now know God saw my shame as His pain, in those moments and the many times I questioned my faith, I only saw my pain as my fault; I deserved it. I had been punished.

I was a good girl. I worked hard. I won awards and did my absolute best in everything. What did I do wrong? Why me? Deep inside, I thought what was happening to me was because I was a bad, disgusting girl who needed to be taught a lesson. If I was a good girl and was well behaved, maybe it would stop.

Fitful dreams filled that night, like many nights before and to come. Over time the emotional nightmare was to build up into cycles of self-destruction. Silent anger would come creeping in, and like a predator in my life, eat away at me until I was completely overwhelmed. There was nowhere to displace the rage - if that is what it was. So, it stayed bottled up, simmering under the surface. I would cry, my frustration and pain becoming a war of spiralling negative thinking and justification for the repeated acts against my soul and body.

Darkness was my only friend and yet my greatest enemy. Its silent tendrils were creeping into my life, creating strongholds that would keep me bound behind my fear for many years. I resented myself, and him - my tormenter. Fear was the constant shroud over my life that ate away at me, accompanied only by my lonely thoughts. I became the shell of someone who I once was. I grew up too fast, too soon.

Sometimes I was present and full of life: in fact, I was unstoppable. Sometimes I was drifting into a sea of numbness, away from the world of reality that never made sense. My dreams were always big and sometimes even inspiring to others, but they were merely keeping me alive. For many years I hid behind these dreams as veils for my imperfections, my shame, anger and guilt.

There is unspeakable joy when I can truly say that I know now my prayers were answered. There were moments of joy, when the love of family and friends were the shards of light that pierced my dark places. I hold onto them. Allow me now to bare my soul and share my memories - my story from darkness to finding my Unscathed Beauty.

always changing names
in our "story" to
protect who a from
what exactly ? '
Accountability . = Truth

Chapter 1
Not a Princess!

Kelly-Anne Princesca Marie Humphries - Kel. That's me. Princesca? Yeah, before you laugh over trying to figure out what the princess part is, well, you should know that in no way would I choose to call myself that. I am far from elegant. I don't even own a handbag or a purse. I am a true-blue, bona-fide tomboy with an appetite like a footballer and a 'floordrobe' that leaves most clean freaks pulling their hair out. Why my grandfather Jack, my mother's Dad, put 'Princesca' in my long string of names, I will never know. I don't have a complex about this - not really - but I'm not a huge fan of the princess connotation. In fact, I don't even own a nail file. If I were to grow nails, I would no doubt stab myself in the eye with my complete incompetence for all things girly.

Well, now you know my name, but who am I really? I won't say I'm *just* me, because there is a great deal to this emotional 'princess'. I'm like an old patchwork quilt that has seen better days. Faded somewhat, a little bit 'old school', busting a few stitches here and there, with stains that won't wash out even with the toughest of stain removers. The old marks, like my scars, are stubborn and refuse to move.

You see, like many of us, I have been broken and beaten, but I have learned to overcome. I know it sounds dark, but I need you to know where I have been, to understand how far I have come. I have been lost in a desert and yet found my way when I didn't think I had the strength to even stand. I have worked hard and played hard. Occasionally, I am swallowed by the murky waters again and feel as if I am right back in the prison of my youth. The only difference is that now I have the tools, the strength and the courage to fight my way out, escape and take other people with me from this prison where I often find myself. With time and love, my wounds have been mended, sometimes with the care of a fine seamstress and at other times with just one of those iron-on patches. Sometimes, my scars start to pop open, but by challenging my fears head-on, I continue to move on, to grow, to learn and unlearn.

Of course, my life started out good – great, really, from my perspective. I grew up in Queensland, Australia - a strong lass, with blonde ringlets, a fierce stubborn streak (which was to be both a blessing and a curse) and a love for beer. Mum has a picture of me trying to steal a bottle of beer from my Uncle John when I was 18 months old. I still like beer, but always in moderation! I am a Leo; some would say I am like a lion with my mane of curls. I find it hard sometimes to find my way out of my hair just to get out of bed! It's the biggest 'fro you've ever seen.

I get my hair from my mum, June Allyson Humphries (nee Griffiths). That is her name, but I've never really known everything about her or *who* she is. What I do know is her heart. Mum has a beautiful soul and is the definition of unconditional love. She is my friend, my inspiration and my confidant, not only for myself but also for the whole family. I respect her and adore her.

I don't know how she did things 'back in the day', living where she did, having her first baby at sixteen, unmarried, and raising me. Mum is as strong as an ox, with wild, rugged blonde hair like mine. She has sparkly hazel eyes and a soft, compassionate personality. She can cook anything out of nothing - a gift I was able to inherit, thank God. The difference between Mum and I is that she manages to keep most of her food on the kitchen bench, yet when I cook it looks like a cyclone has gone through the kitchen!

My story begins with my mother …

• • •

Mum had a tough upbringing, and that's probably an understatement. What she has overcome makes my journey feel tiny in comparison. I love my mum because she is my mother, but I respect her deeply for her ability to persevere in hard times on all levels. She just did what had to be done and got on with things. This is what I have learned from her: Just do it. It is because of her unconditional love and my parents' sacrifices that I have the life I do today. More than that, the strength to stand and my foundations are due to those who poured themselves into me. More than anyone else, that is my parents.

My Mum's mother Enid died in 1975, when Mum was just ten years old. Mum, her two brothers and sister struggled because they were so young; this whole experience shook them to the core. Grandma Enid died from breast cancer after suffering for twelve painful months. When Grandma was finally diagnosed, it was too late for treatment, so sadly she died much too young.

Mum was one of four kids - well, five, but the family didn't know about the fifth, Mary, until much later when Mum was in her forties and she received a phone call from her. Mary is much older than all of them and was adopted out when Grandma Enid was seventeen. That family secret was kept from everyone for about fifty years. While Grandma Enid was hospitalised and struggling with cancer, Mum and her siblings - Margie (in true Aussie style shortened to Marg), Ralph and the eldest brother Robert (Bob) - lived in a children's home in Rockhampton, Central Queensland while their father, Jack, worked away. Being the oldest brother, Bob was the man of the family and the one his siblings leaned on for support. He wasn't always able to be there, especially when the family lived in the children's home.

The siblings spent every holiday with a different family to ensure they weren't staying at the children's home all the time. At first the boys would go with the girls, but after a while the boys and girls were split up and they didn't see each other for long periods of time. It was a blessing that they could go to family homes during the holidays where life was almost normal, except for the absence of their parents. I can only imagine how hard it was for them to have not only lost their mother but be separated from all that they knew.

There were twelve children in this foster home where my mother and Aunty Marg were to live, of these, three belonged to the carers, a husband and wife couple who ran the home. The rest were all traumatised in some way, with an array of distressing stories from their past. The children who belonged to the carers were openly spoiled and received whatever they asked for, which was hard for the other children who were denied the simplest of things.

The carers were far from ideal, with Mum recalling how bad the meals were and how they couldn't cook to save themselves. They would all eat plain, pasty, tasteless food or takeaway, *if* they ate at all. The carers showed little love or kindness toward Mum or her siblings. The male carer was sarcastic, downright nasty and verbally abusive to them all. Mum shared a room with three other girls who were all in a similar situation. The girls bonded together and helped each other through the awfulness that was their children's home experience. While she hasn't told me too much about this time in her life, Mum obviously still bears the hurt.

I have the utmost respect and admiration for Mum in knowing a small part of what she went through as a child and how, despite the lack of love and affection showed to her in her upbringing, she has an amazing ability to show unlimited compassion and love in caring for others. Mum had big dreams like mine. She wanted to be a swimmer and did well at athletics. She was as committed as she could be back then, with little money and a heart to do big things. Mum lived in Rockhampton, in the central part of Queensland - not too far from a pool where she loved to practice her swimming. She managed to practice about twice a week and continued to swim until the end of her school years, but never got the chance to compete.

Mum did running and netball at school but could only dream about anything further than school representation. Sadly, money, opportunity and support were not things she had. The carers in her home didn't allow for extra-curricular activities, bar swimming practice. Even when Mum and Aunty Marg finally moved back with their father, they were still unable to afford these opportunities.

A lot of people in the local church would bring Mum and Aunty Marg in and look after them and the rest of their family. While she is grateful for this now, she says in her youth she never really appreciated those things. Mum believed that perhaps it was a case of simply taking what you could get. I cannot imagine being without a Mum at such a young age.

After three years in the children's home, Mum, Marg, Bob and Ralph went to live back with their father, Jack. It was a hard life. Mum and Marg would do everything around the house including the cleaning, washing, dishes, the yard-work, and whatever else needed to be done. Mum was only twelve and Marg ten. Grandad Jack was a heavy drinker but not violent. He usually spent money on alcohol and smokes before buying food for the household, which led them to miss out on the things they most needed.

Mum was only fifteen when she discovered she was pregnant - and she subsequently hid under her house! That's when her dreams of being an athlete stopped. She had to come out from under the house eventually, but she was so afraid to tell anyone her predicament. I understand the hiding part, but I cannot imagine how she felt being pregnant at so young an age. When she finally told her dad, he said how silly she was for being upset and that they would work everything out. Lucky for me! Grandad Jack let her stay at home throughout her pregnancy and for a time after. I was born in Gladstone Hospital. It was 1981. (I'm starting to clock up my years; you do the maths!) While Mum was young, I think she did an amazing job to help me become the woman I am today. Gary, my biological father, was only 21 when I was conceived, and I would not know him until a few years later.

Mum and Gary never lived together and weren't in a relationship for too long after I was born. They were both young and, as they say, footloose and fancy-free - although fancy is something I didn't inherit. Gary was an incredible football player, and in that regard perhaps I missed my calling! He was brilliant at the game and earned a few trophies in his time. From what I have learned, as a young man Gary was honest, loyal and a great friend to his mates. He was not particularly good at being a dad at that time, but he has since improved. He was at the hospital when I was born and tried in many ways to make things work. However, that was not destined to be

After I was born, and we were still living with Grandad Jack, Gary would visit Mum at 2 am, drunk, and want to be let in the house to see her or me. It happened a little bit too frequently, so Mum gave Gary an ultimatum: 'If you're not going to come visit in the day and be sober, don't come at all.' And that was the end of Gary and my mum.

Gary didn't come around after that for a long time. He *appeared* not to take any responsibility in relation to my upbringing at the time, with his drinking and partying attitude. He didn't help Mum financially. She lived off about thirty dollars a week while having me and then eventually got a sole parent benefit. She reckons that if you do it right, having a child doesn't cost that much. I have no idea how Mum pulled that off on such a limited income; lucky she knows how to cook up a great feed. She said I never went without as a baby. I learned from an early age that if you want something, you go and get it yourself; you must work for it.

> *I learned from an early age that if you want something, you go and get it yourself; you must work for it.*

It was a painful start in the beginning to be a single mum, but I believe Mum made the best decisions she could under the circumstances. I believe Gary, at the time, thought he was doing the right thing, too, and wanted to be part of my life. What he felt and how Mum saw his actions were two very different things. This has often been a point of frustration and anger for both Gary and Mum.

There are always different sides to a story: there is each person's perspective, like two sides of a coin, and then there is the truth somewhere in the middle. I will never know the full truth of what happened with Gary and Mum, and I don't think it really matters. That's their story. I believe each did what they thought was right. It has taken a long time to get that into my head. As a kid, you can go through all kinds of emotions and wonder if it was your fault that things never worked out between your parents. I know from my policing work that there are too many cases where families break up and the child feels they are to blame. It is either that, or it's a personal thought that has nothing to do with your parents and everything to do with how you think as a child. In trying to make sense of the world, children develop this self-imposed blame, or guilt born out of a lack of communication and understanding from all parties. Sometimes it is words spoken over a child as well. I think it would have been much harder for me, had my mother not been so open. I know that what happened with them was a choice that was made by them and I was not responsible. You are not responsible for your parents' choices.

I was six when I first met Gary properly. He was a skinny but solid bloke, with a wiry red beard and hair to match. He had a cheeky North Queensland grin and wore thongs/flip-flops and Stubbies (short Aussie shorts). He looked like the typical true-blue Aussie bloke you see on any postcard. He always carried a token canvas satchel, which tradespeople used to carry everywhere back in the 1980's. His spattering of freckles matched his red hair - the same colour that hides in my skin and pops out when I get sunburnt. My mop of hair also has a wiry red tinge, which comes from Gary's side of the family.

I now know that Gary is very much the sweet Aussie guy, laid back and nonchalant in some ways. But when it comes to his friends, he is very passionate and protective. I think it was partly from him that I inherited my ability to play so many different sports over the years, and at the levels I have performed them. But I don't forget the untapped athletic talent of my mother.

Gary and I have had to work through many hurdles to forge the friendship we have now. The early days were difficult to say the least. Mum's decision to keep us separate for my first six years to protect me hurt Gary and he bore a grudge for many years. I understand why she did what she did. They have maintained a somewhat rigid friendship over the years, which was both awkward and distant, but one that enabled a relationship to occur between Gary and me.

My grandmother Peggy (Gary's mother) pursued a relationship with me from the beginning. She was persistent and came to the house several times to try to see me and give me clothes and other things grandmas like to give. Grandad Jack tried to protect me and turned her away from the house. Mum didn't know this for many years and felt that both Gary and Peggy simply didn't care. So, when she found out, she was angry with my grandad, and hurt, and went to make amends with my grandmother Peggy.

Peggy was the reason Gary and I began to see each other again; she was always there, obstinate and dedicated. The first meeting was awkward, but Grandma's roast chicken alleviated this. A love of chicken is one thing that Gary and I share ... chicken is my staple diet!

I was nervous and cautious during the first few visits with Gary, but Grandma was a fortress. I was to lean on her much later in my teens, when I often visited her and stayed overnight. She was my sounding board and an inspiring character for many people during her life. She was also a single mum from a young age and raised three boys on her own.

Grandma Peg had a mop of wild red hair and was a beautiful woman in her own right. She smoked like a chimney. I used to call her 'Puffing Billy' or 'Puff the Magic Dragon'. She didn't like that because, as I found out later, 'Puff' wasn't just a green dragon that lived by the sea, but was a term linked with smoking opium. So, I can forgive her for chasing me around with her tennis racquet to try to smack me when I called her that!

Gran could wield a tennis racquet better than most people, which is why I had to run fast when she tried to whack me. Gran was infamous, well respected and loved by everyone. She harassed the guys and gals on the local radio station and was always trying to guess the secret sound or make a request. She was a local superstar. Everyone knew who she was and they all knew who I was because she was 'that' proud gran. Everywhere we went people would say, 'Oh Peg, is this your lovely Kel?

Oh look at her, she has grown so big!' The oldies would squeeze my little cheeks, and squish me into their bosoms. I look back fondly now, but I never remembered who all of these people were. Grandma was still winning tennis trophies right before she died in 2012, very suddenly and unexpectedly.

I was grateful to be with Grandma then, holding her hand with Mum, Gary and his family as she breathed her last breath. I felt her sweet soul leave this earth in one of those few moments when the world brings people together to see something both beautiful and painful. I know she loved to dance, and she danced out of this world with grace to Elvis Presley's version of *You Were Always on My Mind* and *The Green, Green Grass of Home*. I credit her with my fighting spirit.

• • •

My early relationship with Gary was a struggle. I wanted to know who Gary was, but he would never come. I would never hear from him except on the phone. I thought he didn't want me. I mean, he was my dad, right? My family tried to reassure me that he did love me, but I was never too sure in the beginning. It wasn't that he didn't care, but he liked his North Queensland tropical paradise and chose to live so far away.

I was confused from the beginning and received such mixed messages from him that my internal chatter would tell me that I wasn't wanted. I couldn't remove the thought that Gary was supposed to be a certain way, play a certain role and he just didn't, or maybe he just couldn't. This is something I battled with until I was probably in my late teens. I think we all have ideas of how people are supposed to act in our lives, and I was trying to understand why this man, who was my dad, kept away from me. I eventually managed to go and visit him with Grandma Peg up in Far North Queensland. Experiencing an incredible array of seafood, trips to animal parks and up the mountains, I had an absolutely wonderful time. That, I believe, was the start of the healing journey, but it has taken many years to come to where we are now.

I came to know Gary properly, eventually, as a genuine Aussie bloke, fearsome in a way; no one would ever mess with his daughter. This ferocity was well vocalised, and he would let me know at every chance that he would break any man's nose who hurt me. He would never let things go when it came to messing with his kid.

The beautiful thing is that Gary has gone from someone I didn't know to the one who held me up and made me feel valued as I was, especially much later in life when I needed someone to just accept me for me. When I was hurting, he listened impartially and loved me regardless. This, to me, is what had been missing and what I cherish the most about my relationship with him now.

But it was to be a long journey, and those early days were tough, for Mum and me. We were fortunate that Grandad Jack provided a roof over our heads, and soon someone else was going to come along to make us feel even safer.

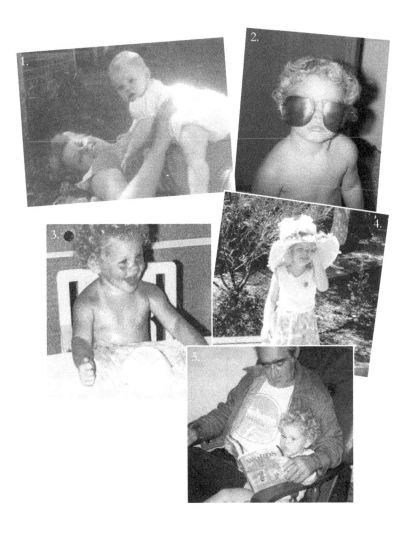

1. Mum and me approx. 10 months old **2.** Cool chick, fun times. 18 months old **3.** Slightly sunburnt after water skiing and making a mess with food (as usual) **4.** Tears at the Easter Bonnet parade after I won best decorated bike. 5 years old **5.** Me with my grandfather Jack, my mother's father. 2 years old.

They always Catch my Tears

Broken bones and Broken skin,
I broke this and that. I broke everything
I cut my arms and sliced my legs,
I even sometimes bashed my head.

I had patches here, and bandages there,
and yet they were there to catch my tears.
I broke my heart and broke my soul,
and when this happened, I broke alone

alone   alone.   There was
              no one...

No one   no sun to bright my dark.
But I never let them into my ♡.
So   I broke, I broke ... But,
      I didn't need to choke,

Because they always catch
              my tears.

Kelly Humphries 2015   They always catch
                                  my tears.

Chapter 2
The Big Catch...

I still remember that first house Mum and I lived in with Grandad Jack in Gladstone. It was one of those old housing commission homes with the iron hand railings and weatherboard walls. It was a simple house, a roof over our heads. We made the most of what we had. The name of the street was Harlequin Street, like one of those old romance novels where the handsome bloke on a horse rescues the damsel in distress and sweeps her off her feet. Funnily enough, Mum had boxes of 'Harlequin' books lying around, plus the famous 'Mills and Boon' books. While I don't remember ever getting swept off my feet by a prince (despite my princess middle name), Mum did, right there on Harlequin Street!

———————————

Mum fell in love with an amazing man, Kevin (Kev), before I had even met Gary. Kev was a blessing to us both. They were married when I was four and the three of us became a family.

Kev and I had an extremely close relationship; it was so rock-solid that, apparently, I was fine when Mum told me I had another dad, too. Because of the period this book covers it will be much easier to refer to Kev as 'Dad' and Gary as 'Gary'. Dad is best described as a caring man with an awesome sense of humour. He is brilliant with his hands, witty and full of charisma. A very typical Aussie bloke often nicknamed 'Harry Have-a-Chat' with a deeply beautiful and sensitive side that I love. He is selfless in all he does, always looking after his mates, even to his own detriment at times.

He does have some questionable dance moves, and I am never sure if his singing voice is good enough for the next *Australia's Got Talent*, but he has taught me to appreciate music and look at things from all sides. I can't recall many days at home where songs weren't playing, and I was often caught singing those songs at the top of my lungs.

Dad desperately tries to get me to just 'let go'. He sees me - he sees my heart - and he has this knack for reducing me to tears, in a good way. He can lift me as high as I can dream of in one moment and reduce me to tears in the next because he really does wear his heart on his sleeve. We spent a lot of time together when I was growing up, and he loved me as his own. Our relationship grew, and Gary resented it. I felt like I was caught in the middle for a very long time, which I struggled with because I didn't understand why Gary was so bitter. It wasn't until later in life that I would have a better understanding of what happened.

Kev, who would never be referred to as my stepdad, has been present since my earliest memories - supportive and loving. For so long, he was the one I would always go to first for anything, even before Mum. My earliest memories are of him hanging out the side of the family car, an old yellow Cortina. Dad was one of those 'old school' surfie guys with long curly hair cut in the traditional mullet style, with big ears and a fierce passion for surfing, fishing and camping. He still does sport the mullet look at times, but this is his way of protecting the back of his neck from the sun. He has leathery skin from all his years surfing and working incredibly hard outdoors. I love dad's hands. They remind me what hard work looks like.

I recall Dad trying to teach me how to surf one day. I wasn't very good but finally managed to get myself into a standing position on the board. I was doing well until I fell off and was thrown into a sandbar and tossed around under water like I was in a washing machine - inhaling water and finally choking and vomiting it everywhere afterwards. What a metaphor for being tossed around by life and overwhelmed. I stayed much closer to shore after that!

There were a lot of innocent, fun times with the family as we grew up, although choking on seawater was in a class of its own. We had fun with our family including uncles and aunts. We were close. Because I was the eldest cousin, I was doted on and loved. Uncle Bob was my favourite uncle because he spent so much time with me as a baby, reading books, playing games and later helping me build cubby houses, among other things. I remember loving my Aunty Margie just as much. She was a tough cookie, made delicious spaghetti bolognaise and gave awesome hugs. I was a grubby kid, always outside and getting covered in dirt. Call me crazy, but I really liked getting dirty!

We didn't want for much and we needed very little. We were taught to work hard and to be creative. I don't remember often going on long, extended family holidays because we couldn't afford that stuff. When we did, it was usually in a tent or the back of Dad's panel van. Yes, we were a special surfy kind of Bogan; in fact, Dad loved his big V8 cars and we grew up like little grease monkeys, listening to all forms of colourful language coming from under the hood of a car. Not to mention the smell of his farts, which would often have us running for the hills or gagging as we covered our noses. I won't say if we have inherited this gift or not; that will remain cheekily hidden!

I was often in the garage or wherever Dad was working, and can recall him and his knack for wielding a hammer. I can see his face now, arm in full swing, banging around in the engine, or swearing and cursing at inanimate objects and getting easily frustrated. Dad constantly yelled at things, as if they could hear him - the cause of many a laugh for all of us.

• • •

I also have so many memories of being out on the beach and camping with Mum and Dad. To me quality time with someone is a cherished gift. One recollection I have is when we camped in an old canvas tent on a small island not far off Tannum Sands, Queensland. We got there by four-wheel drive at low tide and had a mighty storm that night. I remember how scared I was, as that tent shook like it was going to take off.

Another reason I remember this trip is because it is where I first got excited about fishing. I was only four and was sitting on the beach, using my small red hand reel when I felt my line tug. 'Dad! There's something on my line!' I called out. He took it from me and obviously thought there was nothing there because he gave it back. As he watched me I complained that my line was heavy; there was definitely something on it. I could feel my little heart racing and my tears prickle my eyes as he didn't believe me … Mum even piped up, 'Kevin, take that back off her and check!' Funny, this is one of my earliest memories, and I can still see Dad looking out to sea with his hands on his hips saying, 'What? There's nothing there!' I was so excited when, as he took the line back, he realised there was in fact something there - and it wasn't just a small something. Then the action began!

Dad and his brother-in-law (another Gary) spent the next half an hour or more pulling in a large fish. They only had a small hand reel! I don't know how they did it; my little arms couldn't. As it came to rest in the shallow waves, the size of the fish scared me. Dad pointed out its long nose and told me that it couldn't hurt me. He explained that it was no fish, but a monster shovel-nosed shark! They are probably one of the funkiest, funniest-looking sharks around - undoubtedly named for the massive pointed, flat, triangular nose, which they use to get under the sand and dig around for food. They are harmless creatures, similar to rays with their mouths being on the bottom. My Uncle Gary had a Land Rover Ute and the head of that shark was in the back, wedged in the tailgate with its nose in the corner and its tail over the roof, touching the bull bar and strapped down. That night we tried to eat it, but it tasted old and leathery with a tangy, bitter flavour. Mum said it was because it was such an old fish, so it ended up being used in the crab pots. I was ever so disappointed, and still am! Perhaps given my time again I would have begged Dad to let him go! I have never caught anything as big since, and I have never again caught anything on a hand reel. That has never stopped me trying to catch the big one!

• • •

Excitement was never far away as I was growing up, and it didn't come in the form of theme parks or skate parks. We never needed that stuff. We just made our own fun. That's why living in the country had such amazing benefits. From the earliest years I can remember, I was 'rough as guts'. A real country kid. I was always throwing myself into everything, careless and carefree with the innocence of youth. I was one of those accident-prone kids, so many of my early memories are of spending time overlooking the Gladstone Marina and waterfall after getting a bunch of stitches at Gladstone Hospital for one thing or another. I'd be bribed into silence while getting my stitches. 'Be a good girl and you can have a lolly.' I remember being held down by the nurses while I screamed the hospital down, getting my latest wounds cleaned out and all stitched up. The nurse then gave me a handful of jellybeans or little Chico babies from the huge lolly jar (for good reason!) as solace. She probably wanted to give me a sedative! For the tough kid I was I could produce a scream that would burst your eardrums! The big, tough kid with the big, girly scream!

I often felt like I was in one of those B-grade 1980's horror movies where the tape runs out and goes in fits and starts. After my epic sagas at the hospital, Mum would coerce me with Kentucky Fried Chicken and then, Mum, Dad and I would watch the lights on the harbour while eating KFC. Those nights went on forever. I was labelled 'accident and injury prone', and this has stuck with me ever since. I continually say to myself that this is not who I am! These statements can really hold us back and stop us doing so many things. (I am still working on this one!)

The first major incident I remember was when Mum and Dad were building a house at Tannum Sands, just a little south of Gladstone, about 25 minutes north on the highway from Bororen in Central Queensland. Tannum Sands and Boyne Island are twin towns that lie on the Queensland coastline, separated by the Boyne River, which has some pretty good fishing. We have had many adventures at the Boyne River; let me tell you! We could also see the ocean from that house - a two-storey place with a big front veranda.

Picture this…a tomboy, a typical scrubber of a child with wild, crazy blonde hair, freckles and chubby cheeks. I was solid and wore shorts and a shirt and was probably snotty and gross... definitely a tomboy. I played in the sandpit, rather than with dolls. I was the kid who put their dolls in the sand pit and lost all their shoes and clothes. One day when I was about four, I had my first of many accidents that sent me to hospital. I don't know how it happened - perhaps my sheer childhood strength? More like my childhood silliness.

I was playing with beer bottles in the sand pit and filling one bottle at a time with sand. Suddenly I saw blood pouring down my arm and immediately went into shock. Then I let out the highest-pitched wail of a scream you have ever heard - that ear-bursting scream that gave Mum goose bumps and prickled the hairs on the back of her neck! That's when I first learned just how fast Mum could run! I would get used to Mum running when I screamed; a piercing girly shriek will still escape me sometimes even while acting brave. I try to hide it, but it sounds like a mixture of a scream and a whale's mating call! Sometimes it amuses those close to me. I am very tough (I'll keep telling myself this) and can sometimes be quite intimidating, so my girly scream is one of those things that people are surprised by and tend to give me grief over. Who wouldn't, right?

Yep, Mum could run, and fast - something I made her do repeatedly. Perhaps it was just my thing to get Mum to exercise. She even had an awesome technique with knees up, arms pumping and face very red. She never cried when she saw what I had done to hurt myself, (maybe she did when I wasn't looking), but she got angry, which was a bit funny. She never knew whether she should be mad or sad. She would say, 'Oh you're a silly bugger. Bloody hell, Kelly, what have you done now?' I remember this fondly as she would bundle me up and give me a big hug, run her hands through her hair, sigh in pain and frustration, then take a big breath and go about what needed to be done. She is good like that - just gets stuff done.

I have learned this from Mum - just get stuff done. Whether I feel awfully tired or incapable, things still must be done; the world goes on. I guess it's reinforced in what I have had to do in policing - just taking care of business. Mum was sometimes so matter of fact about things that I couldn't 'sook' about it for long. In some ways, that probably prepared me to later stand on my own two feet. When my crying subsided, Mum would get the story out of me, pick me up, throw me in the car (gently of course), put a cold washer over my injury, or gaping hole at times, and Dad would drive us to the Gladstone Hospital (a good 45 minutes' drive). Mum couldn't drive back in those days. Luckily, I was able to time my accidents for when Dad was around to drive us to the hospital, typically in time for dinner. Either that or it just took that long to get through the emergency department. I can remember the old waiting room at the hospital with its long rows of chairs and screaming babies. Certainly, waiting rooms are enough to drive anyone bonkers if you're in pain - to a child the wait can feel like an eternity. I know what you're thinking…it seems like quite an effort to get KFC for dinner and see the pretty lights on the harbour.

I have learned this from Mum - just get stuff done. Whether I feel awfully tired or incapable, things still must be done; the world goes on.

It seemed like it was around the same time every year, the Easter holidays, that I'd get busted and broken, scream my ear-piercing girly scream and then, true to form, Mum came running. She would yell at me, then pick me up, cuddle me, put me in the car, take me to hospital, feed me KFC and take me to the waterfall with the lights at the harbour. This became somewhat of a routine for our family. Some may call me a masochist, but these were days that I remember happily, thanks to the Colonel's 11 herbs and spices.

• • •

We weren't far from the beach growing up at Tannum Sands and often went there to have adventures, swim, and eat fish and chips. I know back then money was tight, but fish and chips were cheap, too. We played in rock pools and hunted crabs and whatever we could find on the beach. Frequently, we took our lunch breaks at the beach during the years Mum and Dad were doing lawn and property maintenance, odd jobs really, to make ends meet. I remember one day going down to the beach and someone must have won the lottery because there was a trail of money on the grass. We just kept walking along and picking it up. I ended up with about eighty dollars, which I could keep. I remember saying to Mum, 'Is there a wicked witch at the end of this?' It was like the trail of breadcrumbs in *Hansel and Gretel*.

While I remember those times hazily, I know how much I valued that quality time with Mum and Dad, just the three of us. I eventually would have to share, as very soon I would be given the duty of big sister. Welcome the joys of a little brother, Brandon.

My family are incredible and now the older we get, the more I appreciate them. While they probably will never know it, they are the reason I was able to fight.

Life Goes On

The grass dies. Life goes on
The trees die. Life goes on
Pets die. Life goes on
We die,
Eventually
But
Not before touching someone's life in a very special way.
And…
Not without the world changing first from your mere presence.

[Kelly Humphries © 1999 – 18 years old]

1. Asleep after a day at the beach, one of Mum's favourite pics. 4 years old
2. Athletics Day, Year 1 when I was cute and could run fast **3.** Bad hair cut
but ready for the first day of year 2 **4.** Dad built me my very own little shop.
Approx 6-7 years old **5.** Mum and Dad's Wedding.

Chapter 3
Boofheads, Bikes and Brakes

Brother, Protector, little blonde-haired dude who stole all the attention ... I loved him from the first moment, as any big sister would. I was five when my brother Brandon (Bungy) arrived on the scene, bringing me all the 'joys' that come with being the oldest. He was a very cute baby with soft, almost white-blonde hair, fair skin, a big smile, big blue eyes and a soft loving nature. As it goes with siblings, as he got older, while we became best friends and would do almost everything together, sometimes - a lot of times - we fought like crazy. He went from cute brother to crazy, annoying, cheeky brother - and I still loved him.

I was 'possibly' the instigator of many a fight with my little brother. After all, I did love to wrestle! Bungy probably took a while to forgive me after I got him into 'deep trouble', one time in particular ...

Dad was digging in the big round rock garden out the back of our Tannum Sands house. I was around six or seven. A large white plastic downpipe for the drain was leaning up against the edge of the garden bed, ready to replace the one on the side of the house. I thought I was pretty clever and creative when I found I could use it as a trampoline! It was quite exhilarating, as we didn't have a trampoline. (I loved watching Bugs Bunny and Loony Tunes, so perhaps I had learned a few lessons. Who said cartoons are innocent?)

Dad wasn't watching ... I started to jump, higher and higher, and just like in the cartoons, when everything comes crashing down, the pipe split and shattered into pieces underneath me, sending white plastic chunks all over the yard as I landed hard on my butt. I was quick to jump up and get on my feet with my hands behind my back. (Surely that was enough to make Dad suspicious!) I figured I was about to die. Dad was so angry; I had not seen him that angry before! He yelled, 'Who did that?' I quickly pointed to Brandon who was playing innocently nearby. He was still in baggy nappies and they were hanging around his knees. He couldn't even climb that far.

Dad was red in the face and my poor brother Brandon got the flogging of his life. I was so scared and upset that I ran upstairs and cried and hid in my room for hours. I could see Brandon from the bedroom window. His butt was stinging, and he was crying. A part of me was devastated yet also pleased with myself because my brother was annoying, and I had just got some sweet revenge. I'm not sure I owned up to Dad until much later. I learned one of the greatest lessons that day about being honest and I remember apologising to Brandon, but I'm not sure he would have understood then anyway. I have never done anything like it again. I felt terrible. I have since apologised again profusely … Sorry Bro! This is probably why he terrorised me for the rest of our childhood!

I suppose in one way it now looks pretty funny, but back then, I should have been given an absolute hiding!

• • •

I was generally a very well-behaved kid, which you may find hard to believe in light of that last story. I wasn't often naughty, and if I was, I was usually fast enough to run away from Mum and Dad if they tried to smack me. I would laugh, Mum would laugh and swear at me, and then usually I would be forgiven. I used this to my advantage many times as Mum went in for the big swing and missed because I was too quick. She could always run faster than me in a straight line, just like a crocodile. So, I had to use my agility, and Mum didn't have that. We Humphries kids have a fierce and feral wit, which has given us the opportunity to joke our way out of trouble on a few occasions. I wonder if Mum and Dad knew how we conspired! Mum's laughing face and Dad's twisted frown did give it away sometimes.

I remember her guffaws and red angry face, though, when Brandon or I were bad. It was worse when it was Brandon who was being naughty. He got the strap a few times and I was so afraid of getting whacked that I would clench my little, round butt cheeks and run off as fast as I could, with knees high and hands over my butt. On the very few occasions that the belt came out, it was my hands that bore the brunt.

I was always getting into situations I probably shouldn't have been in, and this has never really changed. Maybe it started with my first 'boyfriend' - the boy across the road. I'm talking kindergarten boyfriend - the kind of boyfriend and girlfriend thing people go gooey over. It included my own kind of kindergarten nightmare.

The boys from the kindergarten ganged up on me one day and I hid in the tyres in the playground. The tyres were set up like a big caterpillar, with half the tyre in the ground and the other half above. It was awesome but secluded. We used to crawl around and hide in them, having a great time barricaded up in the tyres. That day I wasn't allowed to leave until I kissed the boy from across the road. I was pretty upset by it. I didn't want someone making me do *that! Yuck!* But now looking at it, it was probably a little funny in some ways. Although the teasing part was not, it was traumatising! Then what happened next definitely wasn't funny. The boys then made him show me his willy and I had to show him my vagina! This upset me, but what does a five-year-old know about these things? I was embarrassed and ran away, crying.

I still remember feeling dirty and that I had done the wrong thing. I know now I felt violated. But back then, I just felt I was a naughty girl and felt embarrassed when I remembered the boys pointing and laughing, and my 'boyfriend' was also subjected to their taunts. I was also anxious and I felt a fear I couldn't understand at that age. I didn't tell anyone because I was ashamed and the teasing from the boys stuck in my head.

I was also anxious and I felt a fear I couldn't understand at that age.

My personal boundaries were broken in that one incident, and perhaps that is where a cycle of silence began for me. This is my earliest recollection of absolute humiliation and shame.

It was all a bit 'weird' between 'my boyfriend' and I after this for a while. I don't know what he had felt about the incident, but not long after we were 'besties' again, and it was time for his birthday party.

There I was in my party dress, and in true form I was getting all gross and dirty, playing in the yard with the boys. The fact that I was even wearing a dress surprises me! Probably one of the last times that ever happened! I was also riding a bike with no brakes. I'm sure I was told not to, but it was too late. I was on a downhill run to potential serious injury or harm…nothing new there. (This was the beginning of my downhill relationship with bikes!) Well, I was as directionally challenged back then as I am geographically challenged now. As I sped downhill, too fast, I panicked and steered too close to the fence on my left. I put my hand out to slow myself down because that's what you do, right? Well, didn't I mess things up; it was a barbed wire fence! My poor hand was shredded, and I fell off the bike with a scream! Cradling my little hand in the other with blood everywhere, I ran back up the hill to find Mum.

She was sitting inside with everyone else, and they were eating all the party food! Now I never said no to junk food, but with shock and nausea coming on, I wasn't even tempted! The tomato sauce from the mini pies looked too much like flowing blood from my hand to even contemplate eating. 'What have you done now?' said Mum, with a groan as she quickly stood up. My party visit was over! Luckily Dad was just across the road at home, so off to hospital we went. This time I was stitched in two places! Mum, Dad and I had KFC and went and watched the lights at the waterfall over the Gladstone Harbour and the marina. We may have had fish and chips. Who knows, but I'm running with the theme here.

• • •

Mum and Dad did a lot of work with their handyman/mowing business. Copying their example, I could soon mow a lawn, use a drill, concrete a driveway and build a fence. It was often hard, hot and dirty work. We loaded the trailer and went to all manner of jobs, doing whatever we could to help the family out. I'd have grass clippings down my pants and was downright filthy by the end of the day. In the shower my boogers would be black, and I would have dirt in my ears and in many other places it shouldn't be! While Mum and Dad sometimes struggled to make ends meet, this early grounding in hard work, reward and respect, and our lessons in postal Sunday school, kept us humble and grateful for all we had.

Many times, while Mum and Dad were busy mowing, I looked after my brother. We were best mates most of the time and were always doing things together, despite our love-hate relationship. Secretly I think we fed off each other ... you only have to meet him to know how much of a shit-stirrer he is, but he balances that with a beautiful caring soul. Lucky for him, or he may have got that strap a few more times!

At this time, I also started Year One at Tannum Sands State School. I remember my first day in 'big school'; my lunch box fell out of my bag with the contents spilling everywhere. Seeing all my yummy food on the ground made me cry, but Mrs Lio, a lovable Kiwi with wilder hair than mine, was there to pick it up. Mum and I made friends with Mrs Lio and her daughter Mel, who was in the same year level as me. Mel and I became best friends that day and I spent my childhood growing up with her. She was there when I had my best times and my worst times. Not that she knew at the time about those 'worst times' because when she was with me, I was at my happiest. We would stay over at each other's place often and she would come to camping, fishing, athletics competitions, birthdays and Christmases.

What I remember the most about my first year of school was the first athletics carnival. We were all clustered around the school oval. I knew nothing about running techniques and warming up, but I was fiercely competitive, like nearly everyone else. Aside from jostling and pushing each other around at the start, though, we all just had fun. I won the sprint that day (my first ever race), but there was a little bit of conflict afterwards over how I had run and ended the race! I had been stretching and leaning so far forward that I fell at the finish line! That was to be my technique for a while, and henceforth I was called 'lawnmower girl'. I was terribly upset by the name-calling - I didn't want to be a lawnmower - but I turned this into a fierce determination.

> *The trick, though, is to make sure that you always get straight back up again, dust yourself off and no matter how hard it is, always finish the race, even if it takes you ten years! Just don't give up!*

I was to repeat this pattern in life in general: never seeming to finish my 'races' without falling first! The trick, though, is to make sure that you always get straight back up again, dust yourself off and no matter how hard it is, always finish the race, even if it takes you ten years! Just don't give up!

Fortunately, I eventually lost this nickname, to have it replaced with 'the fast girl'. I loved running and enjoyed the friendships and fun of sport, but I was stubborn. I trained harder to become better at running and made it my mission to 'show them'. Most people were friendly, and I never had any real problems, but even one sceptic was enough for me to steel myself to prove my point. Realistically, I was listening to the wrong person and I never really had to prove myself to anyone.

We can spend our whole lives trying to measure up and sometimes we really do miss what's right in front of us.

At that time, Mum and Dad recognised my talent and passion in athletics. I was so excited about it and ran in every event possible at school. Imagine this: school shirt with ribbons flapping on my chest and my little, fat, white bloomer pants flapping in the breeze! Yes, it was the beginning of great things to come!

• • •

Mum and Dad decided that they wanted to live in the bush. When I say bush, they bought a block of land south of Gladstone in a group of properties called Daisy Dell (which sounded like a big fat cow to me), just near the town of Bororen. It wasn't far from the coast and about 30 minutes south of Tannum Sands. Bororen was only a tiny place, boasting a primary school, service station, post office, take-away shop and produce store. We would often say that if you blinked when you drove past, you would miss it. Our 40-acre property could be reached by crossing a tiny, rickety, old white bridge over a railway line and heading down a dirt road. Somewhere in all that long spear grass, with nothing much but cows around, we were going to build our home. The little white bridge would become a sign that we were nearly home - a welcome sight after the hour-long drive from the city.

Before we moved down to the property, we went back and forth visiting it frequently. Through the long grass, we tried to find an underground water source. One of the methods we used involved two steel wires in an L-shape. You held one in each hand and pointed them out in front of you. The magnetic pull was supposed to lead you to water. After many attempts, I almost mastered the technique, called dowsing. I took a long time getting it right, but I think it worked, as we did get our bore, although it was a long time coming. Water was always such a precious commodity.

We made the move to our little bit of paradise in 1988, and while we weren't going to eat a lot of peaches, we were certainly going to enjoy the outdoors and the simple things in life. We didn't sleep much the night before we left our Tannum Sands house. I was filled with a mixture of apprehension and excitement. It was time to head not only to a new home, but also a new school, a new opportunity and a new life. The move to the bush was going to bring some of the best years of my life.

It was also going to bring a pain that would keep me bound for many years to come.

1. When I met my dad (Gary) at Grandma Peggy's house. 6 years old
2. Brandon (2 years old) and me, Mum, and Dad **3.** My kindergarten portrait.
4 years old **4.** Me and my poor 'shredded' hand after my bike and barbed
wire incident.

Humpy House Hill

I love our bush humpy home
Where we can scream and run and shout
The joy of the fire, the smell of the flame
Excited and happy as we dance in the rain
Running and jumping what a race,
living and breathing with the wind in our hair
Dirty and grotty but so very pretty,
We even had a dunny is our family potty
A shower by the fire in the washing can
Dessert of damper and fresh jam
Camping for a childhood, eating our fill
Basking in the country,
At our humpy House Hill

Kelly Humphries Poet

Chapter 4
Humphries Bush
Humpy House

You could hear it, the rain...you could smell it. The light, earthy smell of that first rain as it touched the dirt. The sound the green tree frogs made in the pipes and gutters of our home was like its very own bush song. The thunder rolled and echoed deep in your chest and the lightning split the sky and danced on the horizon. It was home; it was where we learned to dream, where the simple things in life answered the deep, complex and at times insurmountable problems we were going through. I am grateful I never grew up with a mobile phone but rather I grew up with the song of my childhood and the heartbeat of the Australian bush, which provided me more comfort than any number of Facebook posts. I wish I could show you a moment of this joy, but at least I can write about it...

The greatest decision Mum and Dad ever made was to move to Daisy Dell, the place I will always call home. Daisy Dell is huge! It used to be a massive dairy farm that had been sold off in lots of various sized acreages. The road that leads to our 200-metre driveway is quite long, and a big metal gate hooked up with a chain keeps the cows out.

When we first arrived at the new block, we could see long brown grass everywhere. A dam down the back had water in it, but we discovered later that it seemed to leak, leaving the remaining water sitting in a muddy mess at the bottom.

The rise at the top of the driveway, about 100 metres from the neighbour, became the site for our temporary home. Our permanent home was to be built on a hill about 100 metres back from this. There were a few patches of nice green grass there where the kangaroos had eaten it down. We walked around and decided, as a family, where we would build the house that we all had dreamed about. The spot had beautiful views in all directions. You could see Mount Coulston to the West, just a couple of kilometres away. I was a little apprehensive at the great expanse of the unknown Australian bush, the big snakes, spiders and bushfires, but more importantly, I was full of hope and excitement as I got caught up in Mum and Dad's dreams for our future.

Dad could make anything. He should have been an actor; we all sat mesmerised as he detailed his vision for our future. Dad was just as excited as a small child when he described where all the rooms of the house would be and how the house would eventually look. This excitement was contagious! I thought it was so beautiful that we could see the mountain range from the top of the hill.

It was terribly dry when we were building the house. The brown grass looked like a wheat field, only it was spear grass - the kind of grass you didn't want down your pants because you were forever picking the sharp prickles from your bum! Brandon and I were cheeky and found we could break the heads of the spear grass off and throw them like little darts at each other as we chased each other around. The spear grass was terrible, getting into everything - even working its way into our 'bits and pieces'!

The best way to deal with spear grass when it is at full head is to burn it. It is not good for cattle and luckily; they tend to stay away from it. But as sharp and awful as it was, there were times when I revelled in it; like when the wind blows and the grass ripples like a wave - a rare moment of beauty. I was enchanted, knowing that such spiky and painful little barbs could create something so beautiful. Even the most horrible things can surprise you with their beauty.

Our caravan had an annex and a shed of sorts, which Dad rigged up to protect our things from the rain. It's what I called our

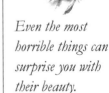

Even the most horrible things can surprise you with their beauty.

Bush Humpy House in the sticks. We cooked over an open fire or inside on the tiny stove. I loved it; it was like camping full time, full on. I still remember the smells and sounds of dinnertime, particularly the smell of the smoke from our fire. Brandon and I were always on firewood duty and were forever chopping and carting wood around. It was needed so we could function - cook, heat water and basically have our life. I was pushing wheelbarrows full of wood around as soon as I was tall enough. I always had splinters and grubby clothes. Nothing stayed clean for very long.

I remember it as the best of times. I thrived in the country. I was a dirty scrubber of a bush kid, but that's because we would run around until the sun went down. Brandon and I rode our bikes and took the dog down to the dam; sometimes we even had our bath in the dam, when there was water.

It was a wonderfully simple life, and that is what I miss even now - the uncomplicated, appreciated moments where the simple things bring undeniable pleasure.

Mum, though, struggled sometimes with the lack of space and trying to fit things in the tiny caravan. The annex was the living area with a couch and a small black-and-white television. Who has a black and white TV? That little TV did serve its purpose, I can tell you.

I fell in love with a bucket bath. We didn't have a shower to start with, so we had a very large pot that we filled with water and heated over the open fire for a hot bath. Every day we boiled the pot of water and Brandon and I lined up. The dirtiest went last as we could only use a small amount of water, that is, if you could get Brandon to stop running around naked for more than two seconds to get himself washed. He was somewhat rebellious.

My favourite thing was when Mum got us all soaped up and poured a watering can of water over us as a shower. It flowed down my back and felt like a big warm hug. If it wasn't a watering can it was a pot of hot water and a face washer. For a long time, Dad brought water home from the city where he worked (Gladstone), as we didn't have a permanent supply. We had all kinds of containers of water everywhere and saved as much as we could.

We lived roughly, by most people's standards - certainly not a typical childhood - but I loved it and never wanted for anything! We were all clean (at least when we went to bed and when we got up), well fed and loved. We lived in the caravan for almost two years. It was fun but hard! I only say that because I see what I have now and can appreciate not having to carry my own water, having a hot shower and water that comes from a tap. Back then, though, it seemed quite easy to get by, as I didn't know what I was missing.

Certainly, we were protected from the struggles Mum and Dad faced with money; it was not something they discussed with us. But it was not hard to see that we had less than others. Sometimes when we wanted things Mum would just say, 'We can't afford that'. I do know that Mum and Dad struggled immensely to make ends meet, which is why we were not strangers to having to earn our keep. This taught us respect, honour, humility and responsibility.

It was cluttered and cramped for those few years before we moved into the house, and yet there were many moments of joy. Mum and Dad would often encourage us to get creative and think for ourselves. We did things like building a cubby house out of trees, playing in the sand, making jumps and riding our bikes over them, playing with the dog and feeling the dryness of the grass under our feet as we walked around like no one owned us. We cherished the small things, like when it rained and having the simple joy of running around in the nude, screaming and yelling like banshees, for the sheer excitement and pleasure of the rain upon our faces and bodies. There was a long period of drought where we had no water and we had to cart it from town and fill up every bottle we had. So when it rained, it was a thrilling, joyous celebration. We had baths in the rain, taking a bar of soap, getting all lathered up and running around like crazy until it had all washed off. The natural things were a joy.

We had wild animals, like dingos, bandicoots, possums, rats, mice and other small native marsupials and Australian creepy critters. We had many snakes in our time, too...

One day, I was swimming down at the dam with Mum and floating in a big tractor tyre in the middle. Brandon was playing at the side. It was a stinking-hot day. So hot that even the local wildlife wanted to have a swim. Suddenly, I saw movement in the water. Ripples emanated from a long, slithering black shape, sliding quietly and determinately through the muddy dam water.

My heart raced and fear hit my guts as we realised this was not a tree snake, but a poisonous black snake coming for a swim - with us! It was one of the biggest black snakes I had ever seen! That thing came swimming straight towards us so fast its head was riding high out of the water. (Maybe that's how they swim, but it looked like it was on a mission.) We were petrified; it was a race between the snake and us. Now at that point it didn't occur to us that the snake was probably more scared of us than we were of it; we just thought it was coming straight for us. We paddled like mad to get out of there! Mum yelled at Brandon to go and stand up on the wall of the dam and watch where the snake went. The snake could probably feel the vibration on the water with Mum and I kicking. Soon enough, it turned and went left of us, but that didn't stop us panicking! It was huge! We half-ran, half-walked and stumbled out of there as fast as we could! What a crazy swim!

We were to have hundreds of incidents with snakes, but fortunately Dad knew what to do with them.

We kids had so much fun growing up and were good shots with a gun, only our pot-shots were with the slug gun. My brother, of course, had more practice than I, but I'd hazard a guess that I would beat him in pistol shooting if we were to have a contest now! There were many times where the paddock was littered with cans with small pellet holes popped through them. Ah, those were the days!

• • •

One year, just before we moved into the house and were still in the caravan, there was a cicada plague. Some can be quite large; ours were mostly about three centimetres long. You could literally put your hand out and be whacked with hundreds of them in seconds. Many farmers around us struggled for some time. Anything green was eaten down to the stumps and you couldn't go anywhere without them getting into your hair and mouth. These little guys would make a hell of a racket. They didn't bite, but we hated them because they also gripped onto your clothes and in the middle of the night you could hear them chirping and find them in your bed and all over the place. My brother and I would ride around the paddock with buckets on our heads, trying to avoid the inevitable mouthful of cicadas.

I can hear the noise they made now, like thousands of large raindrops hitting the plastic. It probably wasn't the smartest thing; sticking a bucket on our heads, but it worked for a while. I think we decided to stop after visibility issues led to us stacking the bikes quite hard!

Probably one of the strangest things that I loved the most about growing up was that we had a real, true-blue, fair dinkum, hot, smelly outdoor dunny - the sort you'd have to check for redback spiders under the toilet seat or snakes curled up in the corner. It was a rustic old dunny that reeked of the outback, old newspapers and ash. It smelled like a dunny and had a corrugated iron roof, wooden seat and a few spiders hanging from the ceiling. I loved it. The dunny is a real part of our unique Aussie heritage, and I am so glad I had that iconic experience.

Speaking of icons, what true-blue Aussie upbringing wouldn't include having a pet kangaroo? We had one… Well, technically he was the neighbour's 'roo, but he made himself at home with us because I honestly believe we were nicer to him. He was a small Eastern grey and was about the same height as us kids, with a beautiful personality, reminding us of one of our childhood TV Shows, *Skippy the Bush*

Kangaroo. So, of course, we called him Skippy.

Skippy was a gorgeous fella. He often waited at the bus stop for us to come home from school or he just turned up randomly, bringing smiles all around. He would hop on over, pick up your hand with his tiny T-Rex paws and turn them over curiously, looking for food. He was a sticky beak and got into everything he could, often causing a ruckus. We loved him.

One day, Skippy came to our little Humpy House and we immediately knew something was wrong as he had lost his hop and was struggling. We panicked at first, and soon realised we couldn't help him despite our best efforts. He spent his last moments with us as a family encircled around him. We guessed he had eaten some rodent bait the neighbours kept in their shed. It was a moment that stands out to me, because it was when I first learned what grief feels like. Animals are innocent and the thought that he was poisoned was an injustice I couldn't understand. It's ironic that I could see an animal as innocent and yet, later, not myself…

We were devastated by Skippy's death, but I was grateful he had felt safe with us and wanted to be with us at the end. This gave me the resolve that animals have beautiful souls that are only broken by how they are treated and raised, which I guess is the same as people. Growing up, we had many animals in our lives, like Skippy, that taught us what it was to be loyal, to be friends, to love unconditionally, and to be responsible for things we were entrusted with. It was a very typical thing for bush kids to have strange pets. We even had a pet chicken, which starred in one of my favourite, yet tragic stories growing up - the story of our Henny Penny who was the 'best-est' chicken in the whole world, however deluded she was about her identity. I swear she thought she was a cat.

Henny Penny was a great black laying hen and a pet you could pick up and walk around with and give a scratch. We all loved her; she was everyone's little chicken. Henny Penny and our pet ridgeback pooch Gina had some jealousy issues. One day when I was walking around with Henny Penny in my arms, giving her a good scratch, Gina got jealous. Perhaps she was just hungry, but she jumped up and grabbed Henny

Penny out of my arms and then dropped her. Henny Penny took off, squawking and flapping. I ran around, chasing the dog that was chasing the chicken. I didn't want anything to happen to Henny Penny, so I was trying to catch her before Gina did. Then Mum came outside and tried to help. She was yelling her head off to get me to stop running. It was a chaotic mess of clucking, squawking, barking, and me yelling and screaming.

We ran in circles around the little caravan - Henny Penny, then the dog, me and finally Mum, yelling in the background! Gina got to Henny Penny in the end, but I tackled her before she could eat her. It was too late! Gina had broken poor little Henny Penny's neck. I stumbled around, trying to catch Henny Penny, who had taken off and still couldn't be caught. Why? Because a chook with a broken neck is the same as a headless chook- they just keep running! She was running around in circles with her head flopped to the side. It was all quite traumatic. I continued to run after Henny Penny, and I couldn't see properly because I was crying so hard. When she finally stopped and bit the dust, I picked her up and ran to Mum and we cried together over our beautiful chook.

After a while when her tears stopped, Mum appeared thoughtful… an idea was simmering under the surface. She decided that we shouldn't waste a good chicken. Mum and I debated about whether we should eat Henny Penny or not. I felt sick and had a morbid fascination with how this would happen. Henny Penny lay there, lifeless, not running anymore. I didn't want to eat her because I loved Henny, and my stomach was in turmoil…but I didn't win this argument. Mum and I sat on our log out the front of the caravan by the fire and plucked poor Henny Penny's feathers out. There were black feathers everywhere. We cried the whole time, so the feathers stuck to the tears on our faces. We were a terrible mess of pathetic tears and feathers…My poor mum, poor me and poor Henny!

Henny Penny became chicken soup. Let's face it; she wasn't going to be good for much else because she was a laying hen. Her revenge, though, was in how tough she was. She wasn't very fat once all the feathers were off and she was as tough as old boot leather; when I bit into a leg it was rock hard. A farm girl has got to eat! We laugh at it now, eating that poor chicken, but we did what we had to. Gina? Well, she was in the doghouse for days! She was also responsible for my next epic hospital adventure.

• • •

I was riding down to the mailbox, with Gina running alongside. The mailbox was a good 150 metres away from our Humpy House on the Hill. I loved riding my bike, but I soon learned that I was a mad woman on two wheels. Maybe I should have taken the hint to never get on another bike after I busted my hand on the barbed wire riding the bike with no brakes! Our driveway at the time was badly washed out from some rain. Gina was a beautiful dog and would always run to the gate with we kids, but this time she got under the front tyre and the bike became stuck in a rut. I couldn't turn, so Gina ran ahead as my bike flipped to the side and I stacked it, hard. I fell, face-planting in the dirt with a bolt from the back wheel piercing my right calf. I sat up and pulled the tiny rocks from my palm, then sat for a moment to get my breath back. I was hurting, but I was OK, until I looked at my leg.

I could see the muscle sinew, quite interesting really; in fact, I was temporarily mesmerised by it until I realised what had happened and the pain started to kick in. I had a large gaping hole in my leg! The sight of the inner muscle was no longer interesting but invoked primeval fear. And it hurt, more than any previous injuries. I did my scream! Oh, that ear-piercing, girly scream, which then turned into tears and sobs. Poor Gina had her tail between her legs, trying to lick my face. I'm sure she was hurting too, having been momentarily squished under the front tyre.

True to form, Mum appeared like a little prairie dog on the horizon, about 100 metres away. I have no doubt she swore a few times, realising what had happened. I saw her sprinting, with no shoes on mind you. It was epic - great technique - and she reached me quickly. She would have won an Olympic gold, I reckon. I was on my bum with dirt matted across my sweaty, red face and caked in through the blood trickling down my leg. My bike was discarded on the side. Mum arrived breathless, which meant she could only mutter the swear words under her breath. She temporarily sorted me out and went to get Dad, so we could go to hospital.

I was bailed up in the backseat of the old Cortina wagon and cried all the way into Gladstone Hospital, with Mum holding my leg and pressing a cold face washer on the wound the whole way. She had to; it was a gaping hole and you could see right inside my leg. I got twenty stitches for this one, which I think was a good effort. I had ten stitches inside my leg in the muscle and ten on top on the outside of the skin. Following this little debacle, Mum, Dad, my brother (who would have only been about two or three) and I went to KFC and then to the Gladstone Marina and watched the lights over the harbour. This one wasn't as much fun as the other times. It was much more painful, and I could barely walk to see the lights!

• • •

I was only in Year Two when I started at Bororen State School. It was small - with probably only 100 kids in the whole place - but I loved that school. It was a typical country school and we all got along extremely well. There was a single schoolhouse and about three other buildings on the school grounds. It was normal for kangaroos to grace us with their presence on the back oval, and all kinds of birdlife were found at our country school.

Going to a country school and living in a country home, where the innocence of the traditional Burdekin plum would stain our lips purple and cause the same colour bruises as we pegged them at each other, has a certain innocence and beauty about it. The plum tree always got us all in trouble when we came home from school with the plum stains all over us. We picked out the grubs and tried to beat the birds to the best ones.

They weren't like normal plums from the shop; they were hard, with a big stone in the centre. When they were ripe and untouched they were delicious.

School was easy; it wasn't coloured by Facebook and how many friends you could accrue. It wasn't marred by cliques or whether you fitted in or not; we were all just mates. There was no fighting for rank or status, and no one felt the need to prove themselves or stand above the other; well, that's how I saw it. That stuff didn't happen until high school. The ride to the bus stop in the mornings or jumping up on the back of the neighbour's Ute was never something to raise an eyebrow at. Life was a tapestry of joy and ignorance.

Daisy Dell was where my soul learned to find its beat among the solitude and contentment of the great Australian bush. Where magpies carolled, the black cockatoos screamed and made the biggest mess, the curlew made its ear-piercing cry in the small hours of the morning and the waves of the spear grass soothed you into a calm sea of tranquillity. Rain brought insurmountable joy to some and an answer to long-forgotten prayers. Watching the lighting on the mountain peaks was better than any cinema experience, as was the fresh smell of the rain when it first touched the dry land.

Small mercies meant big things, and I wasn't worried about doing things the hard way because it was the only way we knew. Life just happened. We just didn't know any better - sweet ignorance. I was happy to be ignorant; it meant that life was uncomplicated... mostly.

Uncle Bob and his kids would often come and visit, camping or just to have dinner and as kids do, someone often got hurt, but we were tough, and we just always brushed the dirt off and kept going, or we dealt with things that troubled us as they came. I worry about our young people now, because I don't feel they have the same innocence we had back then. Young people today tend to be more expressive and emotional about their ideas and feelings, which I think is incredible. The foolhardy innocence of youth, however, in some ways has been lost to the throes of the Internet and social media implications.

Soon I would experience my own loss of my 'innocence of youth'. The simple, exuberant life I knew would change, and it was to be many years until I regained my ability to see things through the eyes of a child.

1. Bororen State School, first day in my new school. 6 years old **2.** At Uncle Bob's house. My new favourite doll **3.** Me and my wild hair one Christmas **4.** With Santa Claus, and the days of innocence. 7 years old.

?

How WAS I TO KNOW?

You STOLE IT ♥

You took it, and you tore it all apart

Where is your dignity?
Where is your ∞?
I NEVER KNEW ? YOU NEVER SAID!

All you ever thought about was yourself instead

How was I to know the lies that you told me?
I haven't had the chance to grow,
I cannot see clearly.

You took away what was mine and you knew it
was evil - SUCH A CRIME ⚬⚬⚬ (SHOULD DO A LIFE OF TIME)

So many times I prayed for you to GO AWAY!
But no matter how I tried it turned out
another way

I cannot deal with my heart torn it 2
You made me scared and my pain you knew
Now its all returned, the pain that your
caused me, it can never be
CHANGED. & you

You will never see my innocence AGAIN

Kelly Humphries © 1998 (18/6)

Chapter 5
Hooked, Lied to and Sunk

Have you ever taken a deep breath when you are standing by the beach and you can taste the salt water on your tongue and savour the briny moisture in the air? Ever feel the wind pick up the wisps of your hair and tickle your neck and the sun kiss your eyelids and face? Do you know what it is like to listen to the tranquil sounds of water trickling over rocks as the tide creeps in? The gentle excitement when a fish starts to bite your line, the adrenaline pumps through your veins and you realise you have caught the big one? Me, my Uncle Bob, Aunty Von, my cousins, Mum, Dad and my little brother would share such moments together.

I remember the sounds of the cousins laughing in the background at Daisy Dell, like it was yesterday. The kind of laughter and voices you can hear when your head is under water, or you're so tired you really don't hear at all…the sounds of being a kid…the sounds of innocence.

I thrived on being outdoors, and more than anything I loved the family togetherness, the laughter of the cousins and the happiness I felt when we were all together. We kids, and my parents, wanted to spend time with Uncle Bob and our cousins - not so much Aunty Von as we still didn't really know her. We were happy, without those family disputes you sometimes see. There was no stress. No fear. Just lots of crabs, prawns and fish!

Uncle Bob would sit with me on the bank of the river and teach me how to knot the hook onto the line and make a trace. Along with my dad, he taught me many things about fishing, camping and life in general. He taught me how to wield an axe and make bush tent pegs, how to clean and gut a fish and cook prawns and crabs and other cool things.

Uncle Bob was our most trusted family friend. He was reliable and a rock for Mum. For Dad, he was a close mate and like a brother. As you know, things were never easy for my mum's family growing up, so our uncle represented what was left of her fragile family. Uncle Bob was always doing things with us, and when he was a single dad we saw him often, spending hours with him. He lavished attention on us, which to any kid is a gift. Aunty Von was his housekeeper who turned into his partner and then wife. It is my understanding that she responded to an advert for a cleaner and babysitter and then, well, things happened from there. Uncle Bob had moved in with her just after coming back from down south, where he had been for a few years to try and sort his personal life out. He couldn't make things right with his ex-wife and had returned to Queensland. We had missed him, but he had only just come back and then Aunty Von came along.

Von represented a divide between our favourite uncle and us kids. We wanted to be around him, but we felt Von hated us, peering at us and looking down her nose at us. Well, that's how we felt. It never felt like she wanted to be anywhere near us; it seemed we were a burden. It *always* felt like we kids were going to be in trouble. So, we didn't like her much, and I felt she took away the relationship we had built with our uncle before she came along.

She must have had a hell of a time with us. On one hand I tried to be nice to her - we all did - and on the other we nastily called her names behind her back. I don't remember ever having that anger towards anyone else. We all struggled to like her and get her to somehow fit into the dynamic that was 'us'. To my siblings and I, Aunty Von seemed very selfish. She often created mountains out of molehills when she was upset and caused everyone around her to be miserable. I could never understand why she wouldn't share her chips and coke, something simple to me.

In retrospect, Aunty Von was a very close friend of my grandmother Peggy. She was creative, and I have no doubt she loved my cousins dearly. She cooked good food, and I know there were a few times of tenderness and connection. My favourite memory of her was of the time she taught me how to make photo frames out of cardboard and material. I still have one today. After that day I tried to see the good in her - I tried really,

really hard. I enjoyed sitting with her and I had a new perspective on her that day, because she actually spent time with me. I loved her. I really did. I just longed to connect with her. I needed her to connect with me.

So, I do have a few fond memories of her, but they are laced with my anger and bitterness. Mum would later remark how she noticed the hatred and sadness I had towards Aunty Von and that she struggled to teach me how to curb my emotions towards her. It did concern my parents, as usually I don't have such strong opinions of anyone. I never really knew why I had that anger until much later when I began to reflect on life and asked a few confronting questions. It was definitely about more than her not sharing her chips and coke!

Uncle Bob, well, he was something else. To us he was amazing: the doting uncle, doting father and ever-trusted brother of my mum. We didn't always see that much of the rest of the family, except Aunty Margie and her husband John, but we counted on Uncle Bob who was always available to help, easy to talk to and made you feel safe. We would talk for hours about everything and nothing. I had really missed him terribly when he had gone away. To me he had disappeared like a puff of smoke, and it was a long time before I knew why.

Uncle Bob was also Brandon's favourite uncle. Later, when my sister came along, he quickly became hers too. Uncle Bob doted on Mum and Dad too and helped around the house to support them as we built our home at Daisy Dell. There were many late-night conversations and sleepovers where Uncle Bob, Aunty Von and the cousins would stay over. We cooked amazing big breakfasts that would set us floating on a cloud from our pillow in the mornings as the smell reached our nostrils. There were pancakes, bacon and eggs and even fish at times if we had caught something. We were wild and free, fat and well-fed, full of laughter and chilled.

Because our home was at least 45minutes away from Gladstone, often we had to go into town for the night or over weekend to do shopping, see family and have dinner. Sometimes Mum and Dad wanted to go out for a party or had errands to run, so Uncle Bob and Aunty Von would look after us. I vaguely remember Uncle Bob tucking us into bed and reading to us before we went to sleep. We watched movies late and had heaps of fun with our cousins. I enjoyed all the wonderful things we did as a family, which taught me a great deal about love and connection. Remembering that connection and happiness in those times are what I would need to draw on in the future.

Even storms were fun! Our caravan was very small, maybe only about 16-foot long. One day we had a storm, one of many that would cause us problems in the bush. Dad went out, driving in star pickets to hold the caravan down and lock it, and us, in place, so we wouldn't blow away. I was scared. Brandon and I were bailed up in our beds, hiding under the blankets. We were lucky because we were safe and warm. I can still feel how our little caravan shook when the storm hit, just like a theme park ride!

I gained appreciation for hard work in building our home, and for the connection and strength of community. Dad taught many things to us kids and one of them was to work hard, taking pride in what we did. We built our house together, and it took two years before we could move in. Dad of course did most of it, but we learned a great many things in the process of this family mission. We all carried Besser blocks or did what was needed around the place. Besser blocks weigh a good couple of kilos each, so you could say I started lifting weights from an early age. Perhaps it was just slave labour! I remember getting sweaty with blisters on my hands from carrying those blocks. Mum and Dad often joked and called me a heifer or sometimes say I was built like a 'brick shithouse'.

Dad showed me how the concrete was supposed to look and the consistency. I'm not sure I was very good at building; my construction compilations looked more like a deconstructed pile of Jenga Blocks. I can still smell the concrete today. We had a system in place; Mum and I would get the sand and gravel ready to make concrete before Dad came home from work. Brandon was too little then to carry the blocks, but he tried.

Building our home became a family affair, with our immediate family helping along the way. It stretched on for many years as Dad continued to build the house and all the extensions to make it liveable. Weekends were scattered with family visits, and our uncles sometimes would stay weekends at a time, helping put big beams up on the roof.

Uncle Bob often had a hand in helping get our house ready. He was super-strong, more so even than Dad, who was a powerful man himself. But you just can't lift a roofing beam on your own. So, when the big jobs needed to be done, Uncle Bob always came to help, which fostered that incredible family relationship. I loved working alongside my uncle and helping my parents. I had a persona where I was tough, but I also had a soft side that wanted to make things right, to fix broken things and try to help people find the best in themselves. I don't think that has ever left me.

I had many ways that I showed people I cared. I was affectionate, gave hugs and loved spending time with people, especially family. From my family I was learning great things, about hard work, being humble, enjoying country life and connectedness. But I didn't know that I was also subtly learning other things …

I was being groomed…but you wouldn't have known that; I certainly didn't, and no one else did either.

I didn't know that those bedtime stories and incredible fishing trips, the giggling and fun tickling sessions I loved and cherished could be manipulated, used against me, and ultimately to betray me and my family.

I didn't know that those subtle touches around my bottom and legs meant anything but that I was loved. 'Oops, sorry.' How did he get so close and I didn't know any different? My boundaries had been shifted - the cord stretched - and I didn't even know. No one saw those subtle moves, or if they did, they didn't know what they were because they were groomed, too. See the game? Can you see the cunning move…? We all fell for it. Checkmate.

• • •

No one knew that anything was off, and if they questioned him, he played the right card to make sense of my emotions in conversations with my family, none of which I would understand until many years later. He was clever, like a cheating card shark, hiding his cards up his sleeve and waiting like a cat to pounce when the time was right.

When someone begs to spend time with you, no matter who they are, then it means they like you, that you are valuable and mean something to that person. Why would it be anything else? Right? He used what I loved to manipulate things to suit him. Things would never look the same... I would never have my full, foolish innocence again, the kind of innocence where you don't think twice about things; you don't think at all, you just do. Like when you jump in a creek and don't think about what's under the surface; fear does not enter your soul for a second. (Not that you should jump into creeks without checking them first!) You laugh without thinking; you do things without contemplating the results or the consequences. You have that spontaneous joy that permeates every fibre of your being (as every child should have). An innocence of childhood where laughing uncontrollably is not questioned, or you can look like a fool and not be questioned about your actions, and not be questioning your own. The silliness is welcomed, and you don't worry what other people think. You are not trying to impress anyone. You already know you are loved...with a love that has no conditions. It is quite simply a childlike, wonderful, happy state of being.

The innocence of those times with my family was the greatest gift I could ask for. Yet my own innocence was quietly being taken from me, and a devil was chasing me down in the middle of my contentment to take what was mine.

I was already being taught things that no child should know. The rust had begun to eat away at the steel sanctuary where my innocence lay, vibrantly alive and safe. The flakes were falling off and I was already groomed, a ripened young apple on the tree of life ready to be picked. I was what had been described by God in Genesis 2:17: 'But you must not eat from the tree of the knowledge of good and evil, for when you eat from it you will certainly die.' I was the fruit of that tree… the forbidden treasure of youth, vitality and innocence. He knew it was wrong…and he could not resist. A young child of seven had become caught in an ongoing web of lies and had fallen prey to the fetid wiles of a manipulative predator.

While Mum and Dad have beat themselves up over whose fault it was, wrestling with guilt, the true art of a paedophile lies in their ability to groom not only the victim but also those close to the victim. How can you possibly reconcile betrayal, not only of yourself but also of your entire family? What do you do when you finally realise what's happening and it seems there is nothing you can do, and it's too late…well, you just stay quiet. That's what I was told to do…what I thought I should do… and is essentially what I did.

One thing I do know: even though I lost my innocence, I did not give him that part of me, which was true and pure, my Unscathed Beauty. He would never touch my soul. I would fight for that, and I know I did.

———————————

Inside

It's what's inside that counts.

People just wear masks that they rarely take off.

Get to know them and it peels off grad…

U…

Al…

…Ly

It just takes a little time.

[Kelly Humphries © 1999 –18 years old]

1. The house being built and a picture of the family **2.** The athletics journey begins, approx. 10 years old. Little Athletics **3.** The dunny in the background, school pic from Year 4.

Chapter 6
Deception

I remember their house in Gladstone. It was an old, creaky house, almost like the Harlequin Street house. The floors were hardwood in places and the lounge room dark and small. The smell... It's the same smell I have encountered in my walks through the hundreds and thousands of places I have traversed as a Police Officer. It is the smell of fear (my own) and the smell of betrayal (his), laced with the musty and sordid smell of my reality back then. The air tasted like the penetrating smell of old cigarette smoke mixed with dust, which lingered in my nostrils. Time stands still for just a second and I can see the dust particles suspended in the cracks of light. It almost looks inviting and then I realise I'm holding my breath. That was the house, which creaked and groaned and swallowed me whole. When I think about it now, it feels like a dark abyss, and a deep fear and crippling anxiety threatens to consume me.

I will never forget those first words, in *that* house, and the creeping fear that etched its way into my soul and down to the pit of my stomach. My breathing would quicken in fear as I heard his quiet whispers, which were to play forever in my head like a CD stuck on repeat - whispers chasing me in the dark. Whispered lies and echoes of his deceit as he convinced me of his own need, and supposedly mine...

I can see it again like one of those slow, old movies where you hold your breath, anticipating, waiting earnestly, in fear or uncertainty, with your skin prickling... It is the slow-motion replay that you cannot stop... through the specks of dust and the sunlight in your eyes. I remember. Did he think I wouldn't?

One day, on one of our family visits at Uncle Bob and Aunty Von's house, I was running around the lounge room in my knickers - a typical Aussie kid thing to do in summer in those days. I was about seven or barely eight, and Mum and Dad were out shopping. I noticed Uncle Bob looking at me funny, like he was thinking about something - pensive. His eyes followed me then suddenly he grabbed my hands and pulled me over to him. 'Come 'ere, Kel,' he said softly. He reached around me with his big hands covering my bottom. His hands were so big they reached all the way around me.

He pulled me close saying something like, 'Kel, you're so wonderful and beautiful.' I felt the prickly heat crawl up my neck, and dark butterflies fluttered down to my tummy. My heart seemed to fall to the pit of my stomach, yet I felt a little excited too. Or perhaps it was adrenaline for some bizarre reason that I could not yet comprehend. At that age I could not even spell 'comprehend'.

I know now that if it looks bad, it probably is. If it feels wrong, it probably is. If it causes you to hold your breath and feel a swirling in the pit of your stomach that is not evoking a sense of joy but a sense of dread, then it's probably not right.

I felt all those things and didn't know what they meant. That choking was fear, telling me there was something wrong with the situation I was confronted with. It was like the fire alarms of my body were screaming at me, and yet I couldn't understand them. I knew what fear was, but this was different, because I trusted Uncle Bob. He always looked after our family. He always treated me as special, made me feel pretty and loved. He loved my family, didn't he? He would never hurt us. That's what I knew for sure, right?

He briefly rubbed his hands on my bottom and said something like, 'I want to teach you how to love, like in the movies.'

'What do you mean?' I asked, confused, screwing up my face. He said something to me about it being a special thing between two people and that I shouldn't tell anyone about special things like that. I didn't mind his hands on my bottom at first; he was my uncle and surely that was OK, right? He had touched my bottom before…just in passing…and it had made me feel special. He said if I wanted to know the secret that I just had to ask him and he would teach me. Now he was rubbing my bum, and I began to feel uncomfortable.

He said, 'I'll show you later if you want to know.' When I heard those words I felt nervous and excited that something special, a surprise, was going to happen - something just for Uncle Bob and me! Maybe we would watch a movie about love together…or he would tell me stories!

When I went to bed that evening, still nothing had happened. I wondered if Uncle Bob would come and say goodnight, and read me a story… Maybe he changed his mind? Then, he did come in and as my curious mind wondered at his earlier comments, I asked him, 'What did you mean about that thing you said before?' As I lay on the top bunk, he reached over and kissed me on the mouth. It was the kind of kiss I imagined lay in the pages of my mum's *Mills and Boon* and *Harlequin* romance books: a long kiss…a disgusting kiss. It was gross, like a furry, prickly ashtray. I wondered if this was like in a movie I hadn't seen. I didn't know what to do, so I just lay there. I wanted to gag and didn't know why he wanted to kiss me like that. My brother and cousin were asleep below. He touched me, his fingers finding their way down my pants. He said, 'I just want you to feel really nice.' He showed me that he could make me feel good and absolutely petrified at the same time. Then he put his finger inside me and it hurt… I was shocked. I'd had no idea that was what he wanted to do. I had no concept of this sort of action.

'You have to be quiet, Kel … really quiet,' he said, breathing heavily like a steam train in my ears, his wet prickly kisses leaving their trail on my face.

He asked me if it was nice… and if I wanted him to do it again, but I didn't know what to say, lying frozen…and he left. I lay awake for a long time not knowing what it all meant. Not sure what happened, and I had the feeling of a burning sensation in my pants. I rubbed my wet mouth on my pillow and tried to get to sleep.

The next morning, he woke me up early because we were going fishing. He woke me up the same way that he had put me to bed. Suddenly the whole concept of going fishing with Uncle Bob completely changed. My heart was racing, and I felt absolute fear, but I was also excited. I was so confused. He had made me feel good - kind of - I was a bit sore... but he said nice things to me and made me feel special, but this?

• • •

The hardest part about this memory is that I realise my body kind of liked the physical feeling of his fingers down my pants, yet I felt dirty, a little bit sore and yucky. What was he doing? And why? I was so damned ashamed, and I didn't know why I felt that way. I was only seven or eight, and simply could not make sense of what had happened to me! I was also scared and felt many other emotions I had no idea how to comprehend. Was I his girlfriend now? What did it mean and why did he choose me? I didn't want a boyfriend, not really. Uncles can't be boyfriends, can they? But I did like being special to someone. What did it mean if he already had her – Aunty Von? Did she not want him? Did he not want her? I did like being our Uncle Bob's favourite.

Suddenly I was seeing everything through different eyes. I had lost my innocence. I felt so grown up. I felt awesome because no one else my age had a 'Special Friend'. I felt like I was the only one. Secrets can be fun to keep, and in a way holds an element of power. The excitement of being the only one to know... But they can also be incredibly distressing and lonely, as I was to learn.

From then on, it was subtle. The raised eyebrows gesturing only to me... The 'Hey, beautiful girl,' look. He would sit, his legs open, and I would see It. It was big. When I saw It, my heart would thunder in my chest and my breath would dry my lips. I felt my face gain colour. What did all that mean? I didn't really know much about It, although he would make sure I saw It. I called it his Willy, and it was gross. But I was also intrigued and scared. His voice, to my eight-year-old self, sounded soft, not demanding or scary. Soothing, like a whisper in the dark…coaxing, lurid, enticing. He laughed, cajoling me in some ways, making light and easing my fears about *It*.

I remember the first time I touched *It*. I was sitting on his lap and felt an uncomfortable lump under me. *What was that? Is that what it did?* What I remember is scattered now, as an adult recalling the scenes of a horror movie and dissecting the storyline, the make-up of the characters and seeking to understand what happened. It was just a fucked-up movie.

When I touched *It*, it sprang to life like a big snake that had been trapped in a bag. It was the devil. 'Look what you made *It* do!' he said as he gasped and sucked in his breath with excitement. I don't remember what happened after I made *It* go all hard and big. What I do remember is how he made me feel. He made me feel like I was incredible because I had made it do this magic thing, which only happened between special people when two people really liked each other; well, that was what he said. 'You're special, Kel. You can make *It* do things!'

I felt numb. I didn't know anything.

I was eight.

After that, my head became a whirlpool of emotions, feelings and unanswered questions, which I could only ask Uncle Bob. He wouldn't lie to me because he loved me. Maybe he did in his own way. If only I had known. How many times have I said this over the years?

He was quick and agile, like a sneaky, cunning dog, a mongrel gradually stealing tiny bits of meat from the family table until suddenly, the biggest piece of steak disappears without you even knowing what happened. I was the steak. The rest of us made up his meal. Little by little he feasted at our table, stealing love and joy all whilst making us feel safe.

But you know from the behaviour of that mongrel, cunning bastard of a dog - the coward - that he was guilty. He couldn't look at Mum straight. I watched. I looked to see if she knew. I wanted to tell her, yet I was so afraid.

That mongrel beast snuck into every crevice of our lives, always there with his smoke-infested breath and saliva hot on my neck. I felt gross, but he also made me feel special. What a dichotomy! Yeah, I wanted him to touch me; I wanted that special attention. He made me feel special, beyond my years, almost like his little girlfriend. But on the other hand, when he touched me I hated it, hated him with every part of me and wanted him to leave me alone. When he did leave me alone I felt rejected and afraid. I wanted to kill him and make him hurt for what he was doing, but I would die if anyone hurt him or destroyed our family.

See how he rewired my brain with his seemingly insignificant offer to teach me things only adults should know? See how he manipulated and confused me? Through innocence and naivety, this country girl with the curls was swiftly caught up in the lies and deceit of a manipulative and sordid predator. See how he tricked my mum and dad? Can you see how the cover was perfected while he waited on his prey? The patient predator or, I could better say, 'the fucked-up fiend.'

I'm not sure I was ever given an opportunity to consent to play in his game, not that it would have mattered, because there is a thing called 'informed consent'. I was not of an age legally where I was able to make those kinds of decisions. I didn't know I was playing his game.

A child learns behaviour, yet I had no idea what I was learning. I had been shown and taught what was OK and not OK. He taught me… and from what he taught me I made allowances for everything. What boundaries I had disappeared along with the shadows of my dignity. I didn't know how to describe what was going on. I didn't have the words to express my emotions. What were they even called? Methodically, he undermined the understanding I did have with how he responded to my innocent questions.

As a child, how do you explain what has happened, unless you have the words? How can you describe your feelings when you have never felt them before and they are washed away by repeated justifications…? 'I feel scared, Uncle Bob; I don't think we are meant to do this?' I remember saying those words, and then my feelings being rationalised and justified by being admonished or downplayed. 'It's OK Kel. You won't get in trouble if you don't tell anyone…'

From that first devastating incident, Uncle Bob became my tormenter, an unrelenting and unfortunate regret and undoubtedly my pain for many years to come. I would never forget the words, the lies, whispered in my ear. They would come back to haunt me when I was most vulnerable, when I felt weak or when I had lost my composure. When I would meet someone in a club or a bar later in life, and they danced and weaselled their way into my pants, their whispers sounded convincingly like something I had heard before… His voice became the voice of many. 'It would make me really happy….' 'It won't take long…' 'Why not? You know you want this. It's a good thing.'

He was always trying to seek me out with his gaze, his eyes etching themselves into my mind and soul; it unnerved me no end. My heart beat faster and filled me with adrenaline. Those intense looks were intended to make me think about what he wanted to do to me in our 'special time' together. They were a signal, a secret communiqué between two people who shared something no one else knew about. It was scary. It meant that he wanted something. He wanted me. I guess to me it looked like he set aside special time to share with me because I was his favourite. He would save me chocolates and always be a bit nicer to me than the other kids.

He would sneak time whenever the opportunity would present itself. He also made it look like he was sneaking time with me, to make me feel special. He was so clever…and yet so stupid at the same time. As soon as it started, it was happening all the time. I cannot count how often. After the first two times in the bunk bed, there were many small and seemingly unimportant touches that were significant to me but hidden from the rest of the world.

At other times we were fishing with the cousins and Brandon. The little ones would fall asleep and I would still be awake, being five years older than Brandon. Uncle Bob fished with me until after midnight, and that's when he seized the opportunities. Even during the daytime, when my brother and my parents' backs were turned, he would find a way to touch me, brazenly and effortlessly.

It was simple really, a touch, a squeeze, a kiss here and a kiss there. Repulsively, they weren't little pecks either, but kisses reserved for passionate lovers. He would quietly beckon me over and touch me or pull me up on top of him and remark at how excited he was. Sometimes he would show me his hardening bulge, or he would pop it out the side of his pants. I don't know that I reacted much, as I was numb to this by now ... and whilst I looked, I tried hard not to see. It made me uncomfortable in the beginning, and this spiralled into a complete lack of feeling. I don't remember a moment where I was ever OK with what he was doing. My numbness was my *not coping*. It was my inability to deal with what was happening.

Sometimes there was nothing between us as I felt him on top of me in the most intimate of positions, as his bulge became a long, rigid and very large, scary thing.

• • •

So many events blurred together like a badly made movie over the next seven to eight years, until I was almost fifteen, with each fearful event chipping away at my soul. I feel like sometimes I want to cut the filmstrip and forget about the parts of the movie that I didn't like. In my head I see a whole bunch of band aids covering those parts of my life I want to forget, which crippled me in the years to come.

How do you reconcile such betrayal? How do you piece together the puzzle when your heart becomes scattered through the Aussie bushland and you don't understand and you cannot find yourself? How do you say, 'I don't want to play'? What happens when your innocent little child self gets taken from you? When all that you know becomes an echo in the background and the reality of your life becomes a numb parallel universe, another galaxy far, far away. The only place that seemed safe was where 'once upon a time' exists and imagination can create whatever world you want ... in a land far, far, away.

When I was a little girl I used to read Enid Blyton books. I read them over and over. My favourite book would have to be *The Magic Faraway Tree*. It is a beautiful story of imagination and wonder. At the top of a tree filled with all kinds of incredible and unusual characters lies a magic land. Every few days there is a different one. Some of them are good lands and some bad. The children in the story, along with these incredible characters, explore all these amazing places. I hid in those books. I would escape into the pages with the children and hide, dreaming of honey-filled biscuits and visits with fairies and strange, wonderful people. Books helped me cope, music nursed my soul and my faith grounded me.

So many times, we can get ourselves caught up thinking 'if only'. If only I had seen what was happening and known what it meant, then I could have stood up and said, 'No! My body belongs to me!'

I was living under a veil of fear, always looking over my shoulder to see who was watching, who was coming, learning to control my emotions so no one could see what was going on. I learned that there was safety if he was happy, and then everyone else would be happy too. So, I would fight for his attention, to make sure I was noticed. This was the cycle: Keep him happy; keep me safe; protect the family; keep the family together; keep them safe; don't tell a soul; keep him happy.

• • •

I sometimes wondered why I still went fishing and camping with him. On one hand, I suppose it was better than being at home with Aunty Von or bored, and I really loved fishing! I know now that paedophiles use what their victims love to manipulate them. On the other hand, I was scared - always. I was always frightened something might happen if I didn't do what he wanted. I wanted to avoid the unknown consequences, so I tried to do all that I could to please him and maintain the status quo, thinking it kept my family and me safe.

I realise now that in doing the things that I loved - fishing and camping - I could also be myself, even with him. So, part of my innocence prevailed, no matter where he took me, whether I was at home or camping with my family.

I was sometimes able to take control by setting boundaries, but this would take some time to learn and was really an element of me coping with what was happening. Some boundaries were set subconsciously as I desperately tried to gain some small control over a situation that seemed so far out of my control. For example, as I got older I asked, begged, even demanded, that he clean his teeth before he kissed me or touched me with his yellow-stained fingers and disgusting breath. I ask myself now if I had a choice. When I look back, I wonder…if I could tell him to clean his teeth before touching me then perhaps I could have told him not to touch me at all! I really was strong enough to tell him to leave me alone; I just didn't know that because at that time because I was so deeply controlled by fear.

I trusted my uncle. My uncle the paedophile: the man who was everyone's favourite. He was, after all, *my* uncle. He was family, and he always looked after me. He always treated me special, made me feel pretty and loved…and then he abused that trust, my trust and my family's trust, in every way possible. I quickly learned to think of him as two separate people in my mind, even though they were one and the same. I now know it's called 'splitting' - a coping mechanism recognised by psychologists as a means whereby victims of abuse can preserve the 'good' in an abuser. Favourite uncle: amazing wonderful uncle. Abuser. Traitor.

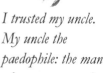

I trusted my uncle. My uncle the paedophile: the man who was everyone's favourite.

This confused me no end: being able to love someone on one hand, like he supposedly did, and then on the other stripping them of everything good…like he did to me. How does one understand this? Certainly, an adult would find it hard, let alone a child. I have learned that this is what happens. In my little kid brain, loving and seeing him as the 'good uncle' still somehow justified what was happening. I sympathised with him and thought he couldn't possibly be completely bad; he was good to me before. I tried to preserve the image of the good uncle on one side and hold onto the fact that there was still a good person there, and perhaps I was not so bad either. It kept the relationship alive with the 'the good uncle'. Then there was the 'bad', 'naughty', 'secret' uncle. The one I had to keep quiet about.

As a child you can only see those unknown consequences as a myriad of 'what if's'. How can you know what someone you love is going to do if they know of your 'dark' secret? Your mind does incredible things in that 'unknown' space. I wasn't in my teens yet but I imagined all kinds of 'what ifs' that might happen if I refused to go with Uncle Bob. Yet there were times that I wanted to go with him. 'What ifs' consumed my thoughts and there was no one I could talk to about them. My little mind worked overtime most of the time. I was completely trapped by my fears and inability to find a way out of the mess I was in. I felt it was sometimes easier to just let things go.

• • •

Uncle Bob smoked White Ox rollie cigarettes, which stained his fingertips yellow. They had a pungent smell I can never forget. To this day the smell of White Ox tobacco turns my stomach, makes my heart rate pick up and brings back a flood of emotions. I feel vulnerable, weak and angry.

I remember how his kisses tasted - gross and disgusting - and I want to gag. When I dwell on these things I get angry because it is these things that cause me to feel disgusted and ashamed, even though I know it was not my fault.

Remembering these smells, of his old house, his car, green ginger wine and his cigarettes brings back a flood of images and emotions. I find myself holding my breath and my head starts to spin as I look over my shoulder, thinking again that he has come for me. I remember the smell of his breath, the way he would press himself against me, and how he felt, as he grew excited. It disgusts me now and turns my stomach to think about him doing that stuff to me. I wish I had known then what I know now. I remember how his hands and calluses felt on my skin with their roughness, and the shyness and fear I felt at his touch.

• • •

When all this stuff with Uncle Bob started, it turned my quiet little world of love and life upside down. I aged about a decade on that first day; it was like I was seeing life through old eyes. Back then I didn't comprehend how it would change the way I looked at the world. Playtime looked different as I lost the innocence of being able to do things with a child's perspective.

Dad had built an amazing cubby house in the front garden with a big sandpit underneath, which I played in most days. I would make cities, plucking off tree branches and Mum's beautiful flowers, much to her annoyance, to create imaginary tree-lined boulevards. Mum would get so mad when I used her roses or new flowers.

I owned few dolls, but I did have a Barbie, which rode in the back of the Tonka truck, her very own convertible, living in a fantasy world with Ken, her lover. Barbie loved to ride with her arms hanging out the side. She made out with Ken in the rear of the truck at my homemade movie theatre, just like how I had been shown - a mirror image of my secret life. Barbie would be chauffeured around my city of mud, toys and Mum's flowers. Then she would have sex with Ken. She was a kept woman and seemed happy being looked after, but she also had no clothes on, and felt vulnerable and afraid.

As I sat in the sandpit, I mulled over things that were happening with Uncle Bob, and what I had been taught about 'love'. I wish it were innocent play. I did wonder at the time if anyone else thought things like me. *Is this naughty? Why am I different?* There are psychological theories suggesting that children naturally 'act out' and experiment with playtime in a sexual manner, but I know this wasn't that. I was truly confused. It saddens my heart as I write this because the more I write; the more I remember and understand. Sometimes it's like a slap in the face when you realise some of these things. Normally, there would be a sweet innocent side to such playing. Some might have found the sight of my naked dolls in the back of a Tonka truck hilarious, only seeing the sweet innocence of playtime. But if they understood my dark thought processes at that time, and why I thought the things I did, the view would have changed.

• • •

Every now and then, when I forgot about 'that' part of my life, I could be normal and enjoy the wonderful things going on in my fun, sometimes crazy, family.

Dad was sometimes a bit of a mad man, especially when it came to storms. He would strip down to his jocks (or if we were in bed, be completely naked in the dark) and run around to try and fix the pipes, check the tanks, and make sure the precious water was going into the tanks and not overflowing onto the ground. We loved it because when the rain stopped, there was always a 44-gallon drum full of water we could play in. I'm not sure we loved the sight of Dad running around in his jocks though. Luckily the trees were big enough that he had plenty of places to hide if anyone drove up the driveway!

I love the rain; it's exhilarating. Running around naked in the rain was absolute bliss as a small child. (I don't do this anymore; it would be slightly scary!) We all did it: my brother, sister and me. As we got older, obviously we kept our underwear on.

We really struggled when there was a drought, not only because we didn't have much water, but basic things got harder: bathing, washing clothes and dishes, cleaning, everything. Water was so precious. Mum would often encourage us to go and do an Indian rain dance. Perhaps she just wanted to watch us being silly and have a silent giggle. Crazily, we danced around in circles and made high-pitched noises like a bunch of yahoos! I'm not sure that we ever actually made it rain!

One thing I can say is that I learned quickly not to let *him*, Uncle Bob, take my fun or my joy. Even as a child I knew that it was not a good thing to feel sad and confused, so I tried my hardest to remember good things and hold tight to the good stuff. For me, the most joy could be found in three things: athletics, camping and fishing!

· · ·

I know every man is not my uncle and I have great male role models in my life. This is about what ONE man did in my life. Don't get caught up thinking that every man is the same. It certainly takes time to heal, and it is hard to let people into that fortress you construct around your heart, but by doing that and letting people in, you will eventually find victory. Sometimes it just takes a little longer than we would like.

Shards of Light

Shards of light like shards of dark,
Pierce right through my aching heart.
Holding tight to what I know,
I'd do anything for that darkness to go.
Shards of light, like shards of pain,
Thank God for you, I can break through again.
Lifting me, holding me yet you never knew,
But your love and goodness, like shards of light, shine through.
Shards of light, shards of love,
From you, from them, from above.
Shards of light hold on tight,
For where there is light, it will eventually … drown out the night.

[Kelly Humphries © 2015]

1. Brandon and I pushing baby Laura around in our trusty go-cart **2.** Dad and I at the year 7 Graduation, dancing the 'Pride of Erin'. (yes it's a dress… and no I never wore it again) **3.** Happy 5th Birthday to Brandon. Mum, Laura and I.

Chapter 7
Shards of Love

I love the taste of camp food and allowing time to drift past without having anything to do. I have such fond memories of sitting by the fire and eating delicious food cooked in the coals. When I settled into bed, I loved the wood-smoke smell on my clothes from starting the fire, mixed with the smell of Mum's washing powder. To take a deep breath and listen to the gentle, and sometimes not so gentle, sounds of the waves crashing on the shoreline, the mullet jumping in the water and the sound of the crabs in their muddy homes was paradise. My escape. A time to feel that life was normal...

Outdoors was where I felt happiest. That's where I strengthened my connection to myself. I probably didn't know back then what I was doing; I just knew it made me happy. I am still the same. I adore getting up at the crack of dawn when I am camping (but only when camping!). It's that crisp smell of the air first thing in the morning, putting the fire on and lighting it with the hot coals from the night before. It's watching the fire and my fishing rod simultaneously while trying to catch something before breakfast - that is if I have the privilege of pitching my tent close enough to the water. It's the wonderful fresh smell of campfire coffee wafting to my nose.

If I'm lucky, I catch a fresh fish, but the real joy is in throwing it straight on the barbecue plate to cook with a dash of butter and salt and eating it straight away! There is nothing tastier than the freshest of fish. Delicious. Simple. Beautiful. Oh, take me there now!

It is hard these days to find places like this, where you can be content and not hear another soul for the serenity of the Aussie bush around you. My family sometimes goes camping at a spot not far from home. It's on a friend's property and has an amazing mix of landscapes. I can walk one way and there is great crabbing and bait fishing, and the other way there is a small beach and large swimming hole. When the tide comes rushing in, it is a great place to catch Mangrove Jack and other estuary fish. The sound of the water rushing over the rocks is a delight.

In the darkness of my memories of Uncle Bob, I will remain ever grateful for the way that outdoor activities in such places gave me moments of contentment, normality, and peace, and helped me escape the shroud of fear I was living in. I guess in a way, the fear came in the form of other things and was hidden under layers.

I accepted that this was my life and that it was normal, albeit confusing, to feel the things I felt. I was in overdrive most of the time, constantly worried. It's called hyper-vigilance. I always knew where everyone was standing; where the entry points of every room were…I was attuned to every sound…and whilst I had trouble hearing, I listened hard…I paid attention to every gesture, movement and non-verbal cue. This is well refined now, after years of policing.

There were other things, like always needing reassurance and approval for whatever I did, to be recognised and feel important. At the very least I felt insecure, but no one knew that then, and I didn't even know what those words meant. I was almost like two different people: the quiet, reclusive girl who would hide in her thoughts and try to make sense of things and the fierce protector - the strong bush girl - who, in keeping secrets, hoped it would hold her family together. I never quite got on top of all this and hid it behind a façade of keeping focus, striving and achieving things. No one could see my hurt or perceived inadequacies if I kept busy and kept pushing and striving to achieve. So, I engaged in the pursuit of perfection, which was reflected in my attitude to athletics, school, life and everything I did. I could have chosen to withdraw and hide completely, but something in me never allowed that to happen permanently.

Sometimes I 'lost my shit' in a way that others could have noticed that something was not right. I only recall one time, and it took Dad to remind me. Trauma has robbed me of some memories of this time. When Mum gave birth to my sister, Laura, Dad had to look after Brandon and me. One night my amazing dad cooked the best mixed grill you could have asked for, complete with bacon, eggs, sausages and rissoles, all seasoned with Chinese five-spice. Yep, interesting and yummy. We were late and Dad desperately wanted to get to town to see Mum and our new sister Laura. I was excited too. We needed to get ready as quickly as possible, but in typical 10-year-old fashion I dawdled in the shower. Dad tried to help wash me, to speed things up. But to his surprise I screamed, cried and threw a tantrum like I have never thrown a tantrum before…all because I didn't want him to touch me. I have since learned the impact this meltdown had on dad; he just didn't know what to do. After talking to dad, I remember this 'tantrum,' and how I was feeling. It sickens me now remembering, and I wanted to tell dad so badly what happened and maybe in a way that's what the tantrum was about. I was in desperate need of help, and I was so scared. Now though, I had a baby sister to protect. I was 10 and while there were signs like these that I needed help, no one knew what they indicated, and I would not let it slip why. If I press hard into my memory, this episode occurred soon after an incident with my uncle. I was coping in my own way…or not.

• • •

Around this time, I took up competitive athletics in Little Athletics, something I quickly grew to love! My friend Mel, aka 'Stix', who I made friends with on the first day of year one, did Little Athletics with me. We won tonnes of medals in our different events and travelled to competitions together all over Queensland, and sometimes interstate. I would do at least five events at every competition. Mel had the long legs that allowed her to pip me in the sprints and the long jump. I, in turn, would beat her in the throwing events and hurdles; we had it worked out. It's what made going through all those other things in my life bearable, and I will forever be grateful for my old friend and the fun we had together.

I loved this part of my life, and so much of it was to do with Mel. We were at training at least once a week, and the weekends were all about competing and trying to beat our personal bests. It wasn't so much about the competition with other athletes that I enjoyed, but rather the pursuit of being my best self.

Mel had this amazing ability to make me laugh in the darkest of times. I have never laughed so hard or cried happier tears than when my mate was around. We were like chalk and cheese. She was tall and lanky, and I was solid and a bit of a nugget next to her. Mel's mother was a Caucasian New Zealander and her father a Malaysian national. Her nickname was Charlie Brown, and in our crazy friendship, so was mine. We were like B1 and B2 from Bananas in Pyjamas.

Mel was tall, with wild, thick, black hair and she had a cheekiness that made everyone smile. She was a gift from God, like an angel sent to shine light into a dark space; I know it. To understand, you would have to know Mel's family. They were a Christian family and leaders in a local church - a part of their life I came to love and share during my childhood. Every now and then I would go to church with them and loved their energy and joy. To me they epitomised the true definition of a Christian family with the love and open hearts they shared with me.

In amusing contrast, some of the most unexpected and naughty things came out of Mel's mouth. We would call each other the most bizarre names. I never knew where half of these words came from, only that these were some of my happiest childhood memories. I was affectionately known as Leprechaun Features, Bum Fluff, Bum Hole, Farty-Fart Bum, Bum Hole Features, Kelly the Smelly, Penis Trotter and Fart in the Bottle.

One day, Mel and I sang a song we made up with all these things in it. Mum was dying from laughter. I'm not sure if she wet herself, but she was close to it. She had tears streaming down her face and was doubled over. Her legs wavered as she crossed them over and staggered, trying not to embarrass herself. I was also laughing so hard I was crying as I was singing, and Mel, well, I think she was relatively straight-faced as we sang about Bum Hole Features and Penis Trotters. As Mum attempted to get us to tame our tongues, we just made her laugh more until we were all in hysterics!

This sort of thing happened often! Mel and I would be on the ground laughing so hard our lungs felt like they would burst and tears streamed down my face. Several times I almost peed my pants! Maybe Mel knew that was what I needed. She helped me understand true joy, no matter how ridiculous and silly, and true connection. Our happiness was found in the throes of childhood innocence.

Sometimes Mel stayed with us at home and even joined us while we were camping. We made up what we called a 'cow poo bong'. It was just a large Milo tin with a wire handle and holes in the bottom. The air came up through the bottom, and ignited the coals that were in the bottom layered with cow poo and grass. It smoked like crazy, chasing the mozzies away. If the mozzies and sand flies were bad, we would say that we were going to 'stoke up the bong', giggling like the little girls we were. We used to walk around the campfire, swinging them backwards and forwards. We both had one and looked hilarious as we swung our 'bongs' while singing and wandering around with puffs of smoke making it hard to breathe, trying to rid the place of the mosquitos while our eyes turned red from the smoke. We made up songs about our mozzie bong too. Yep, we were 'bong' experts. Well, that was as far as my bong smoking ever went, just saying.

Of course, I blame Mel for all our antics. I think I only played a small innocent part (cough, cough). Actually I still have a pretty awful sense of humour, except my jokes are much less ingenuous now.

• • •

Our family had by then moved into the big house. It wasn't finished, but it was liveable with a roof and the rooms completed. Now that Laura had come along, Brandon and I did our best to well and truly look after her. As a baby she was a tiny bundle of a thing, long legged and skinny, taking after our tall dad. I learned about innocence when I spent time with baby Laura. She was the epitome of goodness and purity, though I probably wouldn't have used those words back then.

Laura was a blonde, blue-eyed, delicate little girl with the fairest of skin. I easily threw her up on my hip and walked her around the yard. Most of the time she would have her fingers jammed in her mouth while her big smile hid behind her hand. She was a lanky little lady, and I knew she would grow up tall.

The hackles of my protective nature toward her were well and truly nurtured as I dragged her around on my hip. While Laura, being ten years younger, for the most part doesn't get mentioned much in this book, in many ways she was the very reason I was able to stand tall and write these words. The thought of protecting my precious little sister was a driving force that kept me strong while hidden torment raged in my life.

My most treasured memories with Laura are of when she was still small enough to fit in the clothes-washing basket on the trolley. My brother, who was rather small, and I pushed her around in that thing all day until it lost a wheel. Around this time, we ended up with a pet baby crow we called Charlie, a real character. We fed him rolled-up mince balls and baby grasshoppers by hand. He really was Laura's pet. He sat on the edge of that washing basket as we wheeled Laura around and he chatted or gargled away to her. I'm sure they talked non-stop. As that bird grew so did his ability to speak. He couldn't speak like a cockatoo, but he would gargle out his name and say, 'Hello Charlie'. As he grew up and could fly, he followed us to the bus stop and waited there until we caught the bus.

Our local town was about ten minutes along the highway. We caught the school bus in the morning at the bus stop on Daisy Dell Road, and while we waited we played in the massive meat ant nest and threw rocks at the big tree. Our bus picked us up and Charlie then followed us to school. Before long he went home, but at the end of the school day he would be waiting on the port racks outside the classroom to accompany us home again. Eventually, he didn't need us anymore and went and made his own life, but what a beautiful bird he was. We saw him hanging around every now and then, but it was much better that we had allowed him to have his freedom.

We were never short of pets in our home; we had pet rats, stumpy-tailed lizards (the ones that lay there and did nothing and the head looked the same as the tail), dogs and cats, quails, guinea pigs, and a pair of galahs called Cocky and Joey, and of course Skippy. We had horses on the property and chickens, and hundreds of green tree frogs that I would eventually run out of names for. We all loved our animals. Brandon particularly loved birds and rats. We each had a pet rat, which would be shoved in our shirts as we walked around. Quite often they would poke their head out the top of our shirts, looking around the place, or hide in our pockets. Sometimes they left us little presents in our shirts too…

One night when I was dead asleep, I was awoken by a large, fat, and very cold and wet 'something' slapping me painfully right in the middle of my face. I did one of my piercing girly screams and quickly had the whole family in my room. We have those high ceilings, higher than a ladder, so this frog had had quite the distance to fall! It was quite an awakening. Despite their shock awakening, the whole family laughed their heads off.

• • •

I must share one incident involving my best mate 'Stix' with you, because it is one of my favourites and is something I have always been able to draw upon. I say 'incident' because I think we had conspired well together against my brother, who always did his own conspiring against us.

One weekend Mel came camping at our house and Brandon was being absolutely terrible towards us, as per usual. I was so worked up from his constant teasing and nastiness that I was bawling my eyes out and yelling like a crazy woman at him. We had set up the tent down the garden path and Brandon kept sneaking up on us, yelling and scaring us, throwing things and basically terrorizing us. It doesn't sound like much, but this had continued for hours and we both became very upset with him. So, we came up with a plan of sorts. We decided in all our wisdom that we should concoct a brew.

The idea may have come from the book *"Far Out Brussel Sprout"* by June Factor. I can almost recite the whole book still today!

'Ooey gooey custard green maggot pie.
Four dog's gizzards and one cat's eye.
Four blood sandwiches coated on thick.
All washed down with a cup of hot sick.'

Well, our concoction wasn't as gross as that! The brew we made up in our little cow poo bong tins consisted of rotten tomatoes, mud, both dry and sloppy cow poo, dog poo, kangaroo and wallaby poo, grass, dead bugs and whatever else we could find. It smelled rancid. Being fast runners, we based a plan on being able to catch him; he had been running from us all day. We decided to get our bongs and each go opposite ways around the house to sneak up on him on either side. Then we could peg this stuff at him. Well, it sounded good to us. We knew he was waiting in the bushes, trying to stalk us, so we had to be smarter.

We whispered and giggled as we sourced our ingredients for our crazy concoction, laughing like little banshees. When we were finally done filling our tins to the top, we were ready. It went something like this: 'Are you ready, Charlie Brown?'

'Yep, you ready, Leprechaun Features? Let's get the little Penis Trotter!'

'Farty fart fart!'

Pffft; we let one rip, bums out and ran. It was hard to control our evil giggles as we snuck around the house like panthers, smelling like pig slops and cow poo. It was some awesome stealth I tell you, trying desperately not to spill our cow poo bongs on ourselves. We had worked hard on this concoction and didn't want to waste a drop. We snuck up on Brandon at the front of the house where he was trying to hide in the bushes, sneaking towards our tent. We got him! Yay! It was on.

I thought we were pretty clever until we caught each other in the crossfire! As we brought our arms back to throw this stuff it spilled down our hands and onto our shirts. We had poo, tomatoes and rotten stuff all over us. Oh, but we got him good, so it was worth the yuckiness running down our arms. His back was completely covered! We chased him up the garden path and through the little trails, yelling and screaming and pegging the foul stuff at him. I was so angry with him! The reprieve came from our uncontrollable giggles and hysterical witchy laughter.

It didn't end there; some of the cows had escaped into the house yard and left some wet deposits. I don't remember who started it – me, no doubt. After we ran out of our concoction, we picked up whatever was in the yard and threw that too. It was on; we could not lose to my brother. (Insert evil witch laugh.) We obviously felt the need to fertilise the yard and spread that cow poo from one side to the next, and maybe a bit on the house too. It must have been a sick cow as it was the runniest cow poo I have ever seen…or felt…like watery mud. *Oh, that's gross,* I thought as it dripped through my fingers, down my arm and into my armpits. I don't even remember if it was us chasing Brandon in the end, or if we ended up throwing them at each other in a mighty free-for-all of runny cow poo! The slight hill next to the house became a poo slide and was littered in splotches of brownie green colours of slippery smelly mess. Poo hill!

By the time it was over, Brandon did not even look like he was human anymore! He was brown and lumpy all over like a poo monster from the deep, but so were we. That's the part where we got in trouble. Mum stood there, hands on hips, face red as we joked and poo fell off us. None of us could keep a straight face, even Mum who was trying desperately to discipline us but was failing miserably, going between yelling and laughter. Brandon needed to be hosed off and those clothes never made it to the washing machine. They went into the fire.

I had the best time ever. I'm not sure that Brandon did, but we still sometimes have a good laugh over this incident, so perhaps he wasn't so traumatised after all. I obviously liked getting myself in the poo, and I was ever grateful for these times - the fun of the bush. I was glad for the joy of this friendship with Mel that would continue for a lifetime, even though we don't see each other much anymore. This was the stuff that would set me free from my nightmares, the stuff that would almost make me normal. It was that joy that helped the other 'poo' in my life seem a little less like poo.

Solitude

The trees bend in the breeze to guide me on my journey.
A slight whisper to comfort my lonely thoughts.
The barest of sounds provide yet another moment of joy.
The chirp of a bird, the most absurd sounds.
Providing alliance with my tortured thoughts.
Working for a gentle peace, if only lasting for a second.
A moment in time when my thoughts blend into peace and solitude.

[Kelly Humphries © 1998 – 17 years old]

1. My beautiful sister Laura Humphries **2.** Such fun times, me, Mel (aka Stix) and Laura, who is now more fashionable than any of us **3.** Mel again with her antics and a face covered in red jelly.

Chapter 8
Betrayal, Ignorance or Just Naivety?

I could run. I could run so fast. I remember the smell of wet grass as I put my spikes on. My sprinting shoes made me feel like I could smash records and fly. I ran so hard sometimes I could hear my heart thunder in my head...I could feel the air on my face as I sped around the track, faster and faster. You can't catch me!

I was a sporty young lass and to date, there is not much in the realms of the sporting arena I haven't done - something I consider a feat! This was also one of those wonderful things that would set me free or allow me moments of peace in all the frustration and confusion I was feeling. After all, when you are busy and engaged, you have little time to think, *what's wrong with me?* I was physically very strong, as tough as fencing wire - a 'rough nut'. I always used that as my façade, so people thought I had it together - and I did mostly. You just learn to cope.

At the time, even though it was hard, I tried not to dwell on what was going on and just got on with things. Now I think I held my own rather well. I had fun with my family and made the most of things.

Dad was into Tae Kwon Do and we sometimes sparred with each other. It was always just mucking around, but the play fighting usually started in the kitchen and you should have seen Mum go off. 'Get outside you two!' Red-faced, she would grab her wooden spoon and chase us out of the house. She would smile cheekily as Dad simply said, 'What?'

Dad or Brandon and I would wrestle and roll around on the grass. It was so much fun, but someone would always get hurt. Usually it was after Dad had a few beers. I remember one day when I asked him to show me how to do a swoop kick. He showed me all right; I was on my bum in seconds. It hurt. I got up and had to try it on him. It took a few goes and when I got him down on the ground he said, 'Righto, that's it! I'm done!' He wanted to stop, and I wanted to keep going! I was just getting started!

So, I was practiced in the art of swoop kicking, blocking and punching. I was tough as nails and Mum affectionately called me a heifer. I was not a little cow, maybe a little pig, or a horse, with a tendency to eat like one. I was strong, solid and stubborn. I was also very emotional and became more so as time went on. Despite that, I became more driven. It was like the harder it got; the more I fought to keep my head above water. It's easy to understand now how I became proud. I always felt I had to fight to hold my own. I didn't feel like I had a voice, so I worked hard to protect myself by projecting a strong and capable persona. I was fighting a massive internal battle daily, silently trying to maintain my composure and strength. So, when challenged, of course, I was defensive and sometimes a little controlling - not of other people, but certainly I needed to maintain composure and peace as much as possible. (I didn't want people to think I didn't have things together, because if they knew, I would come unstuck.)

I believed I could take my Uncle Bob out, in a literal sense. Many times, I imagined flogging the crap out of him with all the Bruce Lee moves I could pull on him. I had the tiniest details worked out. Because Dad was into his karate, we tended to watch a mixture of Star Trek, Stargate and Kung Fu Movies. I relished those movies; they made me think I might just be able to do something...anything! When Dad taught me karate, I mentally weighed my options. I often played this idea over in my mind...of punching Bob in the face. Sadly, even those thoughts would disintegrate into some form of helplessness as I realised he could crush me with one hand... He was so strong compared to me, and he was *our* uncle.

Even to this day I think about what I would do if I saw him again... All the kids in our family loved Bob. My whole family, including my

Aunty Margie, Uncle John and my cousins loved him. Favourite, loveable uncle was the ultimate disguise and cover for him. Only I knew what was lurking underneath. He was the demon that controlled my nights and had me looking over my shoulder for the better part of my childhood, and subconsciously into adulthood. In my mind I struggled with the question, 'What will happen if anyone finds out?'

He told me many times, 'This is between us; you can't tell anyone.' - a very typical thing for a man well practised in the art of manipulation to say.

I don't blame my parents because they never had cause to know what was happening; Uncle Bob hid it from them, and so did I. I felt I had to protect my family, including my father Gary, who always threatened to kill anyone that ever hurt me. There was all this stuff around me, all this pressure that kept me from thinking I could tell anyone. There was no way I could reveal my secret. I didn't write my first draft of this book until March 2014, and it has been an ongoing project and a battle of healing. Even when I started this book, my dad Gary didn't know what had happened to me, because I was afraid of what he would do. A ridiculous concept, considering how much time had passed, but understandable when you realise the depths of shame sexual abuse causes. (I have since told him and I will talk more about this later.)

This is the kind of burden a child should never have to bear. When abuse is happening I now know it is ALWAYS wrong and whether the person you tell believes you or not, you should try. Tell someone you trust who can help you on the journey.

Don't do what I did and try and protect everyone, because essentially it did not help the situation. Just be wise who you tell.

I don't blame anyone, except him. Uncle Bob. He broke our trust. I blamed myself for a long time, but he was the one who destroyed the beautiful family relationship we all thought we had with him. He made our family life difficult in later years as we came to terms with what he had done. He destroyed many parts of my childhood and changed the way our family lived and dealt with each other. He alone caused more hurt and pain in that time than probably any other thing, and as a family we are still trying to understand. Uncle Bob deliberately groomed and deceived Mum and Dad as well. That's the nature of paedophiles.

How did he groom them? By offering to help, by being around and available and doing everything he could to be that nice, helpful brother to them. He was the uncle that could be relied on for all the things we needed support for in our family.

In the same way, Aunty Von was also supposed to be a helpful, reliable and trustworthy person. In many ways, she was groomed also; he manipulated Aunty Von into thinking he was someone he was not. But even after Bob was arrested, Aunty Von stayed with him. To me that says that she was both a victim and afraid, but also that she didn't care. But I am making assumptions based on the journey and what I saw. Actions always speak louder than words…

I believe one day she caught Uncle Bob out. I was sitting on the couch, next to him. He was watching an explicit war movie, full of porn and guns. I remember sitting rigid, unmoving; I knew what Uncle Bob wanted. You learn to know these things, or they make it pretty obvious by their behaviour - the touches, the grabbing of my hand to make me feel how hard he was, things like that. This time he made a point of masturbating while he was touching me and watching the movie. I had secretly hoped and prayed that one day she would catch him and know what he was doing to me and she would stop him. This day she did see. It was not well lit, but there was enough light to see. The room was a glowing hazy red colour, like a dirty 80's horror movie. Aunty Von walked in while he was doing his thing. She looked shocked and put her head cocked on the side. Then she very quickly tried to maintain her composure.

She asked why I was still up and what I was doing and then simply told me to go to bed, saying something about not watching 'those kinds of movies'. I hated her even more then. It was clear she knew something was wrong, but she didn't say anything to him to stop him from ever doing this again. Why would she let him keep doing that?

I beat myself up for years and years over this incident. I knew that he was more careful after that. But I tell you what; it hurt even more thinking that she didn't care. It hurt thinking that her relationship with him was more important than what he was doing to me. I found that hard to understand and even harder to accept.

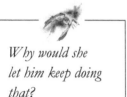

Why would she let him keep doing that?

Why couldn't she save me? Why didn't she help me? Why didn't she come to my rescue? She was the only adult that appeared to have seen something and more than any of the other adults, she was the one who was around the most when things happened to me. Was it simply that she was so lazy and consumed by her own stuff that she chose to ignore it? Did she not care? Realistically, I can never say what exactly she saw, but after a time, and from other people's encounters with her, I am convinced she knew.

I can never understand why people knowingly continue to have a relationship with a sexual predator. Does the fear of being alone outweigh the prospect of being with such a person? I can't answer that. I can only think it's because of a person's self-esteem, upbringing and mental health. Is it love? Well again, does love outweigh betrayal? I'm not sure there is any one answer. That is what he did - betrayed all of us and violated our trust. I think he also betrayed Aunty Von, but I still felt betrayed by them both.

I have only seen Aunty Von once since, and that was at my grandmother Peggy's funeral. When I saw her, and she came towards me, I had no words. I just felt anger because she had come. If I had told my grandmother what had happened with Uncle Bob, Aunty Von would have worn my grandmother's tennis racquet for a necklace, and that would have been the least of her worries.

Years later, prior to the publication of this book, Aunty Von (not her real name) was offered the right of reply and asked what her recollection of events were, specifically on the night when Uncle Bob was touching me on the couch and she walked into the room. She denied seeing anything untoward and said she was unaware of any improper, abusive or predatory behaviour from her husband, until the day the police came to their door to arrest him.

The hatred I felt for her sometimes because of her failure to expose him was so strong. She never seemed to SEE me. If I could have connected with her the way I had wanted to from the beginning, maybe I would have felt SAFE enough to reveal what happened. Not to mention that I didn't feel she would believe me, which is why I hoped she would catch him in the act of doing something. I felt she let me down, like she should have been the adult to help me, and the one opportunity she had was lost. I couldn't know for sure whether she really did see him, or not. I just hoped with some small part of me that she did. It broke me, and it was after the couch incident that I almost lost faith in life itself and felt that there

Any wonder that when a child makes a disclosure, your belief in what they tell you is one of the single most important things you can do to help that child heal.

was very little hope. I stopped fighting and forgot who I was, and what I was made of. For a long time, I was a very lost little girl…I was trapped. I was hurting, and I was stripped of the things that were meant to be my childhood.

Any wonder that when a child makes a disclosure, your belief in what they tell you is one of the single most important things you can do to help that child heal.

When I didn't see him for a long time, I was OK. I would keep going with other things. I enjoyed life like every other kid and I could snatch back moments of my childhood. Like a game of tug-o-war you don't really know you are playing, this cloud of my secret life hung over my head. Again, it was fear and until writing this book I could not name it. For a long time, I thought this feeling was normal. It was a silent anxiety that niggled away at me, and I just learned to do things with it, and in spite of it.

As stoic as I was, there were many tears. There are many ways people choose to cope, but as a little girl, tears were one of my means of coping. Some kids I have seen have very little in the way of coping strategies and it comes out in behaviour, dealt with by drugs or other substances. Sometimes it manifests in mental health issues or suicide. I know I was depressed. Sometimes I was overly happy, and sometimes I recall being so sad my heart felt like it was crushed and I couldn't breathe. Others choose to self-harm so they can feel something...anything. I wasn't someone who self-harmed, but I was always getting injured... maybe it was connected. If I wasn't depressed, injured, or crying then I was worried and looking over my shoulder. I knew in my heart of hearts that he would never kill me, but that image often floated in the back of my mind. My uncle was a dichotomy: on one hand the caring uncle and on the other, the sinister, scary uncle. This created unnerving fear; who was going to be the uncle I got to see today? I remembered seeing photos of him and his big semi-automatics and black guns, alongside dead pigs in the bush. I didn't want to be the dead pig.

• • •

The frustration and the shame in all of this as I look back, is that despite my fear, I also felt elated that Uncle Bob treated me in such a special way. I was his special niece; the niece he would take fishing and camping. He even taught me how to live in the bush. This is the extremely contradictory nature of what I was feeling and seeing, how I acted and felt. Talk about confusing and complicated! He was the uncle that showed me how to string a fishing line, cast a bait net, build a hut, make tent pegs out of wood with a small tomahawk, go prawning, cook on a camp fire and basically survive. All the things I absolutely loved! I relished spending time with someone who was as excited as I was to do something I loved. With these commonalities, however, he was easily creating opportunities which tainted these moments in time with his toxicity. This was the niece that got chocolate, lollies and whatever she wanted, and even green ginger wine, which I have never had since. I didn't know that this was part of what's called 'grooming'. My parents also didn't know what was really happening; remember, they are victims of his grooming manipulations, too.

What hurts my heart is what was concealed on the flip side of this beautiful, innocent-looking relationship; which was just that, beautiful and innocent-looking - to everyone else. Uncle Bob lived two lives but destroyed so many more. He was so bold and brazen in his approach and even came to athletics training and competitions with us. It seemed that wherever we were, he was too. I don't remember anything happening on any athletic trips, but he was very encouraging and helped with coaching as well. That's just how it was; parents and families all got involved in teaching the kids. Everyone felt safe with him.

Thank God I had athletics. Athletics days were fun, with the starting gun firing off at the start line, the smell of the cap gun and the carbon mixed with the air. The fresh coolness of the frozen poppers we had at the end of the day, smashing our personal records in events, and beating our best times and distances was always encouraging. It's funny how many amazing memories I have of athletics, and the incredible people with whom I shared that journey. But a dark shadow was always lurking on the fringes. His.

1. Me in Port Douglas meeting my dad at one of the wildlife parks.
10 years old.

THE TRUTH

IF I WERE YOU
    I WOULDN'T HIDE...
I'd TELL THE TRUTH.
    YOU'LL ONLY GET IN TROUBLE LATER
LATER THE PAIN WILL BE GREATER
    YOU SHOULDNT HAVE LIED.
    ALL THOSE USELESS TEARS YOU CRIED
IT WASNT YOUR FAULT ♡

    JUST TELL THE TRUTH.

Kelly Humphries ©1999

Chapter 9
Teach Me, Break Me and Groom Me. I Hate Me

The world played out around me like a movie; was I asleep or dreaming? I felt like I was outside my body. How does that happen? There was nothing real happening there, I was there but I wasn't. It was like I was in a dream. Floating…voices echoed around me. I couldn't see who was speaking… I could see myself below him; lying on the bed… I was looking to the side. It was sitting like a rigid scarecrow in a halo of black filth. I hated It. Like the movie glasses I saw most of life through, I watched my uncle hurt the little girl I knew was me. 'C'mon Kel, be strong,' I begged. 'It will be OK, Kel.' While I felt intense sadness and anxiety, another part of me felt nothing. Disassociation was my friend and my filter. Disassociation - psychological splitting, messed up, hard-hitting. Where was I? In survival mode, just a whisper, an object; a mechanism.

I was Uncle Bob's little pet. His secret plaything that he touched and felt whenever he could. He was opportunistic and brazen. There were times when we were all at home with him and he would set the kids up with a movie or get them to play outside. Mum and Dad would have left to go and run errands in town or go to work. Aunty Von was always asleep; or she was out doing something. I hated that she slept so much. It meant that she didn't see what he was doing to me. He would tell my cousins that he was going to show me something, something that he couldn't share with them. He would pull me aside from whatever I was doing with them and take me somewhere quiet within the house, like his room, and close the door. There he would touch me and have his way with me, the kids nearby or playing outside.

I know they had burning questions, but something about the

intimidating way my uncle would shut them down kept them silent. I remember once the face of my oldest cousin; I think in a childish way he knew. I looked in his eyes, pleading with him silently. I knew I would not have been able to tell him, but it comforted me for a moment. They were only young then; how could they know what their dad was doing? I was still the oldest and felt I had a duty to protect them all.

I developed coping mechanisms like going numb and disassociating from my body, which I now know is common for victims of abuse to avoid the intensity and fear of what is physically happening to them, and perhaps even to protect their emotional state. Dissociation means a person goes into a state of disconnection. People describe it in many ways, but mostly it is like an out-of-body experience, a detachment of self, feelings, memories and identity. It's a psychological process and can last for the time of the event, or at times it can span weeks. There were times when I felt like a fly on the wall, watching what was happening and mentally not being present, not even in life itself. I would say I was totally withdrawn. What did I miss in that haze?

I still felt physical things, although I was quite numb mentally and emotionally. For example, my uncle had huge hands and while I could detach from most things, I can remember how sometimes he physically hurt me. I would not generally partake in what was going on; I was an object. This enabled me to cope. There are other strategies, such as crying or distraction, which I also used from time to time.

It's a bit clichéd, but I truly wish I knew then what I know now! I could not understand these deep feelings as I was so young, and I felt trapped. Whatever you imagine in your mind is sometimes so far removed from what is real, you don't really know who you are or have any solid ground to stand on. What is real? What is safe? There is, of course, always a way, but when we are so young we are simply overwhelmed and feel no one else would or could understand what we are going through. That is sometimes where that numbness slips in. Not to mention there is the fear of saying anything at all, so it can sometimes be easier to just close off from the world. I remember how hard it was hearing the words I was saying to myself and how my inner self struggled with what I believed about who I was. The little voice inside me went like this, over and over:

- *I don't think anyone would understand what I am going through. Hmmm, would they even believe me? What if they did know? Would they think I was a little slutty girl, a whore, and a dirty little secret? It's gross; I'm so fucking gross.*

- *No one will understand, so it's better to just be quiet. It's easier. I don't want to get in trouble. Everyone will think I'm just a dirty little bitch, so I don't want anyone to know 'that' stuff about me. I don't want to be in trouble for letting him do that to me.*

- *I feel so dirty…*

- *What would people say? They are all going to think I am a liar. Everyone will think I am just a weirdo whore.*

- *People will think that I am crazy, mentally unstable, all fucked up in my head. No one wants to be friends with someone who does the sex stuff with their uncle.*

- *You're so fucking gross.*

- *I feel so ugly…*

These weren't words that anyone used to me; it's just how I felt; words and sentences that popped into my head daily. You know, the worst part of this is that some people do understand. More people than you can imagine … just most don't talk about it. *(Not everyone will get it, so that is where it's so important to speak to people who you know do have an understanding.)* In essence, I was never alone, but fear kept me hidden and trapped while I was sinking into negative, degraded thinking. Realistically, there were always people around who would have listened to me, if I had told the truth about what I was going through.

Even when I thought the worst of myself, there were people who only thought the best of who I was. Perspective is a gift and an amazing skill. Trapped thinking keeps our minds and thinking locked, as it does our dreams. You have to believe you are worth more.

See, you may not know this, but predators train your mind first. They teach you through what they say, how they act, and they manipulate your thinking to keep you locked into a place where you feel they are the only safe person.

How does the nasty, disgusting and manipulative predator turn himself into the sole person you feel safe with? It's clever, but more than being clever, it's cunning. They make it so hard to open your mouth and talk about what is happening through indoctrination and fear. They bind you to them with the secrets and lies. You don't know it's happening, especially when it starts so young. Soon, you know nothing more than the crushing cycle…round and round like a merry-go-round.

When you finally see…when your young eyes have awakened to the world…you begin to know what is wrong. You finally understand you were right all along, but you still can't move. It is like you are trapped behind the glass and you can see the innocence of a young child being stripped bare, right there in front of your eyes, and there is not a damn thing you can do about it.

Then…well, then you cry for her…you grieve for her spirit, her lost happiness. You grieve her lost innocence and smile. You pray that the betrayal was not real, and you pray even harder that you were the only one; that no other child had this happen. Whose fault is it…? Who can help? I prayed my soul out. I cried and I realised there was nothing I could do. I knew nothing else.

We survivors of child abuse sometimes feel we have to take on the weight of the world and do everything on our own. We tend to become control freaks in a way. Anything outside of that causes massive internal chaos and at times crippling anxiety. We do this because if we show cracks, people will find out who we truly are. People will see our secret. People will find out…thus, we strain to protect ourselves. So, we must maintain control; that is the survival instinct in us. That is how we live and how parts of us also die.

Any wonder police work, while a wonderful career for me, was extra hard at times. We are taught everything is either a high risk or an unknown risk. In that alone, I have grown immensely and no longer try and control everything in my environment. It's way too much hard work because no matter how hard you try, the world is bigger than you and *always* has other ideas. *Let go.*

I have had to learn to let go of many things and only accept what I can change. I have found my voice and learned to have the moral courage to stand up for myself and set boundaries. I was too young to know any different when all this started. I had to learn it was *not* my fault, and more than that, I would need to accept it; that took much longer. There was still a time to come where I would take those first steps forward and have the courage to speak. But it doesn't matter how old you are, you have the right to speak if you think someone is doing the wrong thing!

I didn't know this early on, and I couldn't have known any better! It was not a negligent thing on part of my parents. They taught me what was right and wrong. But, it all started when I was just a little bit too young and I didn't have my feet. By the time I figured it out (probably about eleven or twelve) I was already trapped in a cycle, so I learned to survive. I learned coping mechanisms, and I turned into a numb, confused child with a very distorted view of things.

I did inadvertently learn to start to put a few boundaries in place, thankfully. One day when I was still quite small, Uncle Bob lay next to me on a single bed. It was in the early days, and he would usually touch me by using his hands and keeping all his clothes on. He would press against my body to let me know how excited he was. But as time went on, he wore less and less clothes. I lay next to him that day and he had his shirt on but no pants. He was fully erect. *It* was one of the biggest things I had seen. My heart was pounding in my chest and I felt terrified. He was not a small man, and he wanted to put that big thing inside me. I was petrified that it wouldn't fit. What would I do with such a thing?

Before this he had shown *It* to me, but not in the erect state. It was mostly just the feel of him on me, the occasional putting of my hand on his penis and him touching me. He never forced me to have intercourse with him. At that stage he would often show me condoms and insinuated that he wanted to 'get it in'. I never really knew what I wanted to do. I wanted to please him, and yet I knew it was wrong, and I was afraid of how much it would hurt. This double thinking led to all kinds of confusion. That day when he did try to get *It* 'in there', he stopped because I told him it hurt and to stop. For that I am so grateful. I felt proud of myself though not sure why. What I had done that time was to set a boundary with him by saying no. Sadly, I didn't understand that I could also say no to other things.

That one **"No"** didn't stop him trying over the years, but, regardless, using his hands was the same thing. I now know it's called 'digital rape'. Soon he moved onto oral sex, too, and seemed to favour that.

The continuation of things happening, and my experiences as they grew in intensity, led me to be more dissociative when things happened to me. I could automatically switch the disassociation on and off. I could be completely absent if I wanted to, and I would do this many times over the years and not know how or why I did it.

· · ·

As you know by now, we had hundreds of fishing trips. My brother was still a bit too small for some of these adventures, so often it would end up being just me and Uncle Bob - only for a couple of hours. No one was concerned when it was a couple of hours here and there. On one occasion, Brandon and I and one of the cousins were hanging out at the Port of Gladstone, where eager fishermen know that when the moon and the tide are right, the place swarms with prawns - my favourite food in the world, next to mud crabs and KFC! It's also very deep in this section, where the big ships come in and load up with coal. We caught buckets of prawns that night; it was so exciting! I was ecstatic! I ran back and forth, picking up the prawns and trying to get as many as I could.

Looking back at it, I can see Bob was playing the god of my life. He dictated how I felt and what I did. I was very quick to change moods. I could be exceptionally happy one moment, catching prawns and squealing with excitement, and then the next, I was feeling majorly depressed, to the point that I felt incredible heartbreak. I also felt anxiety; it was a friend and an enemy. It was hard because it was all very subconscious. I would not even understand what I was doing or what he had done until much later, and that is why I think it is important for children to know their rights, especially when it comes to their body.

Basically, once I was caught in this ongoing toxic cycle, I felt I had to make up my own lies to keep the secret. Lying about where I had been with him or what had happened on a fishing trip, or rather omitting certain information about what happened that day, or just not saying anything at all. I have never been a good liar, I just don't like it, and it goes against all I believe in, so it was much easier to just let Uncle Bob do the talking. When I was a child, Uncle Bob would tell me what to say or he would harp on about the fishing trip, so they would never really know my thoughts anyway…only that we caught heaps of this or that. Sometimes, I just felt that everything was so busy around me that there was no one who would want to hear what I had to say and anyway, who would even care? That is not anyone's fault, but a result of how my brain was already being changed.

More than anything else, I hated that I lied to myself to justify what I was feeling, and convinced myself that it was OK; that what was happening and what I was feeling was a normal process and that he, Bob, was 'right'. That maybe, just maybe, God really did want us to 'feel good', and maybe He would want us to make sure everyone was happy by not telling anyone about it.

One of the things that I struggled most with was the fact that Bob was opportunistic. I am someone who likes to know every detail of things, but I was living under a level of great anxiety I did not even know the name for. Whenever he could grab the opportunity, Uncle Bob would wake me up. It wasn't that he woke me up that was sickening; it was how he did it. It didn't matter if Mum and Dad were around at the same time or not, he just did it, under the same roof. He would say that he was coming to wake us kids up or he would come in the early hours before anyone was awake. It was only when our family stayed over in town at his place. I would wake up to him by my bunk bed, standing there and his fingers would be in all the places they shouldn't be. I don't know how many times that happened. It would happen in the same room as the other kids. Mum and Dad never suspected him.

I was worried about everything (I still worry about everything).
I worried about being caught.
I worried because I wanted to be caught.
I worried what would happen if we were caught.

It is called a cycle of abuse for a reason. Understanding the cycle is hard, but once you can see it for what it is, there is freedom. While it is not the same event, cycles happen in all forms of abuse, from domestic violence, sexual and physical abuse to alcoholism, and the list goes on. Manipulation catapults you into fear and spirals you into a ripple of unknown and misinterpreted emotions that can take a lifetime to understand.

Shame is learned, it's taught to keep us imprisoned in a space where the perpetrator wins. Don't let them win. You can choose another way.

• • •

I am struggling to share this next part. Just know that, like many parts of this book, I can easily write it out, but then when I think about someone reading it and sharing my story, I still cringe, but I realise and have learned that in order to overcome the darkness I need to step bravely into the light - even if it hurts. I also know there is much worse happening out there, and that is why speaking up is so important. So we are not hiding in the dark. For this particular memory I struggle because there is work I still need to do in this space. I struggle with what I am sharing with you…some parts more than others.

There are things he did that I cannot ever forget. This is one of them. While he had done some of this before, many times, this incident stands out, I think because I was going through puberty. And because he did something else that sickened me… It makes me sick to think as I write this, but I press on, as I believe that this darkness needs to be broken. I will not be ashamed! I didn't do this to myself; *it's not my fault*.

Sometimes the memories hurt more than anything else, maybe it is also around this time that I was beginning to know how wrong it all was, and here I was, trapped with him. In absolute turmoil, reckoning my sins with him and realising how cornered I was…the reckoning which should have been stacked against him, and not me…

I was barely twelve. As I had started to enter puberty, I was petrified that he was going to make me pregnant, so I was afraid to go 'all the way'. My flat chest had small lumps, the beginning of breasts. I had started to grow hair elsewhere too. This particular day, he shut the door on us. I remember the red haze…I don't know why. Maybe it was the curtains or maybe my imagination. Perhaps I am just that angry, all I can remember is this whole scene in red...

He showed me a box of videos with all forms of naked bodies on the front, which he said I should watch with him. I never did watch them, but the covers were enough to make me know what they were about…

especially as he flicked through the front covers. That was when my heart started to race and I could feel the panic rise in me. He kissed me, sloppily, but it was a long kiss and he was pushing hard on my mouth. I remember my heart was beating wildly. At least he had brushed his teeth. He took my shirt off and remarked at how big I was growing. Fucking dirty prick. Then he took my pants off. I immediately went outside my body. I was getting good at that, switching out of my body. So, it wasn't truly happening to me…but it was.

He laid me on the bed after kissing me and then violated me with his fingers and his mouth. While he had big hands, I guess you could say I was used to that by then. He commented on my changing body. He did something strange then, which repulsed me. He licked his fingers after he had been touching me and then spat on himself, to provide lubrication of sorts and minimise the 'pain' I would feel. Then he tried to violate me again, using *It*. I hated *It*. *It* hurt; of course it hurt. He stopped partway in. Maybe he second-guessed himself or maybe he just didn't want me to scream loudly in pain; he knew it would hurt me. It did hurt, and I remember saying something to him about that and asking him to stop. So, he abused me in other ways, digitally and orally, scratching at me with his vile, awful moustache. I hated it.

I remember gagging then, and I gag now. Oral sex is a very intimate thing to do and when I was a kid, I never understood this fact, only that it seemed 'yucky'. Now as an adult, I believe that the intimacy of an act like this should be reserved for lovers, and so I suppose I still hold some shame around this. This is also the very reason I share so much with you. So you know that childhood pain, without help and support, becomes an adult stain. Acts in childhood like these do have an ongoing effect on the adult. We need to be able to speak about this and feel safe to do so. We need to do more about protecting our children and certainly supporting each other through some of these tough things. Unfortunately, I have work to do overcoming this, but I understand now this shame belongs to him, the paedophile.

Finger licking, and anything of this whole nature in general, still repulses me. I have flashbacks - moments that remind me of other moments, perpetuating the nightmare. I have never shaken this.

I lay there while he did this to me, unmoving, no sound. *It* was gross. *It* was sticking up, and looked, well, fucking disgusting. Did I already say how much I hated *It*? I was taught to be quiet about things. The kids were watching a movie and playing in the living room, just a few steps from the door.

I felt disgusting, wet and gross. I was sore and burning 'down there'. I was ashamed and unhappy and felt like I was suffocating. I went to the bathroom, desperate to wash myself off, as I always did. Whenever he touched me, I needed to shower, to purge myself of him.

On the way to the bathroom the kids asked me what I was doing, and I briefly said something about looking at a movie with Uncle Bob. I secretly wished they would catch him out and tell someone. I got helplessly angry with them sometimes. I felt that they knew, and I was annoyed at them because no one woke up when he did things. No one said anything, ever. Maybe I was blaming them. I remember those moments, and I cringe, but I remember taking a deep breath and saying to myself, 'They are so little, they could never help me - how would they even know?' I was so little myself. I only have to look at my lovely niece to realise just how innocent I really was.

But, of course, it's unlikely they would ever have found out, because he was just that good at hiding it, from everyone. Still, I longed for someone to rescue me. Yet with that came the fear of the unknown. I didn't know what he was capable of, if he was caught out. Who would he become? Who would I become? What demon would emerge from within him? What would happen to my family? Would they leave me?

One day, when I was about twelve or thirteen, mum asked me a question where I had the chance to break this shroud of silence... I was at home in the kitchen and Mum was deep in thought while washing the dishes. She turned around and simply asked, 'Has your Uncle Bob ever touched you?' I looked at her and paused for a moment. I knew exactly what she meant, but I was scared. 'What do you mean, Mum?'

She said, 'You would tell me if someone touched you, right? No one is allowed to touch you under your clothes. Has your Uncle Bob ever touched you under your clothes?' Mum was upset, and I could see it; she was red-faced and seemed really stressed, so I thought I was in trouble... I knew later that she wasn't angry with me... but with him. My uncle, the paedophile.

I was paralysed with fear, my heart and thoughts racing. I felt sick. If there was ever a time to tell her, this was it. Would she think I was a gross, disgusting child? Would the family break up? It might mean we wouldn't go camping again or fishing ever again. I didn't want to upset anyone. It would be my entire fault.

I hesitated ... I don't know if Mum noticed. I desperately wanted to tell her. *Mum! I am sorry I never told you then.* I had a moment handed to me and I hid. I froze. I don't have many regrets, but this is one of them... I should have told her. But I kept my silence and said no. I cried later on my own, tears of anguish soaking my pillow. Why couldn't I utter the words? I could have simply nodded my head! But words would not come.

I didn't want to be the one that took Uncle Bob away or broke up the family. I didn't want him to touch anyone else. If I let him do to me what he wanted, he wouldn't hurt my sister Laura or my cousin Caitlin, or any other little girl. (Aunty Margaret was Mum's sister and Caitlin was her oldest daughter) I hoped in my heart that he would never touch Brandon, and I felt he was pretty safe, but there was part of me that still worried that maybe I was wrong. I felt brave in protecting my family, but I felt heavy, laden with this responsibility. If I sacrificed and gave him what he needed, he would have no need to hurt or touch anyone else, I reasoned. But I was wrong. You see, years later I found out that Mum had just learned that Bob had been charged for touching another little girl. It was after this conversation that I realised what was happening was really wrong. It all felt like such a big responsibility on my little shoulders.

Don't Say a Word

Pray like a child, pray from your soul,
Keep your silence. NOW. Choking like a mouth full of dry flour,
Unable to breathe, unable to speak.
Inhale, but don't.
Choking, constricting like a prison. With your mouth sewn shut and yet
you don't know how. Like wool in your mouth, yet wanting to scream
and shout.
But don't say a word.
Shhhhhhh...
Don't make a sound,
But pray
like
a
child.

[Kelly Humphries © 2015]

1. Receiving an Australia Day Award - Sportsperson of the year. 14 years old. I received this 3 years in a row! **2.** My brother Brandon and sister Laura. Happy times.

Chapter 10
Pray Like a Child - Keep the Silence

Dear God. I know I always ask for your help. I always pray to you. I don't know if you can hear me, God, but I am trying to be as good as I can. I try so hard to get good marks at school. I try hard to be the best girl I can be, so it will stop. I don't know why I'm afraid. Please help me. I promise I'll be a good girl. I won't do it with him anymore. But what do I do if he starts it? I need to know what to do, God. Please help me be happy again. Can you make me into a bird and maybe I could fly around in heaven with you? I could just watch. Maybe I could be like a superhero, like Supergirl, like an angel, and I can save the other girls and boys. Are there other girls and boys like me? Please forgive me for being bad, God. I don't want to cry anymore. Thank you for my family, God. Amen

---

I was jumpy and always looking over my shoulder. When the lights went out and Uncle Bob was around, I would wait. It was only a matter of time before the lurking predator came in the darkness; but only sometimes. Sometimes I would wait and wait and wait, anticipating his arrival. Listening for his footsteps. It was exhausting.

It's taken a lot of self-reflection and learning in the field of sexual abuse to understand why abuse victims feel so much shame. One part of it is that being touched in an abuse situation sometimes feels good (I know that statement sounds contradictory; I cringe just writing it!). Abuse doesn't always have to have physical violence attached to it, either. Your body naturally finds ways to respond to intimate touching that perhaps you didn't know were possible. At times your body wants to retreat within and sometimes you cannot control your physiological response, for no other reason than that you were born that way. When you do figure this out, that is, once the violated and broken you realises you were not made to be a sexual being at seven or nine or even ten, then it seems too late. You are stuck, going around and around in a hamster wheel. When you understand, like I did, that it had felt good (sometimes) to be touched by 'that person who betrayed you', then for many victims comes that prison of deep shame. 'That person, that betrayer', might be a relative, or someone significantly older but regardless- this shame can lead to utterly destructive and perverted thoughts that cause all kinds of emotional battles.

Why do victims feel shame? Because what's happened doesn't feel right, as it usually doesn't fit into the understanding of the love you learned prior to the abuse. The very foundations of your boundaries have been violated, along with your understanding of love. You might know what love looks like from your Mum and Dad, or from what you have seen on Disney cartoons with Minnie and Mickey Mouse - an innocent, fairy tale type of love that you hope one day will happen to you. You try and fit what is happening to you into this ideal and it just doesn't work. When abuse drips its stain into the picture, the picture changes. It's where that confusion comes from; nothing seems to fit into place or make any sense. The puzzle pieces don't fit together anymore. Inside you there is this intrinsic sense that whatever is happening is profoundly wrong. Sometimes you don't know why it feels wrong. It's like your head and heart fight for understanding and you feel the need to rationalise and justify what's happening. You hear the perpetrator's voice, your voice and everything else that is emotionally trying to speak to you. It's a confusing space to be in.

In due course you must realise, like I did, that you were not at fault.

In due course you must realise, like I did, that you were not at fault. Your body only responded because that is its natural programming. There was one person responsible for that whole situation: the perpetrator.

Sadly, childhood abuse experiences like this can teach you that to be loved is to be touched, and touched intimately…and so you allow someone to touch you. Someone or anyone. Or conversely, you withdraw so much that no one can touch you and those walls get built high and tough… It seems to be one of two extremes. Either everyone is allowed in, because your boundaries have been violated; or no one is allowed in because your boundaries have been violated! You feel unworthy of anyone or anything, because *you* hold a dirty secret, a secret that if you tell, it could mean that someone would know about what *you* get up to. There is a feeling that to be safe is to be recognised, to be seen, to make someone else happy. Perhaps you find it easier to hide, and not be seen at all. You find safety in knowing that if *they* are happy, you are safe (most of the time). And more than anything - you understand that speaking up about anything could mean the end of your life, as you know it. Well, that is how it feels. You feel like telling anyone means you could die, you might get hurt, you could break the family apart, you may even be told that you're lying.

There are so many reasons you feel like speaking out is too hard. I subconsciously knew all these things by the time I was twelve when I finally realised it was wrong and the secret was a lie. That's when I felt like it was too late. Presumably, I would have been OK if I had revealed the secret about what was happening, but it felt much safer at the time to say nothing.

• • •

As I got older, there were fewer opportunities for these secret, intimate assaults. As they became fewer and more far between, I was able to feel almost like a normal kid again. What I mostly remember are the fun and amazing things that were going on in my life at that time. I relished those moments, but I didn't look at people the same way anymore. I didn't see innocence any more. I couldn't trust anyone. I always looked past what I could see of people's hearts and suspected there was a hidden agenda; sadly, it was mostly with men. What I had been "taught" by my uncle was what I thought all men wanted from me, a pre-teen girl. I thought that was how love was shown.

Sadly, I began to normalise this sexualised behaviour. I felt as if the touching, the small gestures and all the sexual stuff, was a normal thing, and that to show love to someone you needed to touch him or her intimately. But I see now that I had an overwhelming need to justify this learned behaviour, to try make it right. I was telling myself lies to try to understand what was happening and to make sense of the world.

When I prayed, I knew deep down that things were wrong. I still believed that Jesus loved me, despite what I thought was my fault. The things in my life I was doing almost felt like the ultimate sin... I wanted, hoped and believed that one day I would be forgiven for my atrocities. I would argue in my head that I wasn't worthy to be loved by God - perhaps not in those words - but I felt terrible about who I was, and what I felt about the world was depressing. One side of my life was a place of darkness and I felt I wasn't worthy. Nothing was good enough. Sometimes I wanted to run and run and keep running until I could go to that place in my head where I got to camp, eat food and fish all day, laugh and forget the world.

• • •

I have tried to show you the reality of what my head was going through so that you can understand anyone who has ever experienced a similar thing - or perhaps it is you. It is a confusing space. A place when all that is right with the world quickly turns upside down and you either find yourself as two different people walking in two worlds or as a person stuck in a dark space, watching the light through a door crack in the closet you have hidden in.

My hope is that no matter what happens, you learn to walk steadfast in the darkness, knowing that the light is coming, and that you have the tools and understanding to stretch yourself and achieve this freedom. The darkness never lasts as long when you are focussed on the light and each day, with each step, you become more powerful in your convictions.

Some never make it that far and they cannot break the cycle, remaining in a dark space. As a child, I was frequently in the dark. Depressed, angry, sad… and I found my thought processes and self-talk erratic. On one hand I would say to myself, 'C'mon, you're better than this. Don't you remember what Sir said in Primary school? 'Strive to be the best you can." and then blast myself with, 'You're such an idiot! You're so fucking pathetic! Why would you let him do such a stupid thing like that? You're so weak! C'mon Kel…!'

I would always 'brain bash' myself, telling myself that I wasn't doing good enough, for example, in sport. I had to do better! So, in a sad kind of way, I made choices to seek the ultimate best in myself, always, to prove myself by working harder and pushing myself further. I wanted to feel better about who I was. This in itself was not a bad thing because I have acknowledged the coping mechanism, and I have now turned it into a rock of perseverance.

One of my greatest struggles and deepest hurts was that my uncle's manipulation to comply with his wishes damaged my faith and perception of who Jesus is. Luckily it was not destroyed. I know many who read this might not appreciate the faith aspect, but in place of Jesus you can set the idea of someone who represents 'father', a higher power or your version of 'God'. Stay with me for a moment here…

I said to my uncle that Jesus wouldn't like us 'being together'. I told him that he would be sad. For a long time, I didn't understand completely how wrong things were. On some level, I sensed that I was being lied to and had been for a long time. I felt betrayed. I remember my efforts to justify what was happening to make it 'okay' in my mind by making excuses for Uncle Bob, for instance he had a rough upbringing like Mum and needed me to help him feel better. I was so confused, because I knew the relationship between an uncle and his niece should not be sexual, let alone between a grown man and a young girl. My view of love was being deliberately distorted.

His response was something like this: 'Don't you think Jesus wants us all to love each other? He would want me to love you like this, to show you what love is all about.'

I don't remember what else he said, only that he would always turn it around and make it sound like it was right, it was fine, that it was allowed. I was so angry with him that he would say those sickening lies about Jesus, yet he managed to make it all make sense. I knew Jesus would want us to love each other, but not in that kind of way, right?

I hate that he used God, who I loved, and said that it was OK, and what was happening was a natural thing - that it was good to make each other feel special. I always knew in my heart that what he was doing was wrong. No God would want his child to feel abused or taken advantage of.

On the other hand, I felt confused about what was a 'right' love and what was a 'wrong' love. It would be like someone saying; 'Don't you think your dad wants us to love each other? Don't you think he would want us all to be happy?' The manipulation comes through the perpetrator taking that which you hold dear, that safe relationship, and turning it into an unsafe space where the only one that you can rely on is the perpetrator.

I would pray often, as a child does, to Jesus from the depths of my soul that I wanted this to stop with my uncle. I misunderstood or had a *misconception*, that Mum and Dad couldn't help me. I was afraid because there were all these unknowns about speaking up, about utilising this voice inside me to tell the truth. I felt very alone, but essentially, I wasn't. I would ask Jesus why this was happening to me. I remember the smallness and meekness that I felt, the crying in frustration and confusion in simply trying to understand. Now this was something that I would later struggle with; understanding how Jesus, who was all-powerful, would allow something like this to happen to me. I thought that when we cry out for help from the depths of our heart, Jesus was supposed to hear. I had to have faith. I had to believe that no matter how long it took; he knew what was going on.

Despite Bob's lies, my faith in Jesus kept me sane. It kept me focussed and it kept me hoping that God would do something with this. Even though I felt like I couldn't stop what was happening, I understood that it was his choice, Bob's choice, and he was the one who decided this was going to happen. It didn't stop me being angry in many ways, or justifying my own actions, but my love for Jesus, or who I believed Jesus to be, allowed me to stand under what would become a lifelong battle of overcoming and having a constant revelation of myself. For you, it may be another faith, God or belief system. I leaned on my particular faith, and I believed that I would be eventually brought out of that darkness, firmly and boldly into the light.

I always felt like I had an angel. I don't even know if I believe in angels, but there was always a presence. I felt there was always hope. Sometimes I thought that things could have been much worse between my uncle and me. Sometimes I also wondered whether I had done something to make Jesus unhappy with me, and that was why He was keeping me locked in that place. Maybe this was retribution for something I had done. Payback. Revenge. Again, as a child with distorted thinking, what was in my head was at times destructive. Still, something in me held on.

• • •

Being the oldest child, I felt it my job to protect my family, a duty I was born to. This was compounded even more once I knew what our uncle was like and what he wanted. Not to mention there were other little girls to protect. It meant that perhaps no one was really safe - were they? Then again, as a child, I felt if my lips remained closed with this secret,

I wouldn't upset anyone, and our family would be OK. I was fearful of judgement too, of what they would think and how they would treat me. I remember weighing it up as to whether I should tell Mel, my best mate, about Uncle Bob. She was my most trusted friend and I thought it had to be better to lose my best friend in the world than for her to get hurt by Uncle Bob if he tried anything. I worried constantly for her and hoped he would never try anything on anyone else - ever. I wrestled with this, for a long time. We must have been around thirteen or so, and I had many nights of fitful sleep, building up the courage to tell her to be careful around him.

One night when we were camping, Mel and I walked off with our tin can bongs, smoking up the campsite, and I told her. I warned her away from Uncle Bob.

'He is a bad man. You can't go near him and don't be on your own with him, whatever you do.' I said, seriously and simply.

She wanted to know why, and I can't remember if I told her what he did or merely hinted to her that he had touched me. But she knew enough, and she was angry. She said that he had always given her the creeps. I told her that he would never do anything if she were close by. So, she never left my side that weekend.

Not long after this Aunty Von wandered off through the camp, and we saw her going to the toilet behind a stump. Clearly her butt was bigger than the stump. We laughed like the silly girls we were - a welcome relief to the unbelievable tension from me taking that step to break my silence, however small that step was.

I know Mel never forgot, and it was my way to protect her from him. I swore her to secrecy. The next day, we were more subdued; not as giggly as before and there was a deeper understanding of things between us that really didn't need words. My mate had my back and I could vent my hatred of Aunty Von and Bob to her. The selfishness, the greed that Aunty Von showed…her very nature appalled us both. Mel didn't like Aunty Von either. We were very immature little girls in some ways, and very wise in others. Mum found that anger hard to placate, but finally, there was someone who may not have understood fully what was going on, but my dear and beautiful friend Mel stood by me and listened to my hurting heart.

We both grew up then and seemed to turn into adults overnight. From then on, we stayed together as much as we could. If we stayed together, Uncle Bob tended to leave me alone. At the time, he was a coach in a sporting club and would be around kids all the time. So that worried me. In giving my secret a voice, and telling Mel about this 'thing', I felt better, and I felt I had protected at least one person. It was made easier by Mel's poo jokes and endless ability to have me in fits of laughter.

After this I felt brave enough to tell a friend of the family. I don't want to say who particularly, because my secret never left her lips, and perhaps it should have. For now, we will call her Molly. I remember parts of that day very clearly; other parts are a little vague. I was petrified of telling, but I felt I could confide in her. Molly and her partner had come to visit home one day and as my mum does, she cooked an incredible lunch and Molly just adored mum's gardens.

I was walking around Mum and Dad's beautiful gardens, holding Molly's hand as we looked at the flowers and the new developments around the place. I was about twelve or so.

'Molly, I have a secret I want to tell you.'

She smiled and nodded. I have no idea what she imagined I was about to say. I then cautiously told her just enough that she had an idea of what has happening. I really didn't say much at all, because I was almost testing her with my secret; I had never told an adult before. She looked mortified. I could see fear in her face, and that scared me. I almost regretted my decision to tell her at all, and I quickly backtracked and downplayed my story.

She told me that I should tell Mum and Dad, but I said that was impossible because it was too hard and would tear the family apart. I shared that I was scared if anyone found out, what might happen. I burdened the poor lady in a way that I never wanted to, but I swore her to secrecy.

In one way, I hoped she would tell Mum and Dad for me, and then I wouldn't have to. At the same time, I hoped she wouldn't. I just wanted to break free. I was so confused, and in that confusion I was also frustrated, heartbroken, angry and jaded really. Sharing with both Mel and Molly made me feel a little stronger. I felt two people had my back. They were both safe and wise people, so perhaps I knew my secret would be safe. I longed to speak. I did. But I was also scared that something would happen to them, or me. I understand why silence is a solution for some. I also know now how it feels to break that silence, so would never choose it willingly, and I would beg you to learn from my mistake.

My prayer *now* is that Molly would know what a gift she gave me by listening to me that day in the garden. How safe she made me feel and how much we as kids all loved and trusted her. By her hearing my heart and my being able to voice what had happened, even the tiny disclosure that I had made, lifted a huge weight off my chest. I felt so much comfort in knowing that an adult knew. I only wish that as the adult I trusted, she would have felt brave enough herself to ask me more, question me gently, and tell me how I could be safe. That is after all, the real reason I wanted to tell her. I don't think that Molly had the tools to know what to do then, but today, in this time and place, there is support everywhere. I do know now, had she spoken to my mum and dad, they would have acted immediately and stopped what was happening.

I got on with things, and, thankfully, as I got older it became harder for my uncle to find time with me. It allowed me space to start healing and chase a sporting career, which had already begun on the athletics field. I was indeed good at sport and particularly great at athletics. I think I achieved champion in my age group every year. I also made it to the State Championships every year and always seemed to place in the top five for most events. Hurdles and throws were my strongest. I wanted to be the best in all of them. It is what kept me focussed and I loved it. I had already begun a healthy collection of medals, but I wanted to be the best I could.

If you are an adult reading this, know that no matter how hard it is, how much pain you think you may cause by reporting a 'secret', on the other side of the hard, yucky stuff, there is usually ultimate freedom and healing. While you may bear the burden of a disclosure from a child, the burden will be so much more if something far worse happens and you have not shared that 'secret' with someone who has the capacity to at least give you the right advice and do something about it. Unfortunately, there are young people, children, and adults even, that share this kind of 'secret' all the time with the wrong people and the words fall on deaf ears. They are dismissed, not believed or unheard. The absolute courage and strength it has taken that person to share with you has taken an entire lifetime to build. Your listening to them, your validation and your response are a vital key to them moving forward in life. If not, they may turn and shut down from life. You matter in this puzzle. If in doubt, seek appropriate, professional advice as soon as possible.

A Dream

A dream to ignite,
Inspire, desire,
Setting you alight, a fire, a fire.
Hope, passion, joy, obsession.
I dream a dream, my love and passion.

[Kelly Humphries © 1999]

1. Me and my lovely rival and best mate Mel **2.** Family portrait, me with my brother and sister. I was just starting high school.

Chapter 11
Dream My Dreams

I knew early on of this thing called 'The Human Spirit'. I can see it again like it was yesterday. From my seat in front of the TV, I watched the race that brought the world to its feet. Derek Redmond was inspiring millions across the world by defying the pain barrier. A 400-metre runner from the UK, Derek was racing in the semi-final and when he was just over the halfway mark, he snapped his hamstring. His dream was over. What he did next was incredible. He got up and hopped on one leg to the finish line, after promising his father that he would finish the race. His father ran to his side to help Derek finish, while pain and absolute devastation were written on Derek's face. I understood courage then as a child. I felt it in my heart as I cried. I didn't know I had it too. All I knew was that, like Derek, I was always going to finish the race, even if it hurt. One day, I would inspire people like that. Making silent promises to myself, something in me shifted. I was twelve.

I was glued to the television set for days. It was the Barcelona Olympics in 1992. The Spanish theme song, *Amigos Para Sempre* (meaning 'Friends for Life'), was played over and over throughout the games. One day, I saw one of those advertisements come across the screen where they play the music and highlights of the days before. Fascinated by the spirit of the Olympics, the highs and lows, I understood what *Citius, Altius, Fortius* meant: Faster, Higher, Stronger. I held onto it with all the strength I had.

How can we forget the flaming arrow from the bow of Antonio Rebollo, the Spanish archer who lit the cauldron? I remember the face of Kieran Perkins in the swimming, Kathy Watt in the women's cycling and the Australian rowing team, the 'Oarsome Foursome'. When Kieran Perkins won the 1500-metre freestyle in world record time, Australia was on its feet. I was on my feet.

Kathy Watt won a silver medal in track cycling, securing Australia's first female cycling medal. Daniela Costian in the women's discus and Tim Forsythe in the high jump both won bronze medals. I particularly loved the track and field and all the highlights that came on during the Games. I sat there in front of the television, transfixed.

It was in this space that my dreams of the Olympics started to build. I cried watching this and continue to do so every two years now - every Commonwealth Games and every Olympics. This dream is still burning a large hole in my soul, but I am so grateful for this athletic pursuit. It has brought me more friends, connections, joy, opportunities and adventure than I could have possibly imagined, especially in those early dark times. Generally, I really had nothing much to complain about on the surface. It was only in my quiet times that the self-loathing and silent, unexpressed anger bred its way into a cycle of confusion, fear and doubt. I always had a reasonably good attitude about things and tried to remain positive and optimistic on all levels. Music helped.

I was always moved by music. My dad Kevin constantly had music playing on the radio, old records or tapes and then later CDs. I grew up with Bryan Adams, John Fogerty, Poison, Suzie Quatro, Simon and Garfunkel, Dire Straits, Tina Turner, Savage Garden, John Farnham and Jimmy Barnes, to name a few. The whole family would sing all day long. I loved these times. I had a dodgy old CD player and would stick my headphones in and play music, letting my dreams play out in my mind. With that, my passion and zest for life and athletics grew.

It was at high school in Miriam Vale (which only went up to Year 10) that my athletics career started taking off and I was getting a bit of a name for myself in our local area. In fact, I just heard that I still hold several school records after all this time! I was involved in many sports and I loved what I was doing. I packed my life so full, and in doing this, it made everything else so much easier to cope with. I didn't have time to sit still and think. Again, these are the things that I hold dear to my heart, and so if you are one of those people that travelled these sporting journeys with me, I am eternally grateful for your support, love and friendship. I am still not sure this journey is completely over; I am still so incredibly passionate about it and am just not ready to let go yet!

• • •

I was still quite the cheeky child. Things at home were normal on the surface and we were growing up like anyone else. The relationship with my brother and sister hadn't changed, and Brandon and I were particularly bad at egging each other on. He usually got the better of me. But I sometimes could hold my own. One day, I played yet another trick on him, although as I remember he played many more on me. While I found it hilarious, he was to pay me back for years to come.

I had a random idea, kind of like the Road Runner on Looney Tunes, where Road Runner grabs a rope and bundles up Coyote by coiling the rope around him and then pulling it, sending Coyote flying. Well, the only rope I could find was still attached to the trailer. I called Brandon over and wrapped the trailer rope round him and kept going until his whole midsection was covered. Then, well, you know what I did. Poor Brandon. His feet barely touched the ground as I pulled, and he spun out of control. Remember, I was strong for a girl. Brandon spun so much that he spun out and around. I practically peed my pants laughing! Meanwhile he was laughing too as he was spinning… But as he came back around, he came to a stop and fell over, hitting his head on the trailer. Well, crap! I still couldn't stop laughing while simultaneously trying to ask him if he was OK. He was crying and rubbing his head.

He looked at me and yelled, 'I'm telling Mum on you!' He ran inside, and I didn't exactly dodge Mum's hand then! You probably think I was the worst big sister in the world, but don't you worry. Brandon would always get his own back. I cannot count the number of times he would have me in tears.

He was relentless in how he gave me grief over one thing or another; he never had an off button. He went on and on until I was so worked up I chased him around the house (which is what he wanted, of course) and screamed at him or found myself in tears. When I finally caught up, I punched him in the shoulder or we found ourselves in a wrestling match on the front yard, where we fought until someone got hurt. That never took long, and there was never any sympathy for us if we got hurt. At that point, tension broken, we would be reduced to fits of laughter.

My sister reminded me of one time we three kids were all at home and decided to make coconut ice but didn't have the ingredients. So, we decided on an impulsive trip to Bororen, our local town, on the pushbike. It was a good couple of kilometres away through bush, sand and creeks. So we roped up a cushion on the bike rail, where Laura sat. As I recall, I tried to make it as comfortable as possible for her, but I can't imagine it would have been that comfy! We were set to go! Brandon, Laura and I rode all the way into Bororen, and while it was a hard slog, we had a great time, not that Laura's bony little bottom thought so! We did make coconut ice, but we had no pink food colouring and ended up with the green kind! We rode this track often, sometimes a couple of times a month. Sometimes we got ourselves stuck in creek beds, mud and sand, but we loved it!

I love my brother and sister beyond belief. Despite how much we paid out on each other, Brandon and I were very close growing up, talking about everything - almost. I couldn't tell him what happened with Uncle Bob because I felt responsible for him and Laura. The protector in me was so strong. It has always remained that way, and perhaps that's why I chose a career in the police.

Even when Brandon was ten, I knew that all he really wanted to do with his life was to be a dad, and he now has a beautiful daughter, Sophie, and sons, Ian and Eli. He is an amazing father. Laura has grown up to be an incredible woman. They both have wonderful partners, and my sister has just had her second child. I am so proud of them both. Not just a little bit proud, but an overwhelming, and very emotional pride that I don't always understand. I think I realise that while they have had their struggles, in my heart, I feel like I did something good if I was able to keep that horrible part of my life away from them…and they made it. Thank God they made it. In saying that, I also know that sharing my pain with them earlier would have made life a lot easier for me, including my relationships.

There were many young men in my life - good looking, strong men. I had a few boyfriends, but none stuck because I never let them get close, and I never felt 'right' with them. They came and went. Mum always asked me about these 'boyfriends' and wondered why I didn't want to be with them, and I never fully understood. All the partners I have ever had have all been quite wonderful, including my first 'real' boyfriend Kris. He was one of those guys that just wouldn't give up! He was solid - very good looking with a darker, olive complexion and a hint of Asian surrounding his intent gaze and deep brown eyes. I met Kris on an athletics trip. He was a discus thrower who had a rather nice chest, and I thought he looked a bit like Dean Cain (one of the many Superman actors). He is still a good-looking man. I started dating Kris when I was fourteen and continued to date him on and off until I was seventeen. Kris was my formal partner in both Years 10 and 12.

We were a good couple but not destined to be anything but friends, and to this day we have managed to stay friends. He was a very tender, loving guy who showed me that not all men were terrible. I still struggled to find a deep connection with him, and for a long time I thought there was something wrong with me. I liked him a lot and loved him, but not in the way you are meant to love someone you're in a relationship with. I wouldn't say he was like a brother, but like a close friend. I don't believe I could have ever loved him or any other guy any differently. In some ways I blame this awkwardness and failure of my relationships on Uncle Bob. I realised early on that it had a lot to do with a false teaching of what love was and that I never had that innocence of a first boyfriend. I missed out on that part. I held on tight to the hope that I would 'get over it' and find someone to love me right.

I had many failed relationships as I went on, which never helped with the self-loathing, anger or frustration I felt in trying to understand why I could never get it right. I eventually realised I needed to be right for myself before I could be happy with anyone else. I spent a great deal of time trying to understand myself, rather than simply accepting who I am. Once I did understand, and accepted who I was and what I had gone through, I won many battles.

• • •

I was older now, and a little wiser and a little worse for wear, but I was doing well, mostly. My fifteenth birthday was coming up, and I invited a whole bunch of my friends. We had great fun! I had the biggest sponge cake ever, covered in cream. One of my friends grabbed a pile of cream and I bolted, with her chasing after me. I ran out into the dark of the night, and when I say dark, it was pitch black. The party was in our under-cover area, and our family car was parked at the front. My Year 10 teacher, Anita, had also come out to celebrate with us. In country areas we were a tight-knit community and Anita had become a family friend. (She's still one of my closest friends.) She had parked her nice little BMW behind our family car. There were no street signs in the bush, or streetlights for that matter. I ran right into the back of that car at full speed. I could run fast too, remember. I hit the back of that thing so hard I put a large dent in the back corner of the boot. All I could think was, *"Not the BMW!"*

As I hit the back of the car I rolled over the boot and landed on the other side, on my back on the ground. I couldn't breathe or move my left leg. I was hurt badly, and the partygoers brought a torch out and surrounded me to survey the damage. My friend was still holding the pile of cream in her hand as she looked down on me. I was so upset that I had busted the teacher's car! She wasn't mad and rather impressed at how big the dent was. I even managed to take some paint off the car! I bruised a couple of ribs and seriously damaged my knee. It has never been the same, and I can still see the spot on my knee where I impacted the car. My knee was a write-off. It blew up like a balloon and the fluid was so thick on my knee I had to have it drained. It was braced for weeks. Anita got her car fixed and repainted. Only it took more than a bit of paint and some Band-Aids to fix me.

Anita was my Year 10 Maths and Science teacher. Miss Mac was my English and Social Sciences teacher. Both women played significant roles in my life at that time and were great leaders and role models for me. Anita and I became close friends and she has been a constant inspiration and support for me ever since. Mrs Knowles was also influential. As I went through my high school days, I received awards, plaques, ribbons, medals and the like as I became involved in every sport I could. Mrs Knowles was the local newspaper representative and because I was always doing something, before too long, the whole region would know this country teenager and her big dreams, through her newspaper articles and my good friend from the Gladstone newspaper, Mr Cooke.

What I also loved was sharing some of these times with my little sister. When I was in Year 10 at Miram Vale, Laura was in kindergarten. She remembers with fondness how I took her tuckshop lunches to her and we had our lunch together under the big fig tree. Checking up on her also meant that I could share in a treat of powdered sugar lollipops… what a joy and what a precious memory! (Never underestimate the small things. These times helped me forget that in the shadows, Uncle Bob would still be there).

What is Love?

What is love to a tortured soul?
What is confusion? An act? A role?
Is it real, or a drama as such?
Does it even matter, that loving touch?
What is true to a soul who knows only lies?
What is the answer to these unheard cries?
How can you break free from what is not there?
But then how do you know? It's just not fair.
What is the truth? Is it me or You?
I am so desperate for some kind of clue.
You do what your heart says, and maybe it's right.
Then you get stuck in your own crazy fight.
You have so many dreams that you want to fulfil,
You don't need pressure, or love… better still.
You can do it, all on your own. You could also have said no.
If only you had known.

[Kelly Humphries © 1994]

1. After a very successful athletics trip, winning approximately 9 medals.
14 years old.

Chapter 12
Arise, My Strength

'You may take my innocence, but you can never have my dreams'. 'You can touch me and break me, but you can't have what only I see. You may take my innocence, but you can never have my dreams.' To keep my dreams going, and escape the dark times, I would tell myself many affirmations like these, over and over. It was like the movie starring Mel Gibson, 'Braveheart', where he says, 'You may take our land, but you will never take our freedom!' I lived for my dreams and I held on for my freedom. This is probably the reason I lived with my head in the clouds and spent so much time dreaming about the Olympics and the amazing things I wanted to do with my life. It kept me going. He could do whatever he wanted to me, but I would always have my heartbeat, my dreams, and I could always escape inside where my dreams became so tangible. No one could see them except for me. It was either that or I would succumb to the darkness and be overwhelmed and consumed. The thoughts that crashed through my mind during those times were in many ways devastating, and involved every method of escape possible... If only I had known how much of a coward Uncle Bob really was...

The times where he tried things with me were now few and far between. Most of the incidents happened when I was between about eight and thirteen years old. After this, there were probably only a handful of times. This didn't make it any easier, in fact harder, because I was older, and I was realising it was wrong. Only now it had been happening so long, I felt trapped.

Uncle Bob owned an old green Nissan Pintara station wagon with a pinstripe down the side. It had a fermented smell of children, and old food mixed with cigarettes. I felt a crushing weight on my chest every time I saw it. I remember one day seeing a car like Uncle Bob's driving past, and I experienced massive panic and instinctively wanted to run, until I realised it was not his.

One day, he turned up in his car, around my fifteenth birthday. For some reason I went with him fishing down the back of Turkey Beach, not far from Daisy Dell. It had been a long time since anything had happened between us, and while a part of me wanted to go fishing, another part didn't want to go with him. I know I desperately wanted to go fishing, but I couldn't walk anywhere and I was bored out of my brains with my knee so messed up. I also wanted to please him and I knew there was a good chance he would want to 'play' with me. Oh, the fragile balance of trying to please the predator and keep the peace.

I had asked him if we could go fishing the next time he was down. A part of me still saw 'good uncle' even after all this time, and I hoped I could just be 'normal' with him. But our 'normal' was not normal at all. For him, I guess my birthday was a good excuse to do something 'special' with me - another calculated opportunity. I was required to keep my damaged knee still in a brace or bandaged; I could barely walk. What would he be able to actually achieve while I was in this brace anyway? It had been happening so long now... would it be so bad if he did it again with me? The thoughts swirled in my head wretchedly.

I can picture the place where he stopped, but I don't remember how to get there now. We drove to a flat open area among the trees in the bush near a creek. I figured I was going to just sit on the bank and throw lines in and hopefully catch something, then I wondered if or when he would do something. The more we talked on the way down, the more I realised there probably wouldn't be much fishing. He insinuated that he wanted to have full-blown sex as he flicked a condom out of his pocket, raising his eyebrows at me.

Uncle Bob raised the back of the station wagon and laid out a sheet on the back open area so that we could lie down. He helped me get out of the car and showed me where he wanted me to go in the back. He got himself half undressed, with his pants off but his shirt on, and he lay in the back with me. He started kissing me. Part of me felt if I could just do it, maybe it would be over forever. I remember swearing that this would be the last time. I didn't want this. I also hoped that perhaps, because I wasn't little anymore, that he would never want to touch me again. Part of me simultaneously raged at him and thought of all the ways I could hurt him.

He put his hands up under my shirt, and then undid my pants, taking them off over my injured knee. He ripped the packaging off the condom with his teeth as he masturbated and put his condom on. He started pressing himself into me and rubbing me, saying how excited he was. I hated *It*. I think I still had my shirt on, but I felt completely naked and defenceless.

I felt quite anxious and panicky, my breathing getting shorter and more constricted. I felt like I was choking, and I was getting frustrated. I didn't know what to do. Looking back, I think I had a panic attack. There were images rushing through my mind, from one extreme to the next. He had his hands everywhere, and he was hurting me.

I suddenly snapped. I flipped out. I was angry. Usually I had detached myself from what was happening, but I was more focussed now and knew I could not let him do this to me anymore. My moral sense of right and wrong overtook me and I rose up like a tsunami of anger as the waves kept coming, stronger and stronger until they crashed on the shore. I was now stronger, and that anger finally overtook any obligation he had made me feel to please him. He was on top of me, and pushing himself inside me, when I suddenly lost my shit. I yelled at him, 'Why do you keep making me do this? Get off me, get off me, get off me!' I screamed hysterically at him, and with my good leg I kicked him in the chest, forcing him out the back of the car and stumbling back.

I was struggling to get up and move, with my knee the way it was and my pants off, I was desperately trying to pull myself together.

But I did it.

It was an intoxicating moment of Victory. Elation. Fear.

I yelled, 'Take me home! If you don't, you fucking piece of shit, I'll walk, and I'll tell Mum and Dad!'

I was never going to be able to run with my knee as it was, but I decided if I had to die then I would die fighting. (I was highly emotional and scared at this stage, with my head exploding with images and thoughts.) I knew he was more afraid of Mum knowing, and what she would do, not to mention my dad. So, I turned the tables on him. I threatened him. I had these visions of what might happen to me, which was quickly lost in the confusion of his cowardice. He reached forward to grab me after trying to put his pants on, and I pushed back hard as I didn't want him to touch me… I then hit him in the chest as I struggled to stand up because of my throbbing knee. I stood in that long grass, wobbling like a small foal trying to stand and I beat his chest with my fists for him to get away from me. It was the most emotion I think I have ever felt.

I was hysterically crying, furiously angry, and I was grossly disappointed that he wouldn't fight back. At the same time, I was petrified. I pointed my chin in defiance, thinking I could kill him for all he had done. I saw myself punching him in the face (a scene that often goes through my head), and yet my fists remained clenched at my sides and I gritted my teeth. I was angry that he was a coward and angry that I had not seen it before. I was angry that after all I had been through, he simply dropped his head and walked away, as if there were never any consequences for me. Like what he had done all of those years was never going to matter to me. It was like nothingness. So many emotions ran through my head and I hit rock bottom.

Working as a Police Officer, I have come up against some of the most dangerous situations I could ever have imagined; yet I would still say that this is one of the bravest things I have ever done. After all those years of suppression, I suddenly fought back. I couldn't help thinking, though, of all the 'what ifs!' Even on the job, you can get yourself into a frenzy sometimes trying to work out what if this happens or what about that? That day I couldn't stop thinking about what he was going to do to me, now that I had kicked and hit him. For all I knew, he would shoot me like one of those pigs. We were in the middle of nowhere, completely isolated. No one knew where we were; no one could see us. Fear was paramount, but my anger rose up like a bold, shining light of righteousness.

He tried to help me put my pants back on. Clearly, I was struggling, but I remember batting his hands away, yelling, screaming, 'Don't fucking touch me! Get your hands away from me; you've touched me enough already! Never again will you touch me or anyone else!' I then pointed at him and said in seething tones, '*If you ever touch my sister*, I'll fucking kill you.'

'What? What? Why would I even think of doing that?' he said.

He appeared shocked, as if he didn't know what he was doing. I suppose it was his way of trying to tell me that he would never touch Laura. She was only about five years old. I made him promise he would not touch her or my cousin Caitlin.

Uncle Bob dropped his head and appeared to panic. Honest to God, in that moment I thought he was going to retaliate and teach me a lesson for kicking and hitting him. I was half expecting him to rape me. I felt sure he would do something to keep me silent. I stood there waiting, almost in a defiant challenge. Shoulders back and chin in the air. Now, this may seem a little unfair because he had never been violent with me before. I just knew that he was a big man, he was capable and now he was cornered. These were the thoughts that raged through my head because I was just so scared at my standing up to him like that. I had NEVER stood up to anyone like this. He had no hesitation in killing animals, for example, and it could easily be me, who knows? I had no idea what he was capable of if he got angry with me. I was in unchartered territory.

Never again have I been so enraged, and I have come up against some of the nastiest and most awful people society has produced. I also felt angry with myself that I hadn't seen what a miserable coward of a man he was. He actually appeared scared. What? This man who had stood over me and taken advantage of my innocence for all those years was *scared*?

He took me home, in deathly silence, as he came to understand what had happened. The cycle was broken. He made me swear that it was not going to come out. No one would know about this secret. I don't remember much else about this encounter, my head was in chaos, but he never touched me or tried to touch me again.

It was the most awkward 25-minute drive you could imagine. When we got home I very quickly got out of the car. As fast as I could manage, I went into the house and saw Mum in the kitchen. I wanted to tell her. I wanted to cry in her arms and let everything go while she held me. I wanted so badly to pour my heart out to her, for her to stroke my hair and just talk to me as I fell asleep. I wanted to feel safe in her arms, like the little girl I once was, away from all the nasty things in my mind. But he was there, watching me and I felt I couldn't do a damned thing about it.

I felt trapped again, in a different way. I felt sure Mum knew something was up. It was the closest I had come to telling her everything. I was a pathetic mess, but I contained myself long enough to get up to my room and push down all that fear, anger and hurt into the recesses of my mind and remind myself that I couldn't tell them - why I had to keep the secret. I would be the one to tear the family apart. I would be the one who made Uncle Bob go to jail. I would be the one to make Mum and Dad unhappy. No, I couldn't tell them. It would hurt them too much. And what would they think of me? What would happen to the family? Would they even believe me if I told them?

Of course, it was not me who was to blame. It was the adult who had commenced this cycle; it was the adult that had the ability, back when I was little to have chosen differently.

I couldn't get in the shower fast enough to wash away the muckiness and shame I felt. I had so many feelings about not telling Mum and Dad and so much shame and self loathing. They would think I was dirty or a little 'whore' or would be disappointed in me. The water ran down my back, like a warm blanket, washing the tears and the disgust I felt in myself, in him, away.

We survivors fear judgement, just like we fear breaking the silence. But the truth lies in the deepest crevice of the shame we bear and the confusion that lies in its wake.

I washed his filthy smell and scent off me, scrubbing my skin and using as much soap as I could. I cried, and for the first time I thought it was probably easier if I just wasn't there. I had just won the battle of my life and I felt too tired to fight anymore. What did it matter? He was always going to be there, watching me. If I could just disappear... I felt like the layers of my skin were being peeled away and exposing every inch of my soul. I was so broken, and I just wanted it to end.

After my shower, I walked into the garden to calm myself down. Mum was busy making dinner for the barbecue that night and I worried that Uncle Bob might still be floating around the house, ever a toxic presence. Even with all the acreage we had, I felt like I could not be far enough away. I remember so clearly, because strangely enough, when you are at a heightened level of anxiety, while everything outside of your world fades away, every thought, every emotion and sensation seems to be intensified. I wondered how far I could walk before my family would notice me gone. I wondered if there was a tree tall enough to jump from. I wondered how I would tie the rope. I wondered about death, but even that I knew was wrong. If living was as easy as dying, maybe I could just disappear. I wanted to fly away. At that moment I prayed to God, 'Make me a bird, so I can fly far away.' How could I face Mum and Dad again? How could I face *him*?

I was so angry with myself at letting him do those horrible acts to me for all those years. *Now* I understand that it wasn't a matter of me 'letting him.' That manipulative, conniving, cunning man, well-practiced in his craft, wheedled his way into getting what he wanted. It was like buying a car you didn't want from the dodgiest salesman in the world. *I wish I had known how weak you were, how much of a coward you were!* How could I have comprehended that as a child though?

I now know that it was NEVER my fault. I couldn't have known any different as a kid. If you read this and think, *I know what she is talking about* or *that happened to me too*, then you must not blame yourself. It was always his or her choice; it's always the perpetrator's fault. Why? Because they are the adult. While I have a rational understanding about this now, I had to learn this the long and hard way.

I would have told someone sooner if I could have seen what this cycle was, this pattern. I had no idea. I just didn't realise until it was much too late, and I was already trapped. I tried to protect everyone, including my mum and dad, at the expense of my own sanity and innocence.

• • •

The words of my primary school principal at the time were to indirectly have one of the greatest impacts on my life. It was after I had become upset over something one day. He leant down on his knees and was so close to me. I can see his kind eyes now.

'Keep going. You have to strive to achieve,' he said. Then he placed his hand on my shoulder and gave it a gentle squeeze. The kind of reassuring gesture you just need sometimes. It was his way of telling me not to give up yet.

Not long after that, he took his own life. Things in his personal life were terrible and he had split from his wife and kids. To him, it was over, and I struggled with his death because he had believed so much in telling me to achieve, and I felt sad that he would give up on himself. He was someone I had admired so much. I spent the whole day in bed after Mum came and told me, crying my eyes out. (Mum never sugar-coats anything.) I would never forget his words to me. I would say them over and over when things got too hard and when I was battling with the depression and hurt that came from keeping my silence. I promised that I would try really hard and keep going. And I did.

With Me Still

The weight upon my heart bears down on me.
I don't know where to start; I don't know what I see.
Yet the future is in my hands, for me to do with what I please.
I will take the next step
Because my dream is with me still.

[Kelly Humphries © 1996]

1. Year 10 formal. Yes I had a lot of hair.

TOO SCARED

Smothered by an unrelenting fear.
Too scared to scream. Too scared to cry. Too scared
to even shed a tear
A simple mistake. Ever present in the mystical mind
knowledge you should have had.
Fear you don't need
Smothered by an unrelenting desire.
Too angry to scream. Too angry to cry
To LIVE or die...

The questions ever present.
Why oh why me?
Life, a whirlpool of derogatory thoughts & Lies.
A hurricane of doubt.

Smothered by my own misfortune.
Too scared to live, too scared to
Chance, too scared to Love
Too scared to care.
Too scared not to.

JUST SCARED.

Kelly Humphries ☺. © 1999

Chapter 13
Keep on Keeping on, Baked Beans and Barbed Wire

I pushed hard in all areas of my life, and I continued this pattern despite this pushing and struggling forward sometimes becoming a burden. I never fully realised this until recently, in my thirties. I tried not to be a disappointment to Mum and Dad. If only I had known that they would have loved me just the same and would have supported me. I could have talked to myself in a different way and not beaten myself up so much! The voices of people in our life really can change who we are if we listen to them. As a young girl, I couldn't have known any different.

I packed my life full of every opportunity I could. Some of these opportunities were quite unique and included scanning the school noticeboard one day with Mum and finding Olympic Lifting on the list of sports. We looked at each other and laughed. Mum said, 'You could do that; you're a brick shithouse.' I felt my heart rate pick up and wondered how on earth I would do that, amidst my being slightly offended but happy with my mum's term of endearment for me. It's true; I had become physically very strong.

So, we decided that we would try something different. I went to gym with Mum so that I could learn how to lift the bar with the right technique. There was a 'muscle man' of a gym instructor who tried to help us, but he looked awkward. Because his muscles were so tight, he clearly couldn't get the bar in the right position. We cringed. I realised I also needed to be flexible or I would look as awkward as he did.

After Mum and I had watched the muscle man nearly face-plant in the gym with all those weights above his head, he cocked his head to one side and cheekily asked, 'Do you want to have a go?'

At first I said, 'Hell, no!' It took me a while, but I did pluck up the courage and ended up lifting that bar very painfully above my head. There are essentially two lifts in Olympic lifting: The Power Clean and the Snatch. The Power Clean is not like a quick clean of the house and the Snatch is not a term for parts of one's anatomy! It's a technique for lifting the weights from the floor to above your head. You must lift the weight as technically correctly as you can, and with as much weight as you can manage, all while keeping your body weight as light as possible. It seemed I was going to have to give up the takeaway food I loved, just so I could keep my body weight down!

After some months of training at the local gym, I prepared for the regional weightlifting championships. I had to be as light as I could to get into the right weight category. I love to eat, so that was terrible from the start. The heavier I was, the more I would have to lift to match it with the big tough girls in the weight category above. But I hung in there. There were no Olympic Lifting Clubs in Gladstone and no one that could show me how to do it properly, and so I just did what I thought was best. I was used to training, so that part was not hard. I was always out in the paddock heaving things around but had never taken on weight training. Everything to this point was all running, reps and sessions at the athletics track in town. So really, weightlifting in the Olympic style was very foreign to me. Luckily, I knew how to chop wood. I would say that was what made me strong! The wood-chopping chick from the country!

Eventually, we travelled to Rockhampton and I competed in the regionals! I was so nervous, but there was a gent there who was a former Scottish international lifter and he showed me how to lock my arms out to get three white lights from the judges. He told me what to expect and relieved my fears somewhat. In weightlifting there is a platform and the weights are all placed on the bar before you go out there. There is a stage and three judges who judge your technique. You need two out of three lights to be white. You have three chances at each weight. I was so nervous, but after the judges gave me three white lights, I won my first championships and qualified for the Australian National Championships. My training continued. I learned how to hold my breath, which helped fix my chest and shoulders, so the bar would stay high. I learned to focus and how to set my feet solidly and lock myself in close to the bar. It is a sport that messes with your head. I learned more than ever before about 'mind over matter'. One of the boys at the nationals that year had sniffing salts, which were meant to make you focus; I think they made me cross-eyed! Either way, I did OK, and I won myself a silver medal.

I enjoyed my experience weightlifting and I continued to do this for a few short years, competing at all levels up to the Australian Championships. I used Olympic lifting training techniques to get stronger and faster as I became more serious about competing in all aspects of track and field. I was very good at all the events, but I could never pick one to concentrate on. I was best at hurdles and throwing events, including shot put, discus, javelin and eventually hammer throw. Whenever there was a competition I did at least five events. I loved it, and I have won hundreds of medals, plaques and trophies with athletics. Although I am happy with many of my performances, I always wanted more and never seemed to get that breakthrough in sport that I wanted.

It wasn't that I wanted more medals, I was looking for something else … and if I could put my finger on it, it might sound something like 'Unscathed Beauty!

Then, however, I was dreaming of being like Melinda Gainsford or Cathy Freeman. I wanted to be like Joanna Stone; agile, inspiring and someone that made a difference to all the young athletes climbing through the ranks.

I was never totally happy with my results, or maybe just never happy with me. A couple of fellas at school would sometimes give me grief and say things like, 'Where are you going to put that medal?' or 'Are you going to pin that to your chest too?' These weren't big things, but they were said with sarcasm and it hurt, because firstly I felt like I was a nice girl and fairly humble about things, and secondly, these boys didn't understand me and how hard I worked. What they said stayed with me. I knew that I made Mum and Dad proud. Grandma Peggy and my dad Gary were always behind me and the plethora of friends who we had adopted into our extended family. Where was my resilience, that a few boys from school could so easily hurt me? I didn't know.

What I feel was most important was the journey and how I never gave up. I learned this from listening to the Olympic ideal by the father of the modern Olympic Games, Pierre de Coubertin, and holding it very close to my heart:

'The most important thing in the Olympic Games is not to win, but to take part, just as the most important thing in life is not the triumph but the struggle. The essential thing is not to have conquered but to have fought well.' - Pierre de Coubertin

So, I fought well. At the end of the day I had to decide that I needed to be OK with how I played the battle, my decisions and who I was while the war was being fought. Even if it hurt, I knew I would always come out on the other side.

I also felt that whatever I did was never quite good enough or pleasing enough and sometimes barely satisfactory. I was a perfectionist, yet was finding that with big expectations came big disappointments. When you set your goals so high, it can be very damaging if the goal you set is unrealistic. I had small goals, but as soon as I got there I was quickly focussing on the next thing, and only now do I realise how much I should have taken the time to appreciate each stage I was at and what I had achieved.

I found it difficult to take criticism, and I was very hard to correct, although eager to please. Criticism made me angry - how dare I get something wrong. I always tried to get it right the first time and avoid any form of criticism. Why? Criticism, especially given in the wrong way, made me feel ashamed… a shame I hid. It made all those worthless feelings come up that I tried so desperately to avoid. I had fought hard on my own, and I had fought to protect what was essentially the only thing I felt held me together. So, any criticism about anything only added fuel to my fire. For example, throughout my life I have based some of my decisions on what people said I *wouldn't* achieve. When I said that I wanted to write a book, I was told by some people (very close to me) 'What else are you going to do? You are never going to write a book!' or 'Just another thing you will add to your list.' I remember feeling angry and defensive as I heard those words, but I swallowed that. In my head I said, 'Fuck you, I will so…' but to them I politely said, 'You don't know that.' Guess what? I wrote a book. Want to know a sneaky secret…? You say, 'Yes Kel, I would love to know a secret…' There are at least two more books to come after this. 'Yay, Kel…! I will have 67 copies, please!'

Despite this determination and stubbornness to succeed, deep in my subconscious an element of me was (and still is) deathly afraid of succeeding as I didn't feel worthy.

I was just not good enough! I am still fighting desperately to fully rid myself of this and believe that I am worth it! I will NOT let him or anyone else tell me that it cannot be done. I must strive to achieve and maintain that victory over my thinking! I know many kids are the same and give up on themselves; they don't see the point of even trying. I struggled. At times I felt I could keep going, but then I'd think, *what's the point?* I was up and down all the time. I longed to break through with athletics, to throw that big throw, to run that super-fast time. I just could not focus on one thing and felt like I didn't deserve success.

I should note that I was also burdened, or gifted if you like, with two extra bones in my feet. They call it an 'Exostosis'. The bone in my right foot was quite large and sat at the top of my foot, and I eventually had this bone surgically removed because it was so painful. The left one wasn't too bad, and I could bear that one. I had only one foot done, as my family couldn't afford to pay for two lots of surgery. I still have flat feet and a longstanding patella tilt problem with my left knee. I don't suppose it helped much, running at full sprint into the back of Anita's BMW! My kneecap sits on my lateral side and when I do a lot of training or too much of anything it flares up. It's a constant problem! My knees or ankles, and eventually my feet, are usually in strapping tape. So, all these issues challenged my resolve to keep going. Back then I was literally being held together by bandages, stubbornness and desperation to succeed despite my doubts.

• • •

All the physical farm work I did kept me naturally very strong, like carrying big hefty bricks and timber around and riding my bike up and down the road. I dug up the garden, shovelled gravel and sand, mowed lawns and whipper-snipped. This gave me a good back workout and resulted in very shaky arms afterwards. I lifted Mum's bags of groceries and stole all her tins to make dumbbells, so I had some weights to lift. Sometimes Brandon and Laura would join me on the front yard, and while I did push-ups, my five-year-old sister and ten-year-old brother did a kind of aerobics with legs and butts in the air pointing to the sun. We had fun.

I worked hard, dreaming of what I could do with my baked bean cans as weights and our barbed wire fences as makeshift hurdles! I kept training at home in as many ingenious ways as I could figure. I would even hurdle the barbed wire fence - I didn't want to go to hospital for having hurt myself in certain places! At least I would make sure that I got over the fence! Most of it was just how we grew up, so 'training' was also Mum and Dad's way of making us do chores, I'm sure of it! We were expected to help out, and while we may have whinged, we also enjoyed it.

We couldn't always get to official training, so I would throw in the paddock, running around in my funny coloured spandex! Mum learned to coach athletics and became the driving force behind what we were doing. Brandon was a great athlete too, excelling in the jumping events. He was also an excellent soccer player (which I will now refer to as Football). Laura was still quite little but eventually did do a couple of years of Little Athletics, her long legs and height allowing her to win over most adversaries.

I received a lot of encouragement from both dads. Gary, over the phone, would always say how proud he was and did support financially if the need arose, but I had my own struggles with this. We developed a better relationship as I got older, but the old promises not being fulfilled always hurt me and damaged what relationship we had when I was younger. Thank God things are better now; in fact, we are very close, and I believe I have come to appreciate him on different levels for the support he has shown me when I have least expected it. I am grateful because many have no family, or a split family, and no support. I am very blessed in this aspect.

My dad Kevin would often yell at me from the veranda with a beer in one hand and point down the paddock, telling me to do another lap. Or he would be driving us to our sporting events. While Mum and Dad really didn't have much, they did everything they could to make sure we kids got what we needed. They invested in our future as best they could. Mum coached a lot of the kids I went to school with, too. This was great for Mum, who was denied these opportunities as a kid; it was a practical way for her to be involved and I was very proud of her.

By this time the whole community was hopeful that I would achieve my big dream. I felt the pressure of those dreams building. Everyone had high hopes for me and I hated to disappoint. Every week there was training and every couple of weekends I would go away to compete at Bundaberg, Maryborough, Townsville or Mackay in Queensland and to Athletics State or National Championships halfway across the country. I cannot tell you the number of raffle tickets we sold (well, mostly my mum) to help me raise money to go places. Thank you if you were one of those amazing people who showed your support. I qualified to compete at the State and National Athletics Championships every year from when I was twelve. I won many accolades throughout the years, including two Australia Day Awards, scholarships, grants, plaques and medals, for athletics, weightlifting and softball. I did extremely well for a little farm girl. As I neared the end of Year 10 at the tiny high school that was Miriam Vale, I needed to start thinking about where I would go next.

A friend of mine had an uncle who was a teacher and Head of Physical Education at an all-girls school in Toowoomba called Fairholme College. He was coming down to Gladstone to see her family. They told him about how well I was doing, and he wanted to see 'my form'. That started a ripple effect of negotiations between my family and the school, which meant I was able to attend this incredible place. Me? Little farm girl, Kel? How did that happen? Fairholme College was one of the best athletic schools in Australia.

As I remember, my parents took out a large loan to send me to the College for my senior years (11 and 12). I also received a scholarship for athletics, but I never knew how much this covered. In fact, like most kids, I had no idea how much my education cost my parents. Fairholme College was a huge step away from my tiny little country school. I never thought in my wildest dreams that I would ever have an opportunity to go to such an expensive school.

One of the things that I was worried about, besides having to leave my bush home, was that I would have to wear skirts all the time (of all the things to worry about). I didn't even own one! What a drag! I just didn't wear that kind of stuff - too girly! Mum and I had to go shopping and I remember how uncomfortable I was, even more uncomfortable because Mum wanted to get stuff with pretty flower patterns. Ugh! (To this day, I hate flowery patterns!)

We could only get a few skirts because it was already costing a fortune to send me to school. Mum, in all her wisdom, bought me a maroon corduroy skirt and jacket set, thinking it would be nice and warm in Toowoomba's very cold winter. It looked like it was out of the *Dr. Quinn, Medicine Woman* era. I know she meant well…and I remember nodding and smiling politely, saying, 'I'm just not sure, Mum, but OK.' I thought she was a nut, trying to get me in that; it stayed in the back of my closet the whole time I was at the school. There really wasn't much room in my closet. No doubt it's probably still there at Fairholme College, somewhere hidden and infested with moths. Sorry, Mum! Maybe it found its way to the drama school's costume department!

It was arranged that I would buy some second-hand uniforms from another girl who had previously attended the school. She was a strong, solid girl like me, so her clothes would fit. We drove a long way into the bush to buy these uniforms. I had so many questions to ask. I sat there having tea and trying on these uniforms, feeling a bit apprehensive. She assured me it was going to be fine. I'm sure the uniform itself cost more than Dad would earn in a month. But I was so proud of that uniform.

I said goodbye to my Miriam Vale and Bororen community at the School Awards Night by dressing up in the Fairholme College uniform with long woollen skirt, tie, hat and blazer! It was the end of the year and stinking hot and I remember thinking, *how on earth am I going to wear this bloody thing every day?* I did a monologue of a schoolgirl and forgot every line except the first three! I made the rest of it up, but that just made me sweat more! I'm not sure anyone noticed…except my English teacher.

That Christmas was a hard one, but it was also exciting. I was embarking on a new journey with a mixture of trepidation and excitement. I knew I was never coming home again; well, I didn't think that I would, other than to visit my family. We had a big barbecue and I said goodbye to all the neighbours and family. It was time to start my new life.

I made a vow to myself; I promised myself that I would do what my primary school principal had told me. I would make everyone proud and I would achieve success at any cost. To do this I would avoid clique groups and would not waste time on the small things. I was going to train hard and be the best athlete I could be. I would strive to achieve and do all I could to keep my head up.

Bronze to Bororen teenager

By ROY COOK

Outstanding Bororen teenager Kelly Humphries clinched a bronze medal to help hoist Queensland to prominence in the Australian weightlifting championships in Brisbane on the weekend.

Humphries, in her first year in the sport, produced a personal best lift of 97.5kg to take third place in the under-16 70kg schoolgirls division.

She was considered unlucky not to claim the silver medal after appearing to equal the effort of the second-placegetter who had a heavier body weight.

But Humphries' lift for silver was not considered because of a technicality.

Queensland dominated the women's section of the national championships, winning the open (56 points), under-20 (45), under-16 (55) and under-16 (47) divisions.

Humphries, 15, earnt Queensland

selection for the nationals after taking the silver medal at the state championships in June — just two months after starting in the sport.

West Australia's Grayden Spinks blew away all opposition in the men's super heavyweight division at the Australian championships with a total lift of 307.5kg.

Spinks' total was 27.5kg heavier than second-placed Anthony Martin (Queensland) who was followed by South Australian Shane Donaghey, another 25kg back with a lift of 255kg.

In the 108kg heavyweight division, Peter Bandjak, from SA, won with an enormous lift of 342.5kg, followed by Queenslander Craig Wegert (317.5kg) while Victorian youngster McGregor Hall was third (290kg).

Victoria had a cleansweep of the men's teams event, winning the open, under-20 and under-16 divisions.

Humphries' bronze medal completed a big week on the sporting arena for the Bororen farm girl who will attend boarding school in Toowoomba next year.

She broke the under-16 shot put record on the way to snaring three gold medals at the annual Maryborough track and field carnival.

Her 10.68m shot put effort erased the previous record, ironically set by former Bororen athlete Sally Christensen.

Humphries also won the under-16 discus and javelin events at the Maryborough day-night carnival in an ideal warm-up for next week's Queensland Secondary Schools Track and Field Championships in Brisbane.

Kelly Humphries

Page 24 — The Gladstone Observer, Tuesday, October 8, 1996

1. One of my many newspaper articles in the local paper. Very much full of hopes and dreams.

DISSAPPOINTMENTS

Disappointments can tear and break your heart
You just have to make a new start
Lift your head high and start anew
Believe in yourself and what you
can do.

For it doesn't matter how far you fall
But How far High
You can make
it back

Kelly Humphries © 1996.   (15410)

Chapter 14
Jump and Jive, My New Life

My heart hammered in my chest. We were getting further and further away from our comfortable house in the bush. Through the rear window the trees were a blur as we sped past. I was afraid. 'What's it going to be like? How am I going to leave Mum and Dad, Brandon and Laura? I won't know anyone... But at least they won't know him. I can start new and fresh. I won't see him anymore. Thank God for that.' I started to feel hopeful. As we pulled up in the big round driveway in front of the old school house in our dodgy, dust-covered red Ford, a stark contrast to the beautiful and very inspiring school buildings, I was in awe. The original schoolhouse, an old Queenslander, reminded me of the house of my dreams. Despite a few stares at our cantankerous and yet trusty old Ford, I felt excited as I got out of the back of the car in my skirt, stepping into a world of unknowns and my new boarding school home.

For the first time in many years, my heart was full, and I was happy. Finally, a chance for me. I didn't have to worry about looking over my shoulder for him, my tormentor, to steal my joy, my life. He was history and I had achieved a small victory, for now. That opportunity was allowing me to move on, to push on. It was one thing I could do, at which I was well practised. I had come from a place that felt like I had very little (really, I had everything and more) to this place of opportunity and education. This was a place where my dreams had a chance to become a reality, and I swore to make it work. I had come from the depths of this horrible abuse, shrouded in fear, to be given a chance. I was not going to let what he did ruin my life. That was the most important decision I could make, and I could control that much. I was in charge of my future and my own destiny.

Still, there was one thing I knew (well, I thought I did), and that was that in a big place like this, I was a nobody. I wasn't sure anyone would want to know me. Instantly, I was homesick, and within two weeks I was on the phone, sobbing, having my first noticeable panic attack. I felt so alone in this big place! The school was overwhelming, with girls from every walk and way of life, from far across Australia and Papua New Guinea. It seemed like all the girls' families ran big businesses and had big lives. Everyone seemed to have what they wanted. I felt inadequate. I felt lonely. I felt scared. I missed my mum, my dad, my family and the 'Daisy Dell Clan', our close-knit community. I missed Mum's cooking and the smell of the wood stove. I wanted to go home. I would understand down the track that we all had problems. Many girls' families struggled, but believed in what the school could offer.

School was harder than I thought it would be. I had good grades at my little country school, but all these girls were so smart! I felt I couldn't match them and felt as small as a mouse. I felt intimated by some girls. I wasn't used to that. At my previous school I had always been very popular and a friend to everyone. My other school was so small and you knew everyone. I was always busy doing stuff with everyone, playing Football with the boys at lunch or training. We ran around like idiots, played handball and got all sweaty and gross. I was involved and we had fun together. There was no pretence, no problems.

Here were these girls I had no idea about… We were ladies at Fairholme College and ladies didn't play handball, right? Who was I? A little chick from the bush with a big heart on her sleeve; I realise now that I was sadly lacking in self-esteem.

I wasn't prepared for this new thing, this school, and struggled to deal with the issues surrounding us. While I never chose a group to hang out with all the time, I eventually developed some close friends who I would pour my heart out to. They would become the supportive, encouraging people I could rely on and spend my lunchtimes with. They didn't judge me because I didn't have a pair of wrangler jeans or boots, RM Williams' clothes or a fob chain. I didn't have any of those things, but I did have sport! Soon I would learn that handball was a tiny exercise in comparison to the sports on offer at Fairholme College. Ladies didn't play handball, but they played almost everything else, hard, and to a standard I could not fathom. I was excited by the sporting opportunities available. Sport helped me immensely, and my sporting talents gained me some credibility.

In hindsight, I had come from a very bad ending. I had only just told my uncle in August the year before, that he was never to touch me again. Regarding the girls that I felt judgement from, well, no doubt part of it was my own self-judgement. I didn't know that then, but I do now. Most of the girls were amazing, but there were a few, one group of girls, which would challenge me as I went along, in every way possible. I had many tears at night. They would never know how I felt, but often their teasing and smart comments just hurt. Even though I struggled and felt incredibly alone at times, I kept going, smiling at everyone and doing what I could to help others. It got easier, of course. Everything gets easier with persistence. I had no idea that I was, in fact, inspiring many of them!

I only learned this at the end of my senior year. We did yearbooks and the girls wrote positive affirmations about each other. All of mine said similar things, and I guess it made me realise is that you should never underestimate the power of your influence, big or small. I am ever grateful for the time I had at this school and the amazing network of friends that I now have. 'The girls on the hill' we were collectively called - and probably a few other choice names by our rival schools. I loved these friends, and when I listened to their hearts and their thoughts I came to understand that we all had big dreams, big aspirations and ideals for our future. We were all the same, every single one of us girls, but we were crossing paths and travelling different journeys.

• • •

I ended up really shining at this school. I grew in leaps and bounds; I excelled in everything I set my mind to. Despite what I projected, though, inside my head my perspective of things was quite distorted. I may have looked like I had confidence, and I probably had more than most, but I really didn't feel it. I was a mess inside, and while I remained focussed I always had a fight on my hands to keep it together. I would often feel an inner battle and learned to fight and control my emotions and maintain my composure. I often felt like I could never do enough; that is, I couldn't say no. I always had to prove myself. I do think this need came out of my childhood trauma. Trying to please people, to keep peace and avoid confrontation. It is only through my persistence in facing these challenges that I have been able to identify this and move forward.

When I first started in the boarding house, I was in a room with about nine other girls. Every term, we rotated dorms so it was fair amongst the girls, and sometimes there were only two people to a room. You never knew what you were going to get. The first dorm was called 'Lower Black'. Each dormitory wing had a name: Nancy Shaw, Upper and Lower Black House, Cameron House, House Dorm and Spreyton House. Black House was one of my first. Each floor had a Boarding Mistress, and in true boarding house style, we girls gave them no end of trouble. They came knocking on our doors in the morning to get us out of bed and at night to demand lights out. The ladies were beautiful characters; some wielded the iron fist and some were like adopted mothers to those of us who missed home.

In the morning the music would play over the PA system to wake us up, but most of us buried our heads under the blankets and went back to sleep until the Boarding Mistresses came around again and dragged us out of bed! When it was deathly cold, we stayed in our blankets for as long as we could.

The second room I was in only had four girls in it, so it was much better. My bed was adorned with a quilt Mum had lovingly sewed together; with red and cream patchwork squares and my room had some touches of home. There was a picture or two, a stack of 'stuff' hidden on my shelf, a brown paper bag with 'fizzer' lollies, a few keepsakes and lots of 2-minute noodles - the staple diet of boarding students, along with toast! Oh, vegemite toast and chicken noodles, how I love thee! Late at night, before lights-out, we would smash down two to four pieces of toast or a big bowl of noodles. Sometimes, if we were lucky, we had the Continental Pasta bags that stunk out the whole boarding house.

We sat around in the common rooms watching our favourite shows, or if you had assignments, then you ate at your desk and stayed up as long as you could to get it done. I ate like a horse and my favourite meal was breakfast. Sometimes dinner wasn't as good, but we were certainly fed well. In the evening some girls were buried in books, and me, well, usually I was training until late and sometimes only got back just before lights out at about 11pm. I often had a packed dinner from the boarding house kitchen when I had late night training, but I was always still hungry afterwards and needed to get my homework done. I could never eat enough food!

It was funny; I was always one of the last to leave the dining room in the morning. I certainly got my money's worth. Back then there was a push from Rob De Castella, a famous Australian runner, that a good breakfast should include cereal, milk, toast, fruit and juice. When I sat down to eat my breakfast, I would make sure all the items were there; I was in training, wasn't I? I would frequently have my cereal, bacon, an egg or two, two pieces of toast and fruit with yoghurt. Morning tea was only about two hours away, but I was always starving by then. I craved Mum's home-cooked food.

My love for my food showed. I had huge legs, mostly just strong. I wasn't overweight; I was, just as my mum had said, 'a brick shit house'. In athletics I ran around in a two-piece suit, which consisted of a crop top and bike shorts. That was the uniform of the Fairholme College Athletics Club, which was my primary reason for coming to this school. I think I still looked all right in that, mostly. I remember seeing a photo of myself and my thighs were so large they used to touch. I could back squat around 160 kilograms or so, but I still hated that my thighs touched! I was an Olympic Lifter who competed in everything I could, including pole vault. Mostly I was a thrower: discus, shot put, javelin and hammer. I was also a 100-metre and 200-metre sprinter, and did sprint hurdles, high jump, long jump and whatever event I wanted to do. So, I became a heptathlete (a person who competes in seven events over two days and the best overall average is the winner). My strongest events were the hurdles and the throws.

There were trials in every term to play sports, and there was a smorgasbord of amazing things to choose from: Football, touch, tennis; you name it, we could do it. I got very overwhelmed with what to choose! If you didn't do it in school, you could instead do it outside school. Some successful athletes had attended our school, including Liz Hepple (cycling), Cathy Freeman (400-metre Olympic champion) and Danielle Leish (Australian synchronised swimming). I chose Football for my school sport. I had only played with the boys at school, so I really didn't know how to play 'proper' Football. It turned out I was pretty good. Since I was one of the fastest sprinters in the school, naturally I could beat most girls to the ball. Then I would give it away again. Generally, I know this is not the aim of the game, but I lacked ball control at first. The coach thought I was alright though and I got picked in the Fairholme A-team and became their striker. I was never perfect, but I was hard to catch. I just had to learn to control the ball and my speed together, which I did, eventually. In my first year playing school Football I got picked for the Darling Downs (regional) team and played at the state championships.

I started to play with the Reserve Grade and Premier League teams in Toowoomba as part of the Brisbane Premier League and the Toowoomba Raiders Open Women's team. There was an amazing cohort of girls at the school who were incredible players to train and play with, week in and week out, including two girls who would later play for the Matildas Australian Women's Football team.

I made the state Football teams for the next four years, something that I would not have thought possible, since I had only played for twelve months previously. It was something I couldn't live without, once I had found a love for the game.

The following term was the start of the athletics season and I also played volleyball in local fixtures. I loved serving and spiking and sliding all over the floor. I had many burn marks and holes in my clothes from this. Obviously, Mum wasn't happy because I had to buy new ones and they cost money!

I loved school and boarding life. Although I wasn't as clever as some of the other girls, it didn't mean I couldn't be if I set my mind to it. My focus was on sport and not academics, obviously, but I had promised myself I would do my best in everything. I found satisfaction in knowing I had given everything my absolute best, and that is all anyone could have ever asked of me. I packed as much life as I could in one day and felt that I had accomplished something by the end of it. I was also grateful for any opportunity that allowed me to do that.

• • •

Many of the girls longed for home. There were some that owned massive sheep farms and properties on thousands of hectares across Queensland. I was fascinated by this life and loved hearing snippets of these girls' lives at home. I wished they would take me home with them and teach me how to be a jillaroo. I think they must have desperately missed home cooking like I did, because one night, coming back from Football training, I went to the common room and found all the boarders were in the worst trouble I had ever seen, and the meal room was in lockdown. The girls had planned and carried out a dining room food-fight. I'd had no idea about it, which was good in many ways because I escaped punishment. I was directed to go and get my dinner and to return to the common room. On the way I saw how the dining room looked … Awful!

One of the girls, who will remain nameless, had concocted the plan and hit the lights, plunging the dining room into darkness. Then there was a mighty free-for-all. Mashed potato went flying around in the dark. It was everywhere; in fact, every food item possible covered the surface of the dining room. I'm not sure that I had even heard of such a thing happening at the school before or ever since. But there were some hungry girls that night. I had never seen them looking so sorry for themselves, picking mashed potato and gravy out of their hair for days to come. The silence in the air was petrified and I didn't know where to look. It was talked about for many days. The boarding staff eventually found out who the instigators were but couldn't prove who was the mastermind. I'm just glad I wasn't on clean-up duty!

• • •

I often worried about Brandon and Laura and missed them and home terribly, but I grew to love being a boarder. I called the family as much as I could through the week. I had an 1800 reverse call number, luckily! Being busy helped take care of being homesick, and I embraced my life in the boarding house.

I was still trying to continue with my Olympic lifting, on top of the other things I was doing. There was a local weightlifting centre at the Toowoomba State High School, but to get to this would prove difficult, and Mum and Dad couldn't afford taxis for me to go to training. So one of the parents of a day student helped me, bless her. Though I was ranked number two in Australia in my weight category back then, I had to slowly let weightlifting go. I was so heavily involved in athletics and Football and all the other school commitments, so I just couldn't fit anything else in.

My week generally consisted of training nearly every afternoon until about 5.30/6.00 pm. There were two nights of Football training until late, two lunchtime school Football trainings and two mornings of volleyball training. If I wasn't playing Football in the afternoon I was training for athletics. I was preparing for the heptathlon, but my love for athletics was in the throws. Multi-events suited me best. My problem was that I wasn't great at one thing. I was having so much fun doing everything that it never really occurred to me that I should focus totally on one thing.

Hammer throw was one event I had never done before and no one at Fairholme College really knew much about it back then. The long jump coach had some idea and showed me how to hold it, wind it around my head and let it go. I gave it a go and so became a hammer thrower! I then had an awesome coach, Miss Brownlie. She was a teacher in the school but became more than a hammer coach, being a source of advice, reasoning and friendship as the years progressed. I was in Year 11 and breaking records in the beginning, especially in the hammer, despite having no real idea of what I was doing. I qualified to compete in the Australian Champs and for the next few years I improved at throwing overall. I met another coach, Brad, who pulled me aside and asked if anyone had ever shown me how to throw a hammer effectively. Well, no they hadn't really; I only knew how to hold it and let it go. Brad offered to give me a hand and soon became my hammer coach and a friend that I still have to this day. (In fact, if there is anyone who has watched my struggles and seen me rise and fall, it is Brad. Thank you, my friend.)

I have never won at the Aussie National Champs for hammer throw (yet). I always placed in the top eight. I have only missed about five national championships in the last 20 years of my competing in athletics. For four of these, I was in another country, where I competed in their national championships. I competed at international events and did well also, but that was a different field of competitors. I struggled to have consistent training and stay injury free. Something was lacking in my spirit as well, and while I have always been passionate about sport and competing, I haven't found that 'thing' that takes me from that place to winning and placing in the major and international competitions. I am still working on this, and while I have mastered my thinking in some areas, in others I still have some work to do.

Sport ruled my life, and despite my best attempts at being a great student I was just your average student who excelled in sport and maintained a 'satisfactory' report card. I excelled in English and Health, but for the other classes I managed passing grades, having a few C's, a few B's and even an E. One class I failed completely and needed to do something else. I loved learning, but I loved sport more.

The athletics and swimming carnivals were the biggest, most memorable events of the Fairholme College calendar. I think this is where I fell in love with the spirit and hype of things. The atmosphere fostered our ability to strive hard, not only for ourselves but also for our teams or our sporting house. It was the fun spirit of competition, the friendly and encouraging nature of the girls and the desire to see their friends succeed, even when they didn't, or couldn't, that I loved. It was amazing to watch these events unfold before our eyes, like a feeling of euphoria that I never had before… I fell in love with the spirit of our school at my very first event.

Needless to say, the girls were very successful in their sporting endeavours across the board. The adage about surrounding yourself with success would always ring true. When we were all pushing hard and cheering each other on, despite any differences, you felt you could do anything. We were more than schoolmates. We lived together, ate together and experienced a multitude of amazing events together. Many nights were spent crying on each other's shoulders, sharing each other's hopes and dreams and believing in each other. We shared a genuine love that was family. Without each other we would not be the people we are today. There was very little bullying, though it did happen as it does in every school. Generally, it was minor. There was always a constant desire for all of us to be successful on any level. I am grateful for this, the lessons along the way and the friendships.

———————————

The Map

Let your heart and soul guide you on this rough trek through life.
You never know when you need them, for they guide you better than a
map.
A map shows you the roads, but your heart will always tell you which
one to take.

[Kelly Humphries © 2000]

1. Year 11 school portrait. I was so proud to wear this uniform. **2.** My first
night in the school boarding house on Grandma's homemade quilt.

Chapter 15
Succeed if You Dare

The beauty about dreams is that you own them. People don't always need to know what's in your head, but at the end of the day, no one can take those dreams from you. I have been blessed by the many influential people that have touched my life in some way. I have learned who I can trust. But really, I have had to come to a place where I accept who I am and take ownership for my future regardless of anyone else in my life. I won't pretend I have it all figured out, because I don't. But I sure have come a long way. I am an overcomer.

At the end of Year 11, leading into my senior year, I was crowned Athletics Co-captain with my good friend Stacey. It was an honour; I had only been at the school for twelve months. In Year 12, we competed in the Knockout Athletics competition, where schools put their best athletes forward in a nation-wide inter-school competition. The school with the most points won the elusive title of Knockout Champions. We were the best school in Australia at this stage for the ninth consecutive year, winning every year since 1992. We did this at a state level and then travelled to a national venue to compete. This was a tradition of excellence at the school and one that I was proud to be asked to lead as the co-captain.

Getting involved at school and being a part of something that was bigger than me helped me to do things independently and with conviction. I learned valuable skills, like the ability to network and encourage people, embracing differences, and I challenged myself to find things within me that I never really knew existed. These competitions, sporting endeavours, the team and this whole school journey ignited fires in me and propelled me forward to new heights. It is easy to overlook the importance of our school years and the opportunities before us. I had been given the opportunity of a lifetime. School was hard because I was hard. Because I had a passion and I had found something to pour myself into, I embraced life and all it threw at me. I was so grateful for my parents and their sacrifice to send me to that school. It was a wonderful opportunity that was so very rare, and for that I am so grateful.

For many, I think education is taken for granted. I think this is partly because we don't understand our purpose and unique value. On top of that, *I believe we miss out on things because we are conforming to some label we assign ourselves, or we live out poor statements and words that have been spoken over us by others*. I realise much of what I allowed myself to think would not always serve me well. These labels could be anything, like 'hopeless', 'fat', 'poor', 'single parent', or, for me, 'poor farm girl', 'worthless', 'not good enough', 'no one is going to want me' and 'injury-prone'. Sometimes, we may find ourselves conforming to someone else's idea of who we should be and what our lives should entail, rather than what we desire for ourselves. If only we allowed ourselves the opportunity to try and be our best, to achieve new things and learn great lessons, we would move forward and have a greater sense of achievement in our lives. I never wanted to miss an opportunity. I wanted to be successful. I felt better about things when I learned to **be** better at things. So, I worked hard. And I dreamed.

One person who allowed me to dream uncharacteristically, and without restraint, was Mary-Anne, a Fairholme College swimming coach who came to our school from Portland, Oregon in the USA. I found her, and her American accent, enthralling. She told me about her life in America and what university there was like. It sounded incredible and made me so excited. I was captivated. Something changed in me. I didn't know what it was yet, but something inside had come alive.

Mary-Anne gave me permission to dream freely about things that young bushwhacker farm girls couldn't imagine. She allowed me to think anything was possible. It was because of this encouragement that I decided I wanted to go to the USA for university. I started to feed the idea and was looking at colleges, envisioning this kind of life for myself.

I was almost in Year 12 and my imagination was filled with a sea of colour and ideals. It seemed almost impossible for someone 'like me'. Some people quickly tried to quell this dream. Perhaps the negativity was simply because few people had done it before, well, not that they knew of. But I was going to do it!

This was a battle I had to win. I needed a challenge, something that was going to set me free. I had felt bound for so long, like I was under the weight of several chains bolted to the floor. Fairholme had opened doors and provided an amazing platform to commence my 'diving career'. (That is, diving into everything that would come my way!) I was absolutely loving and embracing my senior years and felt it was important to do as much as I could with the life that I was given. This was partly because I knew my parents worked so hard for me to be there and also because I was grateful for being able to attend this school. I also wanted to help and inspire others, so I did not want to fail. I had expectations I needed to live up to and perhaps, on some levels, I wanted to prove something to myself. Succeed if you dare, and dare to succeed.

This American dream I was playing with was exciting and uplifting. I wanted that! I wanted to do something for me that was big and bold. You see, at boarding school, even though I had lots of friends, I felt incredibly alone with my thoughts at times, and there were often tears. I think in many ways I was grieving, as I look back now I was also healing, learning and growing. I have no doubt many of us were crying, for different reasons. Missing home was one of them, but the rest I believe was finally allowing myself the chance to let my guard down.

I still hadn't spoken to anyone about what had happened to me. I just pushed it all aside in the pursuit of chasing my dreams. I couldn't tell anyone about my secret, and despite developing some anxiety and panic attacks I didn't understand, I buried it so far down, and filled my life up with whatever I could to fill that aching place in my heart. I don't think I realised how much it was affecting me and so I pushed it aside and keep doing what I felt I had to. When I reflect back, I believe I had serious depression, but I just didn't allow time for myself to fall into the pit. I still prayed, and I believed that I would heal.

I continued to talk to Mary-Anne and ask her about the USA every chance I could get. She answered my thousands of questions with the utmost of patience and gave me ideas on how I would go about getting there. I lived with my head in the clouds while I allowed this crazy dream to consume me. Was it even possible? When I look back I can agree that I was a solid track and field athlete, and I had learned to play Football and play it well. Yet I doubted myself so much. Will they even look at someone who only picked up a ball and played a proper game twelve months ago? Will they even look at someone who hasn't quite been able to win a national medal in athletics? Do I have what it takes? Nevertheless, I decided I would give it a go. At the very least, I owed myself that much!

I had a few sceptics. While on one hand this fuelled my doubt, on the other it cemented my stubborn conviction (quite the dichotomy). One of my sceptics was a girl I played Football with, who was very talented. I admired her but for some reason spent a great chunk of my time feeling like I had to measure up to her. That was never going to work, because we should never measure ourselves against another; success is different for everyone. Her opinion of me mattered. It shouldn't have, but I wanted her to see me for who I was. I don't know what it was, but I wanted her approval and cried many tears trying to get it. I don't even really know why, but when she was critical of me it hurt, and I let it get me down. What it also did was make me push harder, train longer and try even more. She also taught me a great deal about myself, and how to play the game, showing me kindness and patience. So, I'm grateful. Other sceptics were people I admired and trusted. People I looked up to. Their scepticism hurt also.

It was enough to stop me for a while and push my plans aside, believing what they said, that I was not good enough. Never one to ultimately roll over and die - I always seemed to go the long way around, sidestep and take longer than I needed to while I assessed every angle instead of just taking the leap - I didn't let the doubt beat me. It was only a detour. I started to entertain the idea again that I might have half a chance and there was no harm in trying. I researched schools (universities) in the USA, repeatedly. All I could see was a mass of colour and opportunity. I looked at Washington State, Virginia Tech, Texas A&M, Portland State University and Clemson State to name a few. They looked incredible! I couldn't believe some of the things I saw. There were massive crowds at games, even in athletics (Track and Field), athletic training services where I wouldn't have to pay to see doctors and chiropractors, and full-time athletic training staff who worked to help rehabilitate your injuries and get you to peak performance. They have picturesque seasons in America - not like in Australia. Our seasons, while beautiful, are not as definitive. They have white Christmases, colourful autumns and rich summers. Everyone looked happy. Universities had money, and their athletes seemed supported in a way I had never seen in Australian athletics. They had it all. Wow! What solidified this dream was a single experience, which may not seem like much to anyone else, but a combination of timing, people and events made this moment so poignant...

• • •

Halfway through my senior year, we had a Football finals game against the Glennie School. This was another school in Toowoomba, our fiercest rivals. We had to win against them at all costs. It was a night game and it started to rain. When it rains in Toowoomba it also tends to get foggy and exceptionally cold. It was 0-0 and no one was scoring.

We were all exhausted because of the rain. In the last minutes of the game, we could barely lift our legs. Both teams had been trying desperately to get a goal to break the nil-all tension. The rivalry had created an exciting and almost hostile atmosphere. The ball was passed my way; I could see the referee looking at his watch closely. We only had minutes to spare. My shoes full of water, I could barely run anymore as the last defender came towards me. I was miles from the goal. The goalkeeper was off the goal line and standing out towards the edge of the 18-yard box. I was just inside the halfway line. I knew I could kick a ball, but could I kick it that far? The ball was wet and slippery, too. I could be wasting our last chance!

I remember running as fast as I could to that ball and kicked it hard and high. As I did so, I slid along the ground on my back and my pants filled with dirt and mud. I looked to the side from my position and could see the ball hit its peak and then I couldn't see it momentarily in the lights. It fell over the top of the keeper's head and neatly into the back of the net. It was the best feeling in the world! I lay there for a second feeling elated, big spotlights in my eyes, watching the drops fall from the sky and feeling the rain pouring on my face. It was a moment of complete satisfaction and freedom that I cannot express in words. The world stopped for a second… It was one of the happiest moments of my life. I gave that game everything I had.

Suddenly there was screaming and yelling, and it was stacks-on-Kel. I was smashed and crushed at the bottom of a pile of sweaty, grass-covered, muddy, screaming girls. They dragged me to my feet. It was amazing, except for the mud up my bum! It was real, and it was because we had worked together to achieve this incredible thing, not to mention beating our rival school. I felt elated, and because it was my senior year, I felt extra proud of what we had achieved.

This was an amazing personal victory for me because, in taking a chance on kicking that ball, I took on the belief that there was something greater than anything I could do on my own, and I was still important. I mattered to those girls and at that moment I felt a real acceptance that was not borne out of having to sacrifice part of myself.

It was about giving myself freely and not having to ask permission or look over my shoulder. About taking a chance on something I had a choice in and risking it all. It worked; it really had worked.

I didn't sleep that night; I was too excited. I dreamed about playing in the USA at one of those big universities, in front of the big crowds and really doing something amazing. Something that people had told me I wasn't good enough for; something that doesn't happen to 'abused little farm girls'. I'd had so many doubts and fears, about everything. I had been doing things for someone else for a good portion of my life. I was now doing what I said I would do. I would not let him, my uncle, or anyone else say it couldn't be done. It was about integrity.

The very next day I went to Mary-Anne and I was excited. She never once said that I couldn't achieve this dream. Not once. She said, 'I can totally help you! That's awesome!' I started to write letters and accumulate references. Before I left school the day after I had spoken to her, I sent expressions of interest to a multitude of US schools. My school Football coach even tried to help me with a video that we could never really get to work. I received letters back, including expressions of interest, but I was the most excited about Washington State University. They wanted more information, including a video so that their coaches could see what I was capable of. But the Football season was nearly over.

There was still athletics season to go, and as the athletics captains, Stacey and I were very busy. We both belonged to Black House, and while our house wasn't the strongest in athletics, we had a lot of very good athletes. We had the best war cries, and we yelled so loud we could barely talk for days after. My favourite was the Fairholme War Cry.

Jump and Jive, Stay alive, The Fairholme Team has just arrived,
A woo woo woo woo, Ah woo, woo woo woo.
Don't mess with the best cos' the best don't mess,
Don't fool with the cool, cos the cool don't fool,
A woo woo woo woo, Ah woo, woo woo woo. (Repeat louder!)
~ Anon.

We did this when the seniors graduated, at big athletics competitions and whenever there was a major event in the sporting arena. We all linked together in an amazing array of colours and song. It was incredibly motivating and moving. I loved this. The Fairholme College spirit was something I would cherish and needs to be experienced to be fully understood. It was the same at swimming carnivals. There was this strength of character that filled the place with a buzz of excitement. Everyone was pumped up to compete and score as many points as possible for their house. Everyone was equal. Everyone was important; we mattered together.

I loved the school. I loved going to school. When I hear young people say how much they hate school, I feel sad because I know you can still achieve great things even when all hell is breaking loose in your life. It is hard, but making choices and focusing on your future keeps your eyes on the light and not the dark. One mantra I lived by in school was; *'Strive to Achieve'*, adopted from my primary school principal. My other mantra was, *'I have a choice every single day when I get up, to be my best, for my parents, friends, community and myself.'* When I got upset and felt like I was a waste of space, worthless and incapable, or if I wanted to throw in the towel, I remembered what it had taken to be there, what it cost not just me, but my family, and I knew I wasn't allowed to give up.

After all that I had been through, I wanted to be all I could be, especially for Mum. She was such a driving force because she wanted to be the athlete I was. She had dreamed of being an amazing swimmer, and she could run; she was able to run faster than me up until I was in Year 8. I know if things had been different, she would have made it. I had to fight.

There was so much that happened in high school I struggle to remember all the amazing things that I was part of and the things that broke my heart. As I mentioned earlier, at the end of every senior year, the seniors put a yearbook together. It was a recollection of memories of life in the boarding house and school in the form of a letter to you from each of your friends about the year, their hopes for you, fond memories and wishes for your future. When I read this, even now I get emotional. I must have had a fierce passion then, much more than

I do now because every single person wished me well in the upcoming Olympics and my dreams of going to the USA. Despite what I felt, people genuinely believed in me and I simply struggled to see that when I was at school. Realising this has given me a new appreciation for the girls I went to school with. They all pushed each other to reach the best in themselves, even me. No amount of money can buy that. It is honourable and beautiful. It is what friendship is about - pushing your friends to be their best and helping them find the best in themselves.

People sometimes see more of you than you will ever see of yourself.

I was believed in then, but I struggled to love and believe in myself. I had to fight hard to maintain my direction, my focus. They believed and saw something in me I didn't even know I had. I believe many of us are like this and we always think people don't see us. People sometimes see more of you than you will ever see of yourself.

At the awards night I won the Senior Sportswoman of the Year award for the second year, something that I was immensely proud of, due to the high calibre of athletic women at the college. This finished the year nicely leading into my 'gap' year. I planned to take a year off after school to work and save some money. We all said our goodbyes and that was the end of my Fairholme journey. I was an emotional wreck having to say goodbye to all those girls! They had become my family!

There was a poem written on a big banner at the school, which has stood the test of time. It reminded me to keep going even when I was exhausted. It also echoes in the footsteps of every girl that walks the paths of Fairholme College and every woman who dares to fight. It is an adaptation of 'The Man in the Arena', which is an excerpt of Theodore Roosevelt's speech; 'Citizenship in a Republic', delivered at the Sorbonne in Paris, France on 23 April 1910. Here it is:

The Woman in the Arena

'It is not the critic who counts; not the woman who points out how the strong man stumbles, or where the doer of deeds could have done them better. The credit belongs to the woman who is actually in the arena, whose face is marred by dust and sweat and blood; who strives valiantly; who errs, who comes short again and again, because there is no effort without error and shortcoming; but who does actually strive to do the deeds; who knows great enthusiasms, the great devotions; who spends herself in a worthy cause; who at the best knows in the end the triumph of high achievement, and who at the worst, if she fails, at least fails while daring greatly, so that her place shall never be with those cold and timid souls who neither know victory nor defeat.'

1. Me and my dear friend from the USA. In the background a poster of sporting legend Joanna Stone **2.** One thing I was very good at, the hurdles. I have jumped many in this life! **3.** A very fond image of the girls on the hill (Fairholme College). Something I was blessed to be part of.

Chapter 16
The Domino Effect

'Kel, you do what you do because it's right... There is no point worrying about what you can't control, but you just have to get up in the morning and do what needs to be done. When the hard work is done, then you can rest.' These words from my mum always echoed in my mind. Could I dare to dream of anything more than a farm girl's childhood curse? Would I dare to dream big enough to fulfil my heart's desires? Was there a way to push past all that I knew was dirty, wrong and shameful and conquer the demons that kept me captive? In a poem by Oriah Mountain Dreamer, which my mum gave me, I remembered the words, 'I want to know what sustains you from the inside when all else falls away. I want to know if you can be alone with yourself and if you truly like the company you keep in the empty moments.' Who was I? I don't even know if I liked myself; every single part of me felt self-loathing. Would there ever be a place for me where I could be free and uninhibited? What on earth was going to happen now? I was on my own now, even more than I was before. I pulled in a large gulp of crisp Toowoomba air, and I walked out of the gates of high school for the last time.

I graduated from Fairholme College among a cohort of amazing young and hopeful women, all with hopes and dreams of going to university and having astounding careers. For a time, I just wanted to earn some money. I didn't have a car to start with; it was just my pushbike and me. Before long I was working four jobs. My first job was at a little coffee shop in Toowoomba. I was terrible, and I still have no idea how to make a proper barista coffee. I had only ever worked with Mum and Dad cutting grass, concreting and doing hard labour, so this was all new. Tony, my boss, was patient and even though he had to yell at me a few times, I got better.

Fairholme College asked me to be a coach too, something I had done while I was a student. I sometimes coached up to thirty girls at a time, mostly working with the throwers, but also with strength coaching. I struggled working these jobs, and I still wasn't making much money and certainly not saving any. I was heavily involved in Football and athletics, and it all cost money in fees and travel. Feeling quite lost as to what to do really, I took up my coach's advice to start university studies regardless of any American dreams and I enrolled at the University of Southern Queensland (USQ Toowoomba) in a Psychology degree. I soon loved university life and that took me on a whole journey on its own.

I moved into a little townhouse with another USQ student, Leah. She was an acting student - a top chick who would help me through those two and a half years I was in Toowoomba, she was a great laugh and often came home acting out all these different personas. She found people in the street and would have to become them; watching her play out all these characters was a wonderful reprieve from my life.

I was still playing in the Brisbane Women's Soccer League and liaising with colleges in America. I had started to get my video together. The season was about to start again, and I could actually have a good go at it. I had sent references and my resume through and was sold on going to Washington State University. I had to get a visa, passport and a whole lot of stuff through immigration. Before any of that I needed a final offer from a college. To get that, I had to perform on the field or track and send the video of me doing what I could do best. I thought that perhaps I would aim for a start in the USA at the beginning of the year 2000.

Meanwhile I made many friends at university and started playing for the USQ (University of Southern Queensland- Toowoomba) Women's Soccer and Futsal teams. I travelled with the girls to the Queensland and Australian University games, which were incredibly fun and memorable experiences. There was many an alcoholic beverage on these trips and there *may* or *may not* have been a few games that occurred under the cover of darkness with a friendly rivalry between the soccer girls and a few other university teams. There was *possibly* the annual university games nudie run, and I *may* or *may not* have streaked semi-naked across campus.

Our team placed in the top three university teams at the Australian University Games. A team was also being selected to compete for an international competition and I was named in that Australian squad. It was incredible. I felt even more determined and so very happy to have that opportunity. I never got to attend that tournament though. I don't know why they had bothered making a selection, because as soon as they named the team and made us feel like we had done so well, they said they only took a team away every four years and we weren't going anywhere. It was disappointing, to say the least.

That was not to be my only disappointment...

We were playing one of our premiership games early into the season when I performed a simple step-over of the ball and felt my right knee pop. I tried to keep playing, but as I stepped out, I realised I couldn't put weight on my right leg. That awful sinking feeling in my stomach came on as I fell and was carried from the field by the coach.

I had to go to an orthopaedic surgeon, Dr A, and after an x-ray and ultrasound, I was told that I had dislocated my patella, there was cartilage missing and I would need surgery. During the arthroscopy, and while I was still under anaesthetic, Dr A found that the back of my kneecap was rough, bumpy and causing all kinds of inflammation under my knee. He decided then and there to scrape it clean, make it smooth and remove some cartilage. For an operation that was meant to be a relatively simple procedure and a rehab time that was generally minimal, it took months to heal. It has never been right since and has caused no end of trouble. I have no doubt that it was more the way my body functioned as opposed to anything that Dr A did. It was this event that started a journey I can't say that I was ever proud of. I became anxious because I knew this injury was putting everything I wanted in life on hold. I started to get depressed, but I was coping, considering I felt I had all but ended my career. An amazing, kind physiotherapist, Carol, who was a parent of one of the athletes I went to school with, believed in me and gave me the assistance I needed. She not only helped to rehabilitate my knee over the many months, but she also counselled my head and heart and reassured me I would be fine. Of course, I would be, but my fatalistic mindset was very hard to overcome sometimes.

One conviction I held onto was to never smoke. But I did drink, a lot. For months I couldn't do much of anything; in fact, it was the worst six months ever, and because of my habits at the time, I wasn't saving anything either. While I was still training as best as I could, it was not until the next season that I was able to come back, and even then, I was tentative. It cost me mentally. Once bitten, twice shy. I have had many injuries, but this knee injury had sidelined me from both soccer and athletics. It took some time before the hesitancy of tackling an opponent disappeared. I was not as committed as I should have been because I was afraid of getting hurt again. What a metaphor for life. The problem is, when you try and tackle someone and you're not committed, you will not win the ball, and more often than not, you will be injured. So, it was about overcoming my thinking.

I was doing OK; I really was. I had worked back up to the premier team and was playing great Football. Well, I thought I was. I was still trying to get the knee right, but nothing that a whole bunch of strapping tape couldn't fix. I was still throwing and competing at the state and Australian Athletics championships. I was coming back! But I was still on a rollercoaster and spiralled into the next downhill plunge, one that literally spun me out of control...

• • •

I was on my way to work in the early hours of the day when the traffic starts to wake up and the air is fresh in your lungs. Usually, I rode my bicycle like a bull at a gate to get to work, smashing myself and getting wherever I was going as fast as I could. On this day, I was rolling down the hill, going quite slowly, thinking about how I was ever going to make enough money to go to America. I was trying to decide whether

I needed a new job and how to save more efficiently. Very quickly I had realised that drinking and the whole nightclub scene was bound to send me broke. I had about $1,500 saved up. Not a lot really, but not bad for a uni student. I was mulling this over on my way to the Chinese shop where I worked. It was one of the busiest roads in Toowoomba, where the road trains and trucks go through the city in long lines. I was too afraid to ride on that road, so I rode along the footpath, like most people did.

I saw it happen before it happened; it was like a slow-motion video. As I rolled down the hill a car came from a driveway to my right. I could see it out of the corner of my eye and there was nothing I could do to stop my bike or get out of the way; it was just too quick. An old guy was driving, and while he was looking to his right and moving forward, I never saw him look my way, to his left. Before I knew it, the bumper of his car smashed into my right leg and directly onto my right knee. The opposite knee that had the surgery on it... I was strong, but that hurt like hell. Disassociation was once again my momentary friend, and I felt like I was watching the whole thing unfolding from above, happening to someone else. I felt sick. As much as I wanted it to stop, or to control what was happening, I couldn't.

When people say that your life flashes before your eyes, well, that's what happened. I didn't scream at all this time, but I was in instant shock and fear wrapped itself around me, followed quickly by pain. I was in a cocoon of silence...all my dreams flashed by me in an instant and then crumbled. Just as I had watched this movie play out, I flew over the handlebars and somersaulted in the air, landing on my head a couple of metres from the vehicle. I came to rest on my back. Luckily, I had a backpack and helmet on, which probably saved me. I lived to tell the tale, but I was hurting already.

I opened my eyes to see this man standing over me. 'Are you OK?' I couldn't really understand him to start with. He sounded Russian, or was at the very least of European descent, and I struggled to understand his words through his thick accent. I'm not sure what I said to start with, but then I heard him say, 'I'll call you an ambulance.'

My knee was already too swollen to bend. It didn't look good. I couldn't move, at least for a while. The man was insisting he call an ambulance, but I panicked because I had no money and back then ambulance fees were paid differently. I am sure it would have been fine, but in my mind, there was also simply no way that this man was going to do anything for me. Talk about stubborn.

As my pride reared up its ugly head and irrationality fought with reason, I said I would call someone. I would have to go to his house, 30-40 metres away, and make the call. He even offered to drive me to the hospital. I was so angry and emotional that I yelled at him. 'There is no way I am going to get in a car with you because you've already run me over!'

Weeping and screaming in pain, crying, snotty, and hyperventilating, I managed to hop to his door. I tried to call my housemate and that didn't work. I made several other unsuccessful calls. I didn't know who else would be around at that time of morning to help, or what phone number I could remember. Finally, I thought to call the Fairholme College boarding house, whose number I knew off by heart. I spoke to the head of the boarding house, Mrs Smith. She was tough, but she always looked after us. I had maintained a friendship with these amazing ladies, and often when I was done training, I went to visit them. They were more than boarding mistresses; they had become friends. I didn't know who else to turn to.

I hopped back out to the road to gratefully wait for them, that anger rising in me. I was crying and weeping pathetically with sadness, pain and a fear that came from somewhere helpless I thought I had left for good. It was the worst feeling ever and flowed from the depths of my soul. They were not just tears of pain. The poor guy who ran me over would not leave until they arrived. I was so angry with him. I could not stop the crazy thoughts going through my head. I was in shock and nauseous, with shivers like a fever, and I was sweating. Lying down on the pavement, I was overcome with dizziness. My chest hurt, and I felt like I couldn't breathe. I wept like I have not wept before. I was broken, in all ways. My dream, my America, my chance! My heart was hurting so much more than my body.

It was with relief that I saw Mrs Smith and Miss Burns arrive. We students affectionately nicknamed them - very originally - Smithy and Burnsie. Smithy was in charge of the boarding house and Burnsie was one of the boarding mistresses. I laugh now, but I remember thinking, *Oh my God, how on earth am I going to get in there?* They arrived in a tiny hatch. It was a task getting me in there because I couldn't bend my leg, and I got angry with myself because I should have called an ambulance! I was literally 200-metres from the hospital, which was the most ironic thing. I felt like a contortionist. At the hospital I was put in a wheelchair; it wasn't even one that held my leg up. I couldn't bend it, and by this point I was in agony and felt like I was going to pass out with the pain. I don't remember any green whistles or injections to help with the pain. I was given paracetamol tablets, which did little to make me feel better. More than anything I just wanted to stop crying! I was angry because I was ashamed of my tears! I didn't know someone could cry so much.

I was emotional and irrational. In my mind, my whole life and sporting dreams were over: my ideals, other people's dreams and expectations, my integrity... They would all be so disappointed in me. Mum for instance... I didn't want to disappoint her. I wanted to make her proud. She never got to do any of the things that I did. More than anything I cried for the sacrifices they had made for me, everyone who had supported me, the money provided to me to help reach my goal. All those kids that looked up to me. I had invested my heart and soul into this. In a self-serving kind of a way, I felt that if I could make them proud, I too would finally have a sense of achievement. I now could not picture a future for myself, which caused me to completely implode.

I felt small again, weak, helpless. I was back in that dark place. The police came and took details from my hospital bed, but they didn't seem to help. I felt disappointed. They must have thought I was nuts telling them I felt like I had seen it happen, like I was floating in the air. They probably thought that I had taken something or smoked some kind of illegal substance. They were very polite, however.

I was left alone and felt confused. Praying like a small child with all my heart and soul, I reached out into the void and felt myself falling, clutching at nothingness.

My orthopaedic surgeon, Dr A, came in after a long wait. He was a great doctor, but I tell you now, he was rough. He had to check the integrity of my knee. He was pulling and yanking it around, looking to see whether it needed screws. It hurt so much I almost wet my pants. I gripped his arm tightly, and begged him to stop, crying hysterically. I felt childish because he looked like he was going to smack me in the chops. He said, 'Let go of me!'

I said, 'I'm sorry, but it hurts!'

He did eventually stop pulling at my leg and then explained what was going on. The impact of the accident had cracked my tibial plateau down the middle. It's the big bone under your knee, and the head of the bone was split in half. There was also some ligament damage in the knee. Thankfully, it did not need screws. I would, however, need a cast for six to eight weeks. It was the middle of the soccer season. I was trying to get to the USA. I felt like now, it was really over for me. It had been my good, strong leg and now it was damaged. I couldn't see past the accident. How could I start this whole process again? What would happen now? Since sending the video, there were many colleges I was waiting to hear back from. If only I had a better understanding of faith and some perspective, perhaps things would have been easier.

I wouldn't even be able to look after myself. I had to call my grandmother Gladys. She lived with her partner Bill in Toogoolawah, a little town to the west of Toowoomba. Gladys was my dad Kevin's mother, and they were the closest family geographically to me. She said they would pick me up and take me home with them until Mum and Dad could come and get me. (Mum and Dad lived a good 6-hour drive from Toowoomba.)

I stayed in hospital overnight and slept a little, but mostly I just cried.

Grandma could do very little with me. Getting dressed, showering, everything was hard. My cast extended the whole length of my leg, all the way to my buttocks. Mum and Uncle Bob came to pick me up. I don't remember much about that journey, but later as I reflected with Mum, I remembered how I had felt seeing Uncle Bob: *I was afraid.* It brought *everything* to the forefront. For the next few months I was at my absolute lowest. I had a lot of time doing a lot of nothing. So naturally I had way too much time to think.

When I finally got that smelly cast off, my leg looked like a stick, or rather a dirty great spider's leg. It had completely atrophied. I hadn't been able to shave it in weeks. I thought I would never be as strong as I used to be, and I was back up the path in the garden praying in desperation for God to make me a bird, so I could fly away. It was hard because I felt like I had come so close and seen a glimpse of something and then it was gone again. I had put my heart and soul into being the best I could be and had shared my dream with my family, friends, colleagues and community. I was ashamed and embarrassed. I had told them all that I would get there, and now I felt like a failure. Over and over I asked myself, 'Why? Why now? Why me?' I was angry and yelled at God, 'Don't you think I have been through enough?'

Mum was angry too and took me to see a solicitor. I felt very vulnerable, but we made a third-party claim over the incident. The man who hit me did not give way and, while I should have been on a road while riding, I was not travelling any faster than a person walking. What if it had been a small child going past?

The claim took some time to happen, but my solicitor was awesome and made things easy. Pretty soon I could come back to Toowoomba and moved back into my little townhouse. My main focus was rehabilitating my knee; I had already missed a good chunk of the Football season. I became very good at juggling with my left foot (that is juggling a ball) because my right leg was still in a brace for a long while. I hadn't written back to any of the universities in the USA and figured I had probably lost my chances.

This resourceful and generally optimistic farm girl from the bush couldn't cope anymore. I felt overwhelmed and descended into a deep depression and suffered major anxiety. A doctor diagnosed depression and prescribed a course of anti-depressants. 'Here, take these tablets.' This made me angry, but I didn't have the strength to fight on my own. There was a huge cushion in my bedroom. That cushion and I made myself well acquainted, and I spent many hours just curled up and crying my heart out, praying for help. I describe how this was for me in the prologue of this book. I couldn't bury these feelings like I used to and simply did not know a way out. It was like my cup was full and my emotions just flowed over because I couldn't deal with anything else. I prayed. I was scared. I felt weak. Incapable of anything.

I was in such a dark place that I wondered if this was how things were always going to be. I didn't want to live anymore. I stared at the drawer in the kitchen and considered how sharp the knives were. *Would I be missed? Maybe it would be better if I weren't around. I could make the pain go away. I could simply disappear.* Then I thought about my family, and I loved them so much I really could never put them through that. They deserved better than me making a cowardly decision to run away.

What about all the things I could do in this world? If I could get better, maybe I could be one of those people that inspired other people. I could still help and maybe that was worth something.

But I couldn't help anyone really until I could help myself. I needed to fight for me - again. For now, though I was stuck.

Panic attacks left me faint and sweaty. I experienced sharp and rapid breathing and felt disoriented. Somehow, I was still working at three jobs, but I wasn't managing the juggling act and had to resign from my job at Hog's Breath Cafe, just to keep my head above water. It was awful because I loved that job. I was a kitchen hand and was generally covered in half of the kitchen foods when it was time to go home.

I was also still coaching at Fairholme College. I knew the way to ride there, and there was no way that I should get lost on the same route that I travelled every day, right? But I would lose my bearings and get lost every couple of days. One day I would be fine and the next I would be in the middle of a park in Toowoomba, not knowing how to get home. I would find my way eventually, but it made for some very long days combing the streets and trying to find the route home.

I was often too proud to ask for help, with my tear-streaked face and puffy eyes. I learned to snap myself out of it, calm down and finally rationalise my thinking. I often had to sit and take deep breaths, say a little prayer, then swear at myself, give myself an uppercut, cry some more and then get back on my bike.

I started to write, a lot more. I had written poems in high school, but this time I was like a machine. I would write up to four poems or more a day as an outlet, trying to stop this hurricane of emotion swirling around my head. It reminded me of the time a category two cyclone hit the house and the doors on the bedrooms were bowed so much you could see the bend in the glass. As the eye of the cyclone passed over the house and there was a calm, I could see the debris, sticks, leaves and everything else flying around in circles. It seemed like I was watching the world spin past me in a single moment. It was like my nightmare, a reflection of how I was feeling. Spinning around and around without hope or control in a downward spiral I felt powerless to control. It would take more than duct tape and a prescription for anti-depressants to fix this. I was often taken back to that moment in the front yard of our house, the day it stopped - the day I told him never to touch me or anyone else again. Who had I become? Where was my fortitude? Where had my resolve gone? What was wrong with me?

The truth is, there was nothing wrong with me. I was just sick and exhausted. I felt like I was the only one in the world who had these ever-present feelings. Thankfully, somewhere in the mess there was a light that would not let me step off the edge, and I kept writing. I would keep going because that's what I did. I couldn't throw my life away. But in some ways, I still was. I had to make a decision about me. I needed to step up in life and make a decision about what I was doing. I played Ping-Pong in my head, the thoughts raging back and forth about *how* I needed to be, *who* I needed to be and *what* I even believed in anymore. If I knew anything it was that my family believed in me … I held onto that.

It's Like Asthma

It's like asthma, constricting.
It chokes like the smoke from a black chemical flame
Licking the edges and burning, igniting my shame.
Choking, the vomit resting in my chest,
Threatening to come out, among the angst, the angst.
It's like a gag, choking, tears prickle my eyes
The raging fire inside, inside.
I can't do it, I don't know, what to do, what to do?
For the first time in forever, I'm drowning. I have no clue
It's like there is no air in here, and I break out, I shout!
I don't know how to make it stop; it burns, it spins around.
So tired, so damn tired, do I fight or succumb?
Why does it feel like I am the only one?
It ebbs and flows like the tide of an ocean of destruction,
Picking at my heart, like a cancerous devotion.

[Kelly Humphries © 2015]

1. Year 12 formal picture, with long-time friend Kris.

Chapter 17
Coping or Not

I could hear the music pumping, blaring loudly as I surveyed the dance floor. The beer had finally done its thing. I was wasted. All my mates were with me having a blast - good mates. But boyfriend ... partner... pfft. Nobody wanted me, not like that. The room spun as the lights pierced the back of my eyes. I was angry. I needed a fucking drink. 'Hey, do you know that guy?' I saw dark eyes homing in on me from the other side of the dance floor. A cowboy ... boots, jeans and a fucking big hat. As he sidled up next to me I knew what he wanted. They all wanted the same thing, right? Maybe he would turn out to be one of the nice ones. Maybe he would still be there in the morning when we woke up. Fuck my life.

My body started to respond to rehabilitation and I began to see a light at the end of the tunnel. But I continued to cry for a long time. (I know, I cry a lot; don't judge me too harshly!) Rehabilitation of my right knee took so long, and it took some time for my muscle to come back. Some unhelpful person shared with me that broken bones heal pretty well for the most part, but ligament and tendon damage is much worse. My tears were more of frustration than anything else. I felt out of control. I soon realised that the eye of a storm is the calmest place to be. This stillness enabled me to see things right in front of me. I started to look at things differently, and this now is the way I deal with my anxiety: I just pick out one thing at a time and pull it out of the mess flying around. When I start to see the parts of the cyclone slowing down, and the storm abates, I know I have won.

I knew I was broken, so I needed to be fixed. I couldn't afford to get someone else to do it, so I felt I had to do it myself. I kept telling myself that broken things can still be beautiful.

I got a job at Woolworths, which turned out to be one of the best jobs I have ever had. I worked there for 18 months. I loved that job. I chatted to everyone coming through my checkout and soon had my regulars. I started to laugh again, and even better, I had a car.

I don't often laugh at myself, a habit I am learning to do more and more. But sometimes I had to laugh at the people who came through my checkout. That should be another book; there were some unusual characters, I can tell you. There was this one guy, a customer; he was a chicken farmer. He asked me on a date and I had nothing better to do, and while I advise you not to date people coming through your checkout, I decided to go out to dinner with him. His car smelled like chickens. Ironically, we had chicken for dinner and the conversation was very stilted and awkward. Even though he seemed nice enough, it felt weird and I knew in my heart it wasn't right. It didn't help that his cologne mixed with the hint of 'wet chicken feathers' really made my stomach do flips and flops, and not in an 'I love you' kind of way. I don't think I ever dated another person who came through my checkout. You could say I chickened out…

I didn't stop looking and searching for something, though. Chickens were not the answer, but the ache in me was not for food. I looked for anything to fill the void. The need for acceptance, validation, reassurance, anything. I dated many men, unfortunately, and I struggled with each one. I was drinking a lot on the weekends, Thursday nights especially, and any other time I wasn't working. Every couple of weeks, I would be with a different guy. This is not something I have ever been proud of, and not something I would recommend to find who you are. But I was unfortunately very numb to it all and felt that this was what was expected of me. I was trying to cling on to anything, and I felt completely alone.

I had to have approval, yet hated that I needed that reassurance. Now I can see I needed people around me to assure me I was OK. I allowed myself to get into all kinds of situations, which I felt I could handle with my tough intimidating façade. Then I got scared and withdrew into myself. I felt out of control most of the time, when I should have been in control. I often let myself be pressured into having sex. It is hard to explain this, but it was like I just needed that connection and I was seeking a fairy-tale love. Yet love was not sex.

Generally, I would 'make out' with these guys and it would lead to other things. I would then 'freak out' and try to get out of the situation I had put myself in. Sometimes it was OK and didn't upset me too much, but I still felt dirty. Sometimes I felt pressured. Many of these guys would say things to me that sounded like the things my uncle used to say to me, and then I would end up feeling awkward or pressured into having sex with them. I felt such regret and then I was afraid. Sometimes they wanted more and I didn't know how to deal with that. It just added to the low self-esteem I already had. That, clouded with my childhood battle, only created a recipe of short-lived relationships, some bad one night-stands and poor choices.

When I slept with a guy, I felt rising anxiety and never fully understood why. I got angry. Sometimes I just accepted that it's what they, blokes, wanted and it was easier if I just let them have it. Sometimes it was what I 'thought' I wanted too, but it was never satisfying, wonderful, fulfilling or anything but self-destructive. I certainly didn't like one-night stands of temporary lust and the feeling of disgust I felt at myself the next day. It rarely felt good or right. *(Disclaimer: I know that not all men are all about sex and pressuring women into having sex. This is my experience with some men. I know many wonderful men who are incredibly thoughtful and amazing.)*

In many ways, it mimicked some of the behaviour I had displayed when I was with my uncle. I had tried to convince my uncle to stop for years by telling him why it 'was not a good thing'. I gave every reason under the sun as to why we should stop, and he always had an answer that I didn't know how to argue against. So even though I would say it's not what I want to these guys, I would then become silent and it would happen, even though I never actually said yes. Just like when I was with Uncle Bob. It left me feeling dirty and confused. I always felt like I had to have a shower afterwards and often had a ball of anxiety trapped in my throat for days. I never understood it, and it is only with deep and very vulnerable introspection that I can really see what was happening. That is a hard burden to carry and even harder to admit. But it is the truth for many adult survivors in learning to understand who they are and why they have struggled in certain areas of their lives.

As I look back now and press into this, I realise the damaging long-term physical, emotional and psychological impacts of what I had been taught as a child. By me trying to take this entire burden of abuse on my shoulders, without speaking to someone about what I was feeling, I had formed habits and behaviours that I would spend the rest of my life undoing or unlearning. If I had sought counselling and support earlier, I believe I would have had better strategies in place and would not have had to fight so hard to survive on my own.

When I think back on this blur of a nightmare, the sad revelation is that I can pinpoint a few occasions where I would be able to prove a date rape in a court of law. This revelation has only come now in my thirties as I pull apart these emotions and force myself to face the demons of my past, and I now know what date rape is because of my policing background. How many people out there have had non-consensual sex with someone and thought that it was in fact OK? It's not!

My lifestyle was killing me. My anxiety and depression were far worse when combined with alcohol. I just wanted that happy, romantic guy to come along and whisk me away. All those romance novels and books I read talked about the excitement a woman has when they meet someone they are attracted to; that ability to have a passionate love with a man... It was how it was supposed to be, right? I had good male role models in my life. Mum and Dad had a great relationship, so what was wrong with me? I had no idea, so I just kept trying to find that thing. I pored over romance novels and believed that there was at least one right person, that Prince Charming who would just love me for who I was!

I must have been an OK catch, an easy target, or both, or none of these things, but why me? I would go over and over this. I often had random thoughts that I may have been a lesbian, but goodness me, I couldn't be, right? I remember thinking about this often and being curious. Some girls I had grown up around had female partners. I was always very drawn to them and had no real desire for men. I mean, I liked men; I appreciated when a guy looked after himself. It was there, but not like how others described it. My breath never caught in my throat. My mouth never went dry. My heart wasn't racing either. People talk about these shy glances, waves of passion, orgasms, amazing sex and love.

When I was with a guy I'd be thinking, *Geez, is that it? Is this what I have to look forward to? Bloody hell!* I thought I must have been doing it wrong! How can I not know? You can't do it wrong, can you? The guys I was with were not exactly amateurs. It was me! It had to be that there was something wrong with me, or I hadn't met a guy that could 'do it for me'. I pushed the idea that I was a lesbian away quickly and settled on the fact that I hadn't met the right guy and that perhaps I just couldn't do 'it' right!

I didn't know then what I know now. I basically had to relearn all that had been taught to me, and I had to pull it apart, one awful layer at a time. I understood that sometimes children who were victims of abuse need counselling to help them realign their thinking processes as to what love looks like. So, I tried to allow myself to learn, but I never felt like I won any victories in this area until I was about 26; but that's a story for another time!

I hated my life. Constantly fighting for control. I felt like I was back at Fairholme College playing water polo. I was never very fit in the water. In water polo you tread water for ages waiting for the ball, and then you get pulled under the water by your opponent and must keep afloat at the same time. Every time you get the ball you get dunked, get a mouth full of water, choke, have your ball stolen and then spend the next ten minutes extracting water from your lungs and go do it all again. (Sorry for my poor depiction to any prospective water polo player.) I couldn't win.

None of the drinking or anything else healed me or made me feel better. It just got worse. All I knew how to focus on was my sport and holding tight to my dreams, my memories and the things I knew were real. I was losing my fight to keep my head above water and was sinking to the bottom of that pool, the world passing me by while I drowned. I was scared, and I felt more alone than ever. I had no idea what to do. I knew in that moment that I needed help.

Most of the time, I was waking up tired and went to bed tired. I felt nauseous nearly always, and I was short of breath, panicky, nervy and jumpy. I was almost completely detached from myself, absent. I simply couldn't do it anymore. I needed help.

• • •

I was coaching at Fairholme College still and was talking one day with one of my dear friends who had been my multi-event athletics coach. I needed to talk, and she was there for me; I will be forever grateful. I told her how crazy my life had got, just in a general conversation. I don't know how it came out, but I mentioned to her about my uncle. Holy crap, that was an emotional moment! Tears sprang out of me everywhere, like a burst water main. I thought I had buried that deep, oops! I had let my secret slip!

She listened to me with an open heart, no judgement, and while she said she didn't know how to help me cope, she gave me some good advice. She recommended I talk to someone I trusted who could help. So, I sought out another friend, Mrs K, who was the school Guidance Officer. I had never really had cause to see her before, but she was someone I knew I could trust and who could help me. I needed to let go of my pride; there was no way I could feel any worse than I did, and so I let go of all that contained me and reached out.

Mrs K was there to take my hand. I told her what had happened to me as a child, with my uncle. I told her all that I could bear to say. That is and was really very little. There was so much left unsaid, and for that silence and me not telling her everything then, being vulnerable and allowing myself to be open would cause me to struggle later in life. (Don't ever be afraid to be vulnerable, and see it as a sign of strength and courage, not shame.)

I told her I was out of control and didn't know how to deal with it all. We talked about what the last horrible six months were like and that I thought about suicide. It wasn't really an option despite the thoughts plaguing me for some time. I knew I had a purpose; I just couldn't see it. I was lost. I felt weak. I had worked so hard to be strong to protect my family. Having been given that diagnosis of depression was another label I didn't need; especially in addition to the self-imposed labels I had already put on myself or allowed others to speak over me. I knew how I felt in the park that day not that long ago - petrified, panicked and undoubtedly very much in need of help - and I promised myself that I would only stay on those tablets for as long as needed. I would only allow myself the time to get better and would not be dependent on any medication. I wasn't sure I could do it alone. That's why I needed her.

Through talking with Mrs K, I began to see more clearly. I felt better immediately, and I only had to see her a couple of times. In hindsight I should have continued to talk to someone, if not her. I knew that what I told her was OK, and it was a safe place to be vulnerable. I could take that armour off that I had been carrying with me for so long. I was tired…really tired…and for once in my life I could truly share that load with someone who knew how to help me carry it.

I don't remember much about what I said to her, only her kind smiling face. I do have a vivid memory of once drawing a picture for her. She had asked me to draw a bed and put myself in it. When she looked at my drawing, she remarked that it showed how little I thought of myself. I had drawn this gigantic bed and I was tiny in comparison. It was a lot to do with my self-esteem. It was very revealing, to be honest, and a little scary.

I felt that the dark space I was in get a little lighter.

Mrs K told me that I should consider reporting what had happened to the police. I know I had worried myself stupid that he might try something on another little girl. The guilt that if he did touch another child and I hadn't done something would probably be far worse, and let's face it, I couldn't get much lower than what I was already feeling. He was involved in sporting clubs, and even though I didn't think he would do anything to a little boy, I could never know. I decided to go to the police. I still had not told my family, which was a concern for me.

I was having nightmares…repeatedly. Strangely, one nightmare was the same every night, for about six months.

I remember it clearly, like it was yesterday. It started innocently…

I was watching my sister Laura play in a field of beautiful green grass. She was with someone, but I didn't know who. I sensed my brother close by. Then I felt this darkness and fear clutch at me. There was a presence that was so dark and sinister I could not escape my terror. It was suffocating. I went after Laura. She was there playing innocently, laughing in the beautiful green fields, then she disappeared. I ran to find her, desperate to warn her, to keep her safe. I ran to every person I could; yet no words would come from my mouth. I had no voice and seemed invisible. I searched high and low, feeling the breath of this thing as I screamed silently, my warnings trapped in my throat. I saw glimpses of Laura as I chased after her, her blonde hair disappearing around the corner of buildings, trees…her giggles fading off into the daylight as the sound of heavy breathing bore down behind me like a wolf after its prey.

Next, I was under the schoolhouse at my old primary school. There were lots of people around and I couldn't find her anymore. She wasn't there. She wasn't anywhere. I was filled with a profound sense of loss. Part of me felt like it had completely died. I felt broken. The predatory breathing had stopped and there was only sadness and deep loss. I wandered from the schoolhouse towards a beautiful fountain, the spray from the middle sending off water in multiple directions in an amazing pattern. At the fountain edge I peered into the water, and there at the bottom was my sister - her big beautiful blue eyes boring into the depths of my soul. I didn't know if she was dead or not…it was almost like she was trying to say something. I looked up and I saw my uncle on the other side of the fountain.

I then would wake up in a sweat, crying my eyes out. Over and over, every night… Until I'd shared with Mrs K, I'd felt no one could help me. No one. I didn't know what that all meant, but I knew I had to tell someone about him. This dream plagued me, and I believe it was the catalyst for breaking my silence. I was nineteen and Laura was nine at the time, only one year older than I was when Uncle Bob started to touch me. He couldn't be trusted with me, so how could I trust him to keep his promise to never touch my sister? I had to speak up and speak out. But how was I going to do that? With Mrs K's support, I knew the first step in making this public: Tell my parents.

Lost & Lonely.

HOPE

ABYSS

CHAOS | DARKNESS

DROWNING

STORMS

It's so dark in here, I cannot see the light
my heart thumps so loudly; what of my desperate
plight?

An aching need to break free of the cold forbidden
Chains

a desperate cry for help as the unforgiving reins.
I am so helpless now...
I need some human touch...
I don't care why or how; free me from
the devils clutch

The need lying empty → LIKE
on the bathroom floor ME

I am so sorry God

I just
cant
take No
more

Kelly
Humphries
© 1999

Chapter 18
Breaking the Silence

The to and fro battle I was playing in my head was an immense struggle. The conversation I was having with myself was sending me nuts. 'Dad's going to blame himself ... He could kill him. What if they blame me? Surely not? I have been desperate to tell them all my life... C'mon Kel... You are strong enough to do this... Mum will be so angry with him; she will be heartbroken. It's her big brother. He fucking lied to us all! He even lied about that other little girl, and he did it to me. God, I am so gross. They are all going to hate me for breaking up the family. Mum will be mad and angry with me because I never said anything. I'm sorry! I'm so sorry, Mum and Dad! I don't know how I can tell you without you hating me, but if it saves Laura and you hate me for what I have done, at least she will be safe. I hate that he lied to you, Mum, Dad ... Please don't stop loving me.'

Mum and Dad had talked about coming down for a weekend to the Fairholme College fete, one of the biggest weekends on the Fairholme social calendar. I felt this would be the perfect opportunity to tell them about what had happened. But then Mum called and said they couldn't make it after all; they didn't have the finances. I was disappointed to say the least. I knew they couldn't afford it, but I stressed the importance of this social event. I needed them to come; this wasn't something I could tell them over the phone. I honestly didn't know what to do.

I trusted my flatmate Leah, so I talked to her. We came up with a plan so that I could talk to my parents alone. If I could convince my parents to come down, Leah would take Brandon and Laura to the fete and we would catch up later. So, I called Mum and, oh geez that was a hard conversation. It was terrible. Mum and I can be so connected sometimes; we often read each other's minds. She already knew I was deeply troubled. There have been times when Mum has called and said, 'You had a terrible sleep last night, didn't you?' And sure enough, I wouldn't have slept. At other times something would happen, and Mum would already know. Mum tried to make me tell her over the phone what was wrong, and she got enough out of me to know that I needed to tell them something and they needed to come. But she kept asking if I was pregnant!

That week stretched into an eternity. I talked myself out of it several times. I didn't sleep, and I couldn't sit still. How was this happening? He was the favourite uncle. The best uncle you could have. The uncle the kids loved. This would tear my family apart! Rock my family to the core! They wouldn't believe me. NO!

I went back and forth in my head until I was so exhausted I made myself sick with worry, working myself into a frenzy of emotions for the days leading up to their visit. Mum and Dad found some money somewhere and made the trip. The day came. Of course it came; the end of the week is always there. Tomorrow always comes. What I did not know was how they would take it. I had been determined to never tell them, but I knew they had to know, especially now... After my nightmares, after all this time, I could not keep this toxic, destructive secret to myself and risk letting him anywhere near my innocent, little, sweet and adorable sister - or anyone else for that matter.

They arrived the morning of the fete, looking tired and drained. Right away, as soon as they had a cup of tea, my housemate Leah took my brother and sister off to the fete and left Mum and Dad home with me. Small talk filled the painful and awkward silence. We all knew something was going to be said - eventually - but they were polite and waited until I was ready. This was hard because Mum was, and remains, really impatient.

I had an appointment lined up for us to see Mrs K. She was taking time out of her weekend to meet us at around 11 am. The clock was like a time bomb as the seconds stretched painfully along. It was fucking terrible. Vomit. I knew I had to spit it out. The thick silence was awful with so much tension in the air. Tears began to spill from my eyes and all the hurt and pain I had been holding onto came in a raging flood from the deepest part of my soul. My lips trembled, and I choked. I can't even write this properly; that's how hard this all was for me...

I was feeling sick in the pit of my stomach with the kind of fear that brings strong men to their knees. I wanted to throw up; I had the night before. I wanted to run. But I had to save the others, the other girls. My sister. I knew that. It was bigger than me. It always had been.

Mum eventually dared to ask, 'So ... what did you want to tell us?'

'I don't want to tell you anything because it's too hard,' I replied.

'Well, just spit it out. ... Are you pregnant?' Her face was bright red, and she had tears gathering in her eyes. I remember shaking my head, my words getting stuck in my throat as she started to probe.

I finally said, 'Do you remember that day when we were in the kitchen and you stopped and asked me if Uncle Bob had ever touched me?'

'Yeah, I do... Kelly, he didn't, did he?' It was said in a way that was more of a statement than a question. It was a confirmation of what she already suspected. I don't think I got the actual words out, but just nodded and started to cry.

Dad, who had been sitting tight-lipped, exploded. 'I knew it! I could just feel it!' He went bright red. He didn't cry, but he was angry and holding back his tears and a barrage of emotions. I had never seen him like that, and it scared me. He was the one I needed to hold me together.

Mum came over to me as I sobbed uncontrollably. She just held me and said, 'I never wanted that to happen to you. I know, Kelly... I know all about that stuff because it happened to me, too.'

I was even more upset then because I had no idea about that. It was the hardest day for us as a family. Dad looked like he was going to be sick.

'Your father didn't know about that yet,' said Mum quietly.

It was a double shock for Dad. I went and hugged him tight. 'Daddy, it's not your fault or yours, Mum.' I didn't want them to blame themselves for something that I felt was my fault as much as it was my uncle's. I have obviously since understood and worked through this a lot more and know that I didn't make that choice; it was solely his. I just had to learn how I would cope with it and what decisions I would make by having this 'thing' in my life.

Mum said she knew it wasn't her fault, and that it was always the abuser's fault for what happened. She said she didn't feel guilty for what happened to her, and then for what happened to me. I guess she'd had some more time to work through things. I now know that wasn't completely true, but she said that so I wouldn't be upset. I at least knew on the surface of things that I was not to blame...I told myself that, and yet I didn't truly believe it for a long time.

'How long did it go on for?' Dad asked me.

I didn't want to answer his questions because I knew it would make him more upset. 'I was about seven or eight years old when it started.'

He got up and began pacing the room. I was so distraught, I kept crying. I felt so sick and kept saying I was sorry, over and over again, while choking on my tears.

Mum and Dad were both struggling with their emotions. I was drained but relieved. I just wanted them to be OK. I wanted to know they weren't going anywhere. I wanted to know they still loved me. I watched them. I was afraid. I was desperate to know that they would be OK with all of this.

'What are you saying sorry for? It's not your bloody fault!' cried Mum as she wrapped me in her arms. She held me while I sobbed - the same way that I had wanted her to hold me that day in the kitchen. I held on to that moment and wanted to let myself go completely. But I couldn't lose all my composure; we still had to see Mrs K. I was filled with gratitude that Mum and Dad had come down. As soon as I knew they believed me, I felt like a fool for thinking that they wouldn't. Then I was angry with myself, and I felt indescribable shame. I felt awful and beat myself up for telling them, and then for not telling them sooner. It was madness because I didn't know whether I should be angry with myself or proud.

I was angry because I had allowed that silence to dominate and control my life, and yet ashamed of who I was. That's because in the beginning, while I didn't act like 'the victim', I really was a victim. I needed some emotional support and I know there are countless families and situations where family is not a viable support option. I may remind you later, but if you don't have supportive family, get around the right people who will support you.

It took us all a while to calm down.

'I spoke to Mrs K at the school, the guidance officer. And we have been talking about me telling the police,' I explained. I told them she was waiting to meet us.

We went to the Fete after we had all gained our composure. Brandon, Laura and Leah had been wandering around, waiting for us to get there. We met up and I took everyone down to see Mrs K. She spoke to my parents by themselves and then I came in, followed by Brandon and Laura. I remember Brandon was extremely angry, so he must have understood something, and I think more than anything it was the betrayal of the uncle he loved and looked up to, and how this trusted man had hurt his sister. Laura was still a bit young, but it was explained to them in an appropriate way and they understood what they needed to at the time.

It was even harder for Mum and Dad because there was a barbecue planned for the following weekend and both Bob and Aunty Von were coming to the house. I don't know how my parents were going to talk to him, let alone face him. Due to the report I was to make to the police, my parents couldn't say they knew anything because it may have caused problems for the investigation to follow when the police caught up with him. They had to bite their tongues.

I never knew how Mum and Dad dealt with my disclosure until much later, when I started to talk with Mum over the writing of *Unscathed Beauty*. She shared so much of her heart with me. Until then, I never knew she had not told anyone what happened to her until that day in Toowoomba when I was nineteen. It was the first time she had ever raised her voice and spoken about her childhood abuse. Her story is undoubtedly more difficult than mine. However, we all have stories and I am not sure that there are better or worse stories; it's a matter of perspective. The key to anything is in understanding your emotions and what kind of person you become while dealing with any event. That's why I am so proud of who my mother became, in spite of her own adversities.

As Mum and I have talked over the years, little by little; the layers have peeled away, and there have been some difficult conversations between us. Mum eventually shared with me her nightmare, her darkness and who her predator was. I will allow her to share her own story in the next chapter.

I hate what happened to her, but I am again in awe of the woman that she has chosen to be and how she has overcome. She is the mother of three beautiful children. She is also the friend and confidant of many, and shows her love and compassion to all who cross her path.

As I write this, I once again realise that talking about what had happened to me, and knowing that Mum knew what I was going through, was incredibly empowering. It made me realise that inadvertently I had achieved then what I hope to achieve through this book: Mum had permission to talk. Now she shares with her close friends to help them on their healing journey. Mum writes the next poem, and the next chapter is co-authored with Mum. It is her empowering story and what she has learned from this journey.

———————————

Blameless

They say that to forgive is to understand,
But how can you understand the betrayal of a man.
A man you should be able to trust,
Selfishly caught up in his own perverted lust.
A life is changed in dramatic ways.
Terrifying nights and haunted days.
Unable to realise you are not to blame,
Your life will never be the same.
What doesn't kill you makes you stronger.
Sometimes you don't want to be stronger any longer.
But you look inside and what do you find?
Strength you thought you had left behind.
Even if you feel lost, betrayed and shattered,
It is what is inside that truly matters.
Take control and break the cycle of shame,
Step out; break free, for you are not to blame.

[June Humphries © 2016]

Chapter 19
Through My Mother's Eyes

I am June Allyson Humphries (nee Griffiths). I am Mum, and I am protector. While things didn't always go to plan as they did in my head, I believe, despite a tough upbringing, the things that happened in my childhood have made me stronger, able to love more deeply, laugh more readily and appreciate all that I am.

In my early childhood I grew up innocently like all kids should, full of hopes, dreams and ideas about who and what I could be. I was my father's daughter and he (Jack) seemed to do a lot for us, right from the beginning. We had lots of animals, like goats, cats, dogs, turtles and so many more. My dad worked on the railway for long stints at a time, leaving my mother Enid at home with us kids. Life was fun with a menagerie of animals, but hard. Mum struggled while Dad was away, with little to no money; yet we always seemed to have clothes and food.

I loved sport and always wanted to be an athlete; that was my big dream. I wanted to do every sport I could possibly be involved in. I dreamed about either being a police officer, or a teacher - steps my daughters have both fulfilled, as our youngest Laura is a teacher and Kel became the cop. My dad said I could do better than being a cop, but I had always thought it was an admirable and respectable job. I never got to be either of those things. I never got to be the athlete I dreamed of being, which I regret in some ways. But in other ways I am grateful for what I was able to achieve.

I remember there were always periods of darkness around home, but we found moments of light, which we embraced. There was also a time in our childhood when Dad disappeared for a while.

Cycles certainly have a way of repeating themselves, and I know this throughout my own life and having the unique perspective of watching a daughter go through the same dark emotions I did as a child. You see, my Dad left Mum and my older brother, Bob, before I was born, because he was charged with a sexual offence of some kind, serious enough that he went to jail for a few years. From memory, the child involved may have been fifteen or so. Mum was left on her own to fend for herself.

When Dad came back home from jail, my parents had three more children: Ralph, Margie and me. I have no idea how Mum survived that time and what she did for money. There were no benefits in those days. It put our family on the edge, and I didn't know at my age what any of that meant.

I don't think I was a very nice child growing up, but then again that is my perspective. I believe certain situations made me an angry and frustrated child, with no one I felt I could talk to and share my secrets with. Though I was well liked, I always felt I was not part of the crowd. I kept busy. Perhaps this was my way of coping with how things were in our lives back then.

I grew up quickly. Mum got sick when I was about nine. Well, that's when we knew that something was wrong. Mum showed me a large, red lump on her breast. At my age I didn't have a clue what that was. Not long after that Mum went into hospital. As kids we didn't have a single idea what was going on, only that Mum was sick and needed to stay in hospital. She was there for twelve months. We were sent to live with a family from a Seventh Day Adventist church, because Dad worked away for six weeks at a time and there was just nowhere for us to go. We lived with this family while we waited for another home to become available.

We then went to a children's home where there were already eight children. When she was physically able, Mum had day visits with us, which was wonderful. She could use the hospital kitchen, and we kids were so happy when she would bring us a big round cake with a hole in the middle to share.

My mum had a big heart. From what I remember, she was an amazing woman. I know she wouldn't have taken her hospital time lying down and doing nothing. I imagine Mum would have done Bible readings, talked and entertained those in the hospital - cooked for others and did whatever she could to pass the time. We missed her terribly, but life was quite stable for us for a time. With Dad always away working there had not been a lot of stability in our life. So, for us, routine and rules were good, even though the carers we lived with were quite awful. It was also a time of great confusion for us kids. We were not at home but in a home. We were not happy, really, and so the one person that we hoped we could depend on was our Dad.

My dad would come back to stay at the boarding house on a Sunday afternoon, his day off, and we could visit him from the children's home. He would cook amazing food in the kitchen - a skill he inherited from his Welsh background, which I believe I got from him too. I loved eating all the vegetables. We had every vegetable possible! He made Yorkshire puddings and corned beef that tasted amazing compared to any food in the children's home. He was the father that I trusted and loved.

It was then that I became confused about things with him, and my understanding of love and life became tangled as I went from a teenager in a children's home to the object of his affection. I remember a time before Mum died, when he came back from working on the railway. Dad sent the two little ones off and kept me back in the boarding house with him. That's when he started things with me, and this would be my own private nightmare, which I kept a secret, under lock and key, for about 30 years. This is my first memory of my dad ever touching me. I was eight years old. It was just touching, but touching me everywhere. I guess I felt scared, and I didn't know what else to do because he was my dad. I was trapped.

One day in 1975, when I was ten years old, the people who ran the children's home told us that our Mum had died. Dad was furious because he felt it was his job to tell us this news and not them. We weren't allowed to say goodbye or go to her funeral. I didn't have much closure on her death until recently, when I had a dream. In it we were all standing around Mum's hospital bed and Mum prayed a blessing over us. She put her hand on each of our heads and said how much she loved us. She hugged us and told us how wonderful we all were. I believe this was a memory I had repressed, and so I felt my closure had finally come. That was only ten years ago, and Mum has been dead for 40 years. I miss her, and I always will. Not having her around has given me a resolve to be the best mother I can for my children - to instil in them all I can, as I understood from an early age just how precious life can be.

As we grew up, we continued to see Dad at his boarding house, and the touching continued. Sometimes Dad gave us money and we could go down to the local shop and buy a comic book or whatever we wanted. But generally, we never got much of anything from him. In fact, we always struggled because Dad's drinking was much more important to him than anything that we needed as kids.

We all moved to Gladstone, in Central Queensland, two years after Mum died. The family was reunited, and then it started again. Dad called me out of bed in the middle of the night, grabbed my hand and said, 'Your mother would rather I did it with you than with a black sheila from out west.'

Dad was having some relationship with a dark-skinned lady out at a place called 'Duaringa' in the outback, where he was working on the railway. I don't think it was so much about the colour of her skin, but that he would have used anyone to get what he wanted. As he took me to his bedroom I was scared. I cried the whole time while he did it to me. He asked me why I was crying and if I was worried about getting pregnant, and I said yes. What else was I going to say? I was only twelve or so, and I hadn't even had my first period when he raped me. He said that I couldn't get pregnant because he was impotent. I didn't even know what that meant. He hurt me, and he used me.

I was very confused after all this, much more confused than I was before, and I struggled thinking that sex was love, and love was sex. Maybe he was angry, and maybe he resented us. But for me, nothing was ever the same after this, and I struggled with life for a long time.

I was confused and had no idea about love. I was twelve; how could I? My dad's actions caused upheaval in me and I had no one to speak to. I had no one who could explain things to me. I was looking for that thing that would bring inner peace and happiness; I searched high and low for it. I never felt like I had a lot of close friends, but instead that I was like a butterfly and flittered around with many people I knew I could have good times with. But there was no one I felt I could truly share my heart or thoughts with. I wanted to tell my secret to someone, and find answers, but I was ashamed. He was my father after all, and in those days, you just didn't talk about things like that. It was kept quiet, and keep quiet was what I did. I sealed my lips and my heart, and as I got older, I searched and went looking for a love I didn't know. I had no idea what that was, and I didn't have the maturity to know either.

My Dad and I, despite what had happened to me, were still fairly close. I loved him because he was my dad. He also taught me and gave me a passion to love many things like the garden and cooking, and just love for life and people in general. I could talk to him about my life and he was very astute about some things. He was surprisingly very intuitive about feelings and emotions and could seemingly understand me, which was more than anyone else had. There was also the dark side of things, like when I needed a book or pen for school and simply couldn't have it. I wanted to have an education but couldn't because we didn't have the money or the means. What we had were excuses.

We couldn't do anything as kids; we just weren't allowed, and we couldn't afford a lot of things that other families could. I dreamed about doing all kinds of sports, everything I could, and Dad would never let me. I wanted to do athletics and netball, but Dad wouldn't help. My sister, Margie wanted to do the school musical. She could sing like an angel, but he wouldn't help with transport or practices. I know that doing that one musical would have changed her life. Margie still has a beautiful voice.

Dad would not allow us anything because it infringed on his personal drinking time. It made me so angry! He didn't seem to care, and I developed a strong resentment towards him, on top of an already very confused mentality about what had happened. I wanted to swim. I wanted to be a lifesaver and have my bronze medallion. But I just stopped going to the training and simply became angry, confused and frustrated at life. I got angry with Dad, and I just didn't want to go to school anymore. I quit halfway through Year 10, and I never looked back. It was also when I gave up sport and trying to pursue anything.

I may have regretted leaving school, but I made the most of what I had. I got a job at a supermarket and made ends meet in this way. I turned fifteen and met Gary, Kelly's dad. I think, if anything, I fell for his 'bad boy' persona. But underneath all the bravado he was a decent man, just immature, as we all were in those young teenage days.

I missed a period and was feeling sick all the time. I went out with a friend and had one or two drinks, and the next morning I thought I had food poisoning. Something wasn't right. I went to the doctor and found out I was pregnant! It was one of those things where I just didn't think past sex as having a consequence. I had been still searching, still angry and trying desperately to find that love and security I was looking for. When I ended up pregnant I was not unhappy. I just hadn't known that there would be a consequence for what I did. I simply didn't think like that then.

I didn't want to tell my dad. I was so fearful that he would tell me to have an abortion or give the baby away. When I finally did tell him, he told me that my mother had the same thing happen to her when she was sixteen, but she had to give the child away. I didn't believe him. I later found out that I did indeed have a bigger sister, Mary, and she was adopted out. She later found us, and we were happily reunited. I was already two months pregnant at this point and didn't know it, but Dad did the right thing and went to the doctors with me for check-ups. He was surprisingly good with me.

It seemed only a short time later and I was heading to Gladstone Hospital with contractions. There were so many doctors because I was in labour for 36 hours. Once I had my baby in my arms, my motherly instinct kicked in. We called her Kelly. I breastfed for three months, and while she was a reflux baby and there were a few problems, we got her onto some formula and she was fine.

I was very protective of her from the beginning. When I first held Kelly in my arms, my baby, my child, I wondered how such an amazing thing could have happened to me. As I looked down at her, I felt a sense of wonder at this little bundle of love and swore I would do everything in my power to protect her from all the things I went through. I would give her everything I never had. I prayed I could give her a childhood of love, joy and happiness, and I prayed I could protect her from 'that predator'.

Kelly was looked after by the whole family and all of my friends. She was well loved and protected. There was always someone looking out for her, and she had lots of kids around to play with. I had to tell Gary to go. There was a myriad of reasons why Gary and I could never continue with our relationship. But a big thing was that he was always turning up drunk at the house and simply wasn't ready to be the dad I needed him to be. I made that decision because I thought it was the best thing for Kelly. I made sure that Kelly had everything she needed, even before I had what I needed.

I met Kevin when Kelly was nine months old. He embraced her and loved her as if she was his own child. We had great times camping and fishing. We got married a few years later. My brother Bob by now had moved to Melbourne with his wife. Kelly met her father Gary and we made things work for the best in our humble little lives.

We now have three kids, Kelly, Brandon and the youngest, Laura. We tried to give our kids the childhood we grew up experiencing, with things like gardening and the weather in the bush, how to cook and make things, and just an appreciation for the small things in life. Kevin and I have been so proud of our amazing kids. Kelly was always the sporty one and excelled in everything she did. Brandon was also sporty and was excellent at high jump, distance running and soccer. He was also very creative. Laura wasn't as sporty but still had a go at everything. She was the artistic one, with a creative flair that far surpassed the other two. She even had music lessons and deportment classes.

I know that Kevin and I tried to give all our kids opportunities to find their niches. I believe that despite the hurdles they have faced, all have excelled in anything they have put their minds to. Kel is strong. Looking back over her childhood and teenage years I can see why she had such a drive. I'm sure she could have chosen many things to numb the pain, but I am so grateful that she found a love for sport, rather than a love for other things like drugs, which could have taken her down a very different path.

Around Kel's fifteenth birthday, Bob wanted to take Kelly fishing and I couldn't go. When they got back, I saw her slam the car door and stomp inside. I never pressed the issue on this occasion. Even if I had realised what had happened that day, I'm not sure I would have known how to ask that question. But I did ask Kel as she walked past me, 'What, no fish, then?'

She said no, and I asked Bob then, 'What happened?'

Bob said something along the lines of 'Just a difference of opinion…' It felt like much more than that, but he never said anything more. I knew Kelly was angry. Something wasn't right. Kel went to have a shower, and Bob didn't stay for a coffee and went straight home. It wasn't like Bob to go straight away, so I knew something was wrong. I did try to ask again later, but it didn't seem right. Kel was rather defensive, as she can be sometimes.

Something did happen that day. I never knew until later, when Kel told me, that she had fought with him and told him he was never to touch her again. It was the day that she stood up for herself and took her power back.

Kel left home when she was fifteen and never lived with us again.

While it was hard not having her here and only having her home every now and then, she was competing and travelling all over Australia, doing all she could to become who she dreamed she could be. She seemed to be in her element. I know how much she loved her time at Fairholme College and excelled in anything she put her mind to.

She was bold and driven, but every now and then the tough outer layer would crack a little, or a lot, and she would cry and call me in a panic. I didn't see these panic attacks as anything other than nervous episodes. She'd had a couple growing up, but I wasn't concerned, attributing them to her environment, as they seemed to happen before a big competition. I recall it got worse over the years. I would get more calls when she was riding her bike to work. We never thought for one second that it was anything deep-seated, and definitely not because she had been through the very things I had sworn to protect her from.

I encouraged Kel to go and talk to someone about why she was having these panic attacks. I started to get concerned as she was sometimes confused or disorientated. Kel was very good at dealing with things on her own, but we didn't know the extent of what she was dealing with.

When Kel was hit by a car, I had to call Bob to help me get her from my mother-in-law's because Kevin was working away. When we arrived and put Kelly in the car, I had my second inkling that something wasn't right between Kelly and Bob. It wasn't the first time I'd seen Kelly upset with Bob, but this was the first major display of emotional recoil. I didn't put two and two together then. She had a full leg cast on, and Bob was trying to help her get in the car. I remember the look on her face was absolute fear and anger. It was a 'don't touch me' look. Most people wouldn't have seen it, but I did. She was my daughter and I knew. I just didn't recognise it for what it truly was until a few months later.

I remember the anger that Kelly had toward Von, Bob's wife, as well. It was almost hatred. There was an underlying tension I couldn't fully understand, but now I do. None of us particularly liked Von because we thought she was very selfish; but I didn't mind her generally. But Kel truly struggled with Von, even though Kel was not one to hate people.

She was always full of love and compassion for others and certainly tried to find the best in people. It all makes sense now.

Kel was home for six to eight weeks while she recovered from the car accident, and then we finally got her back down to Toowoomba. After some time, we received her call to come down to Toowoomba because she was upset and wanted to talk to us. Kevin and I talked at length about all the things she might possibly want to discuss. By the time we were done talking, we had concluded that Bob had touched her in some way. We knew this based on some of the things she told us on the phone. But also, we had already started putting a few things together, like how much Kelly hated Bob's partner and how Kel reacted to him in the car that day we went to pick her up.

It was with great trepidation that we made the journey south. It was awkward from the moment we got there, knowing that some almighty news was going to come out of our daughter's mouth. I could see how much Kelly was struggling to get the words out. I wanted to take all the pain from her; I would have done anything. I have seen my kids, all of them; go through different struggles as they grew up. But as a mother, who wanted to protect her children, hearing the words that my brother had sexually abused my daughter for seven years or more was heartbreaking. I felt I had failed. I should have known. I should have seen it.

I had wanted to be the one to break the cycle, and I had wanted to say something to someone when it happened to me - and I couldn't. That was 30 years ago. So many emotions went through my head; so many things that I felt I should have done. So many things I could now see clearly, and I was angry. I was sad. I was hurt, and seeing my daughter's tears as she repeated over and over how sorry she was broke my heart. I was sorry. Sorry that I couldn't protect her. Sorry that I didn't know more or see more. Sorry that no matter what I felt I had done right, that he, my brother, had found a way past that.

He was going to be sorry! I couldn't believe he would do that to our family! Had it all been fake? Was all the attention he gave our family nothing more than a guise for his selfish intentions?

I had to help Kelly understand that I understood her pain. When I told her that I never wanted this to happen to her because it happened to me too, the pain on Kevin's face was something I would never forget. You see, I had never told him. I have only ever seen Kevin break down twice in our married life, and the first was when his mother and father split up. The second emotional breakdown happened when no one was looking, at home, when we had left Toowoomba and Kelly and come home.

———————————

My Pain, My Stain

I approach, I choke, and the tears prickle the backs of my eyes,
I wonder aimlessly, lost, scared, my therapist by my side.
I scream inside, I cannot hide; all hell breaks loose within my soul.
To break the silence; give in to this chance, to run and just let it go.
No one would ever really have to know.
Decision pending, heartbeat breaking, as the vomit rises in my mouth,
Fear like nothing.

[Kelly Humphries © 2016]

Chapter 20
Reporting

I felt like someone had died. I was sick to my stomach. I don't even remember how I got there. It was clinical. Fucked really. Like you knew what news awaited you on the other side and you didn't want to know the answer. Whose idea was this anyway? I was afraid of the police. I was afraid of what they would think of me. What if they didn't believe me? They would just think I was disgusting, and it was my entire fault. I didn't feel like I could go through with it, and yet I had to. I remember sitting there while the officer typed my statement, the keys tapping away sounding like hammering in my ears. The tension was so thick it felt like a plastic bag was shoved down my throat. She was asking me questions, the answers to which were so fucking hard to remember. Some things were so vivid, but I didn't want to say what he did. I did not want to describe in detail ... Help me, God!

I remember that day. It was a hard day, but I did one of the most empowering things I have ever done for myself: I chose to tell my story. I had to take control and give my life, my vulnerability, my shame and my guilt to a stranger, a police officer.

I attended the Toowoomba Police Station and spoke with Plain Clothes Officer Julie from the Child Protection and Investigation Unit. I sat with her for a long time while she typed a statement as I recalled as much detail as I could from my past. Fortunately, she knew what she was doing. She was reassuring, empathised with me and made it easier to do what I found so hard.

It was difficult, as so many incidents had etched their way into my life, and I had never kept a record or diary of every event. I would have had hundreds of pages to pen if that were the case. Most of what happened I could not remember, because my childhood years just seemingly blurred together. I realise now, from writing this book, just how much of my memory I am missing; that evidently is a direct result of childhood trauma. While I have been frustrated with my memory over the years, I now understand. With added stress, some things are just harder to remember than others. This was the first and only time I told someone what had happened in such depth, and it was physically and emotionally exhausting to say the least.

Even when I was talking with Mrs K, I never actually talked about the different incidents, where, or how many times. It just happened and that was that. I didn't reveal the grim details of all those secrets. But the police wanted all those details. In fact, they needed them, and the more accurate I could be; the easier it would be for them to prove their case in court.

I was being asked to bring up all this buried pain. I obviously didn't want to do that, but it was a process I needed to go through. Mrs K, bless her, stayed with me while I gave my statement. I was so ashamed and embarrassed. I was telling someone I didn't know about my yucky past. But you know what? Plain Clothes Officer Julie was amazing, and like many who work in child protection, she never judged me or made me feel like my story was not important. If she ever reads this, I want to thank her for her professionalism and ability to get the job done in the best way possible, while empowering me through the journey.

I will also add that I have taken many statements and seen many statements being taken, and I can truly vouch for the credibility and integrity of every officer I have worked with. When we are with someone who has gone through a traumatic experience, it would be a very rare occurrence for us to be judgemental. Officers who work in child protection are more understanding of your situation than you will realise, especially if you are a survivor of sexual abuse. Be honest and open and you will find wonderful support.

I couldn't remember bits and pieces of what I needed to report at the time, and it made things very difficult when trying to put my statement in chronological order. When you are someone who copes by being numb to what is happening, it can be hard. I could remember enough for the detectives to put together the details and from there ascertain just what offences they were looking at and how they would proceed. The detectives were incredible officers who gently obtained what they needed, in a respectful way. The way they supported me through this was quite wonderful, and I was able to put my heart and my pain on those pages.

I was done. Mrs K and Julie left me alone to read it.

While I was trying so hard not to cry, the tears came anyway - the kind that were silent in the knowledge of what I had done. Perhaps that is part of the reason it has been so difficult to write this book. I have read this book again and again. Reliving every memory makes it all seem too real sometimes.

I took a deep breath and grabbed my tissues. It was the first time I had seen it all laid out in front of me, in writing, clearly depicting what happened, and not just as a splatter of poetic words on a page from pouring my heart out. So much went through my head and heart at this point. Sadly, even though Mrs K came with me, I still felt like I couldn't talk to anyone about what really happened in such a way that would process the events: why and how it all happened. So many questions swam around in my head, and while I had answers for some, others just cascaded into waterfalls of shame and doubt. My inability to understand why someone who was supposed to love me, and love my family, would hurt me in that way drove me insane. Sometimes I hate that I am a deep thinker and mull over and over things. I am learning to embrace this as a gift, but sometimes it makes it harder for me to let go.

As I finished reading that statement, I felt sick. I was emotionally and physically exhausted. It was my family being torn in half…my tormented life being put down on the paper for all to see…my shame and guilt staring at me in the face. There was still a chance I would have to repeat all of this to a court.

I took courage in the knowledge that I was standing up for all those people who were 'at risk'. I was doing the right thing; I was going to protect other people, other little girls from him. Yes, I had to do this at any cost. I signed my statement and walked out of that office.

I regret not reaching out to my family more through this process, especially in the beginning. Thank God, I had even a small amount of faith because in so many ways my prayers were answered as I went through this journey. I clung to those prayers like they were my lifeline. It was all I felt like I had sometimes.

The next couple of days were an awful blur. There was one thing I wanted to do, and then again, I didn't want to…which was a little bit tricky, and a little bit scary all at the same time. I wanted to know why… and to do that I needed to speak with him, Uncle Bob. I needed to speak to him, and I decided that I should record the conversation. For a short time during the process I felt like I was some kind of secret agent. I felt a bit cool doing that, and then the impending craziness about what I was doing hit me and I freaked out. I was afraid of what he would say, and even more afraid of what he wouldn't. I wanted him to confess…to tell me what he had done. I hadn't spoken to him in years. *What?* How on earth would I do that?

I really didn't know how initially, or what I was going to say… I didn't want it to be staged. I just knew that my objective was to get him to admit what he had done to me.

I can't begin to tell you how strange it was to record this with the equipment back then. We have much better technology nowadays. It was one of those old phones with the circle dial. As I watched my finger make its way around the as I dialled each number, every second seemed like an eternity. My heart was falling out of my mouth! What if he found out? I was hoping that he would answer, because I just wanted it all to be over. He finally answered. (I am so glad Aunty Von didn't answer!) So many things were racing around in my mind! My heart was beating in my chest so loudly; surely, he would hear it.

This would probably be the last time I would speak to him, so I decided to just go for it. I wanted answers, so I swallowed the bowling ball in my throat and found something in my spirit that helped me to calm down and stand firm in my conviction.

If there was ever a chance to prevent further harm to anyone else, to have justice for what happened to me, and understand why, it was now - this critical moment. I needed to be as normal as possible; I didn't want him to suspect anything. I started with small talk.

'How you doing? What have you been up to?'

He asked me why I was calling, and I said to him that I was struggling - which was true. I was honest, really honest with him. Whether I was recording what he said to me or not was irrelevant now. I needed him to know that he had 'messed me up'. I told him that I was struggling with depression and anxiety, I was angry, and I had even thought about suicide. If there was some part of my uncle that knew who I really was, my heart, and how I had been trying to deal with life, maybe I would even get some closure. I even hoped that some part of him really cared for me still. If he knew my heart at all, he would hear me, I prayed.

I think it probably helped that I cried, and they weren't fake tears. Not at all, they were fear; they were failure; they were anger; they were shame and guilt; and they were brokenness. I never lied to him during this conversation. I told him that it was because of him I had been struggling for so long.

I said, 'All that stuff that you did to me when I was a kid, why? Why did you do it?'

I wanted to know the answer; I desperately wanted and needed to know why!

I don't remember if he answered me, but I do remember he said, 'Well, I'm sorry. It shouldn't have happened,' and that was it. That was all he said about it. There was no real explanation. Should I have expected one? Did he even know why he did it? Did he know why that desire in him was greater than the desire to love and serve his family? Did he think loving me was love? The questions that raged in my head only served to make me anxious and upset. I was crying like an idiot, and I'm not sure he really knew what to do.

It was more a statement than an apology. It sounded to me like he didn't mean it at all. He didn't really sound sorry. I was so upset and said, 'Okay, well this is not really good for me and I need to clean myself up. So, I'm going to go now. See ya.'

That was my last conversation with him. It was as good a confession as I could obtain, but I prayed it would be enough. I certainly never got a lot from this, but he did apologise, if saying sorry, by definition, is an apology. Was it heartfelt? I don't think so. This would never make up for any of the years of hurt, or how he took advantage of my family's trust. I was exhausted, and my heart felt like it was weighed down by a thousand tonnes of sand.

I was so much like my mum, and my story here is so much like hers it is uncanny. Mum talks about her dad as a weak, cowardly man. She says that she never understood why he did what he did, but she still loved him as a father. I suppose I can understand how easy it would be to separate the two people that he became to her. The father and caregiver, and the predator and tormentor; yes, I understand it well. Grandpa Jack was smart and witty and taught Mum many things, just like Uncle Bob, who taught me many things.

Still, the confusion was something that Mum never understood and she never forgave what he did, despite his taking time to ask for her forgiveness. At least he was able to seek that forgiveness before he died an early death linked with alcoholism. He never got the satisfaction of that forgiveness.

At least I had something - some kind of conversation that indicated his guilt. For now, I held on to hope. I went home and lived in a numb haze while things sorted themselves out.

It all went quiet for a while; the police had a few things they needed to do before talking to Uncle Bob. I continued to do what I did, getting on with my messiness. Only now I felt lighter and lighter as the days wore slowly on.

I felt I had done the right thing for myself and could begin the process of moving on. What was present was an anxiety about what was happening. When were the police going to arrest him? How long did I have to wait? We were kept informed and that helped ease things, but things took time. Mum and Dad also knew briefly what had been done regarding the phone call and now the investigation. They too had their own journey of healing to go through after learning of the betrayal to our family.

Emotionally I was exhausted; I was at a point where I felt I couldn't do anything awesome at all. I needed some rest. I felt like I had been carrying a thousand bricks on my back, and while I could finally let go of the load, I felt like I was still covered in all the dirt and sweat. I needed a 'shower'. I needed to wash my heart, mind, body and soul free from all he had done. The things that used to hold me together - sport, writing, optimism and all the pursuits I took part in - didn't sustain me any longer or take the pain away. My ability to endure was shot to pieces.

One thing that I learned is that sometimes the best place to win your battles is from your knees, when you are the most broken, the most vulnerable and the most afraid. Then you can finally accept yourself, starting from the ground up, setting a strong foundation and building from there. Every now and then you go back to the foundations and rebuild, because if the foundations are crooked, rotten or broken, then, like the story of the three little pigs, the wolf will blow your house down.

• • •

During all this process, I was still in the middle of knee rehabilitation, and it was taking months. My physiotherapist at the time was as frustrated as I was. I still couldn't use it well after six months. Between my injured left and right legs, I literally had no leg to stand on! (Pardon the joke.) I don't know why it took so long, but it scared me because in that time and space, I wondered if it was time for me to retire from sport. At nineteen! I already had injuries to every other part of my body. I felt old beyond my years and things just seemed too hard. Was my time up? Others had bowed out of athletics due to injury; perhaps I needed to think about a different kind of future. What would I even do with myself?

I certainly thought I was done, but I had to hold onto *something* because something was better than nothing. I felt that if I took my eyes off that something, I would drown. While it was not much to hold onto, my something was still there. So, while I didn't know much outside of sport, I made a commitment to myself to at least get better. I had been on anti-depressants for quite a few months. I had to be stronger than my circumstances, and so, as I committed myself to rehab of my knees and my body, I began to feel better. I pressed into the things I knew I could do and that helped my mind. I committed to writing, spent time throwing hammer and discus - even if it was basic moves - small, repetitive and annoying … and I began my recovery journey. I wrote quotes and printed pictures. My room became a montage of sports quotes and pictures of men and women of Football and athletics from across the world. I surrounded myself with mantras and ideas of success and held on for dear life. I wrote songs and sung them, wrote out my goals and read letters from my high school mates who believed in me more than I did. (Thank you!)

Bit by bit, day by day, moment by moment, I healed. The Football season was coming around again, and I spent a couple of days just praying, writing and focusing on what I really wanted in my heart. I dared to dream again. I was at the point where I needed to decide whether I would let this thing beat me or not. I could turn back to alcohol, but I already knew that made me feel dead inside. It didn't even numb the pain because it was still there the next day.

I thought, *you know what? I'm better than my uncle. I am better than the pain and heartache he caused me. I need to rise above this. I have beaten everything else and I will beat this, too.*

I managed within two weeks to turn myself around. I made a choice to throw out those anti-depressants. (The same choice may not be right for everyone.) I made a choice that was about me because I knew that I was stronger than the person he was, and who he made me feel like I was. No more and no less of a person, but stronger, however you look at it. I was not going to let him get in my way anymore. I would win. Fuck you, Uncle Bob. You will not defeat me. I was initially relieved the day I got a phone call from a detective in Gladstone where Uncle Bob lived. She broke the news to me that they had made the arrest. Oh, I felt so many emotions. I let go of so much pain and hurt. I still felt like I was walking around holding my breath, but it was a resolution for all of us.

Mum, Dad and my family were never quite the same after this. It brought us together on some levels, but in the beginning, I sometimes felt a sense of loss and brokenness. Our favourite uncle had broken the trust of our entire family. We had to stand together, but I still felt like we were miles apart, and it was too hard to even talk about it. So, like for many who speak out, it was mostly avoided and brushed over.

As a family, I'm not sure we knew how to deal with it at all. Individually, we had our own battles and wrestled with guilt, shame and blame. Sometimes we think that it's much easier to sweep things under the carpet than it is to deal with them, so I still felt it was my battle to face alone. Not because Mum and Dad were not there for me, but because I still felt it my responsibility to protect them. I didn't need to do that, not anymore. They were adults and while I didn't know it then, I could not be responsible for their emotions or how they felt. I could be understanding and considerate, but they are responsible for themselves and we were responsible for being there for each other. What I felt we did have was a deeper sense of fear and dread about things.

It took some time before we were all able to rise out of the ashes. Mum had never spoken about her own story and hurt. Dad, well, he had to deal with the devastating news from both of us. We were always so close, Dad and me. I cannot imagine his thoughts. I wanted to protect them, even Gary, because I knew that he would lose it completely if he were to know. So, I told them I was OK. I told them I was coping, that life was always good, even when I hurt. I tried, as I always did, to protect them.

I was even more relieved when the police gave Uncle Bob his court date and he was sentenced to a period of imprisonment on the 02nd day of March 2001. I am thankful that I was never required to give evidence, as he pleaded guilty to a number of counts of 'Indecent Treatment of a Child' and other similar charges. (This meant that I was spared the further ordeal of having to go and give evidence in a courtroom.) He was convicted of his crimes and sentenced to four years imprisonment to be eligible for parole after serving 18-months in custody. He was also required to report to police periodically for several years after the conviction as part of his sentencing, meaning Police would be watching him. I was not excited about the sentence at all; his measly 18 months actual imprisonment for the abuse, personally felt like it was a life sentence for me. I would have to find a way to deal with what he had done for the rest of my life.

At least he wouldn't hurt anyone else and I had done all that I could to make that happen. In that I found reassurance and some closure. I felt guilty though, because of the rest of the family. Uncle Bob had two boys, and at that point Aunty Von had fallen pregnant. However, I now know he alone was, and is, responsible for his own choices. Bob was arrested, charged and pleaded guilty to the multiple charges against him. Bob's wife, Aunty Von, says she believes Bob was innocent.

When asked why she thought Bob had pleaded guilty to charges and gone to jail, she said Bob told her they could not afford a defence lawyer and were therefore unable to fight the charges in court. Aunty Von said she found it difficult to understand why I had not reported the abuse and sexual assaults sooner, as she remembers me as an outspoken child. Aunty Von still believes Bob's denial of guilt and stood by him.

Here are my mother's thoughts surrounding his betrayal.

My mother's perspective
– June Humphries

After hearing the news that my brother had been sexually abusing our daughter, we got home to our own house, to the place where we could let go, and my husband Kevin broke like a small child... I broke too, and felt part of me had died right along with my child. It really felt like she had died. I didn't know who to even talk to, and if it weren't for a few close friends in our life at that time, I'm not sure how we would have coped. I felt like a part of Kelly was now gone forever and I experienced an indescribable grief.

Kevin and I both struggled to get over this, with our family dynamics changing over the next few months. Kevin changed the way he was dealing with our other two children, Brandon and Laura. It wasn't much, but he became so alert and aware. They were close, Brandon and Laura, but because of what Bob had done, Kevin felt like he had to treat them differently, watch the way he was affectionate with them and guard himself. He lost the ability to love them innocently like a father should. Bob took that away from us. He took away the memories and tarnished them with 'what ifs' and 'when did?'

Bob made me think over and over again where I went wrong, and I clutched at that guilt for a long time, right along with my own pain, which resurfaced from what had happened to me with my father. How could this happen again? How was it even possible? I know I couldn't have changed it, not really. My Dad... he was not especially manipulative; he just did it. Bob, on the other hand, had us all convinced that he was this amazing, loving, caring uncle and brother.

I was so hurt and felt so betrayed, as was Kevin. We were alone, growing up as kids. My mother had died, and my father was immersed in alcohol. We struggled and fought in a life that sometimes was quite unbearable. He was my big brother. He was supposed to protect me, us, our family. He was the uncle and brother that our family looked to for support, friendship and love. Essentially, he really was all that was left, and I thought I could trust him.

Our children, Brandon and Laura, were also hurt; child abuse affects everyone! While they never fully understood all of it, they really missed their uncle, yet were also angry for what they understood he had done. Laura would have only been about nine and Brandon about fourteen. Because Kelly was not home, she faced her own battle, and while we would have loved her to stay home, I knew she needed to handle this journey in her own way.

I was not sure then that any of us really knew how to deal with the issue. I know Kelly was seeing a counsellor, the same one that helped us with understanding where she was at and that she wanted to make a police report. I was so proud of Kelly for taking those steps to tell the police, although I never wanted her to go through it, ever. But more than that, I knew that no one else should either. Still, one of the hardest parts was the knowledge that Kelly was going to do this, not because I didn't want her to make a report - I absolutely did - but I was afraid of doing something to jeopardise the report process. Bob was coming down to have a barbecue the weekend after Kel had told the police. He was bringing his family and we had to continue on as if nothing was wrong until the police were ready to make their arrest. I didn't want to see him ever again, after knowing what he did to our little girl. The same little girl that I swore I would protect; the same little girl that I held in my arms and had wishes, hopes and dreams for. I didn't know how I would react when he came, and I had no idea how Kevin was going to be towards him either.

I tried not to call him about the barbecue, but he called us. They came but didn't stay long, thank God. I couldn't even look at him without being angry. Kevin was upset, more upset than I had ever seen him over the whole thing, in fact, more than I had seen him upset over anything at all. I know how hard it was for him, and he really protected all of us in this. But I know what he was thinking as he was sharpening his fishing knife. We were all just so hurt and felt so betrayed over what Bob had done that Kevin and I both experienced every emotion we could go through.

Kevin wanted to kill him, literally. He talks about how he was the one that had to sit and talk with him at the barbecue like nothing was wrong. He had a thousand questions he wanted to ask, a thousand things he wanted to know, but he couldn't say anything. It was an hour of torture waiting until Bob and Von left. Kevin also thought Von knew what had happened all those years; she had to. He believed that because she was around so much while everything happened. It left him hating her as well and feeling like he could really teach them both a lesson. It is absolutely human to feel those emotions, and I am so glad that Kevin and I could talk about it, because we had a long and arduous healing journey to go on together. After all, we had just lost a brother, a friend, a mate and a vital part of our daughter we thought we had protected - her childhood innocence.

I knew that I had to keep quiet because of the investigation, but in my heart, I was broken. I felt convicted in my heart because Bob had told us that the incident with the other little girl he was charged with was all a lie, and the police had it wrong. There was a story around this and while I can't tell it here, he was my brother and I wasn't sure what to believe. But I had hoped that there was some sort of mistake, and I believed that he would never do anything to harm one of our kids. Any kid for that matter.

It was after this incident with that other girl, that we did all we could to never leave the kids alone with him. There must have been something in it and we just wanted to be careful, yet he was still my brother. Usually someone was around, whether it be the other kids, Von or someone else. Wanting to believe in blood, in the trust of family, we honestly believed that Kelly and all the other kids were safe. I guess I didn't think for a second that Bob had already been taking advantage of Kelly, and I had no idea that she was stuck in that awful cycle of abuse. I told her that day in the kitchen that she needed to be safe, and I prayed that she would tell me if something was wrong, and I believed she would. I didn't think for a second that the power of that betrayal and his manipulation would be so much stronger and so heavily ingrained. I didn't know I was already too late.

I know how this makes me look, but trust me, had I any idea I would have done everything in my power to stop it. I believed in my big brother and I trusted him, because I loved him. He betrayed me too and it kills me to say it and even write the words. I never took it for granted that we grew up without our mum. I miss my mum every day, and I clung to my big brother for support, for friendship and so many things. We were close. We tried to embrace his wife as well, and I too believe she knew something and never said anything. I will probably never know the answer to this; whether she knew, or she didn't.

It changed us, and it changed Kevin. I know he felt like he had to be more aware of his own actions, and he certainly had to get over the hurt. Their relationship, Kelly and Kevin, changed in subtle ways, but there was more of an understanding of some things.

In hindsight, we remembered random comments by Bob about young girls, which were at times blown off or addressed, but we felt guilty. It was a sign, but we didn't know that at the time. That was the betrayal. He groomed and manipulated all of us, which makes me again question what is right. Where was my brother in all of this and who was he? What kind of man had he become? He was our protector, and now he was my daughter's predator. I was angry, and I had no idea where to put my emotions for a long time. There are some regrets, but I can look at them now as something different, especially as I start to see Kelly come back to life with passion and the ability to stand on a stage and tell people how to be strong, how to chase their dreams and not let these same regrets hold them back from their true purpose in life.

When Bob was arrested, I had mixed feelings. I was relieved that he could not harm another child, and I was heartbroken at losing my brother. In reality, he destroyed two families' lives. I felt relieved when he pleaded guilty - for us, for Kelly and to close that chapter of our lives. Kevin and I coped by talking about what happened with some close friends. They really supported us, and without them we would not have handled what had been thrown our way. We really were blessed.

I have prayed, long and hard for reasons, for my pain and my daughter's. I have asked why? I have questioned my own motives in the storm of uncertainty and even whether I am a good parent. We both have, Kevin and me. We never wanted to let her down, or any of our kids for that matter. I felt that in some ways I had failed, especially when Kelly sent me one of her recordings of the first time she told her story in front of her Toastmasters group at Police Headquarters. Kel called me the next day and asked me how it made me feel, and if it sounded OK... it made me feel awful. Guilty.

She said to me, 'Mum, you know it's not your fault, and it's not mine. You never got to have your voice, and now you have given me the tools, ability, courage, fortitude and strength to be a voice for both of us.'

I know it was not my fault, and there is probably nothing that I can or could have done to make it better; all I know is I did my best.

No one should have to suffer in silence. It's time. Maybe I needed permission to share my story. Maybe I needed courage. I spoke because I needed to let my daughter know she wasn't alone, and neither are you.

Kelly asked me what my message would be for others, and besides sharing my story, my hope is for victims of childhood trauma to learn to speak up, move on and find inner peace, with the knowledge that what has happened to them it is never their fault, they are not alone, and they can achieve their heart's desires if they can find the strength to believe in themselves.

While we are very young

While we are very young
dreams will fill our minds
Our hearts and souls ablaze
love of the very best kind.
Our dreams as kids often fade
but you know they never die.
So believe in what you know
Don't give up the chance to fly.

Kelly Humphries
© 1999

1. Soccer representative team, Darling Downs District. 16-17 years old
2. Toowoomba Raiders Soccer Team (Reserve and Premier League Teams).

Chapter 21
Fresh Perspective

I was tired. I felt like I had run a marathon. It felt like those mornings where you hit the snooze button on the alarm five times... until you drag yourself up, bleary-eyed and dizzy with no sleep. Even though the motivation was not there, I knew that, day-by-day, it would get better. I could do this. I had finally learned enough about my coping and how I operated to know I needed to set myself challenges and hold onto them, to pull myself out of those low places. It's how I overcome emotional hurdles, by keeping my eyes on the next big challenge.

I focussed more intently on my rehab and I held on to the hope that the USA might still hold a place for me. I needed a new tactic - a new strategy. I just knew it wasn't going to work the way I had planned, so it was time for a new plan. I had given up on the big US colleges. As I got better, mentally and physically, there beckoned a light, and it came with having perspective and seeing past my circumstances, my immediate crisis. So, I began writing to some of the smaller colleges about what I wanted to do. I dared myself to dream again. I had won a small victory. I was back, albeit a little worse for wear, a little rough around the edges, slightly emotional and sensitive, but I was back.

I decided to concentrate my efforts on just a couple of small colleges in the USA. Meanwhile, I had started playing for the Raiders Soccer team in Toowoomba again. I was only playing reserve grade, so I had to work back up into the premier side. I was doing fairly well, actually; I surprised myself. And while I was being held together with a bundle of strapping tape, I got around the field and held together, both inside and outside. One day at a time, one letter at a time, I got closer and closer to finding myself and to the reality of my crazy high school dream.

Most people in my life were supportive and encouraging as I went through this period of healing and chasing this ideal I had set for myself. Some didn't understand why I wanted to go. To be honest I don't know why either; but I knew I had to.

It could have been an escape from the darkness that found me when I closed my eyes, or the racing of my heart and difficulty I found in facing the truth ... I believed, though, and when I believed in my heart, my spirit soared, my eyes lifted and my heart didn't race in fear but with anticipation.

I was set apart in my goal because it was different, and I hoped I could inspire the kids back home to get involved and do awesome things with their lives. I think it was a noble cause back then. It was my pursuit of perfection. Trying to maintain this perfect image on the outside. When I was told 'no' I did the opposite and always found a way; I kept going against the grain. Some sceptics said that I was silly and that I shouldn't even consider trying because I had only played for a couple of years. That just solidified my resolve. With all the injuries, some said, 'Don't you think you have had enough?' Most had already written me off. I don't blame them; I had almost written myself off.

• • •

I got a package in the mail one day from one of the schools I had been talking with. They had a Football program and a track and field program. I remember getting the envelope in the mail and the feeling I got when I had it in my hand; my heart raced.

It was a small college in Jamestown, North Dakota, aptly named Jamestown College. Their colours were orange and black. It looked like a lovely little college with magnificent buildings and beautiful grounds and an awesome looking athletics field. Most colleges had the red tartan and a big grandstand. The Jamestown College track had black tartan. It looked awesome, immaculate and pristine. Though I didn't know how cold it could get in North Dakota!

Well, all this information was nice, but how on earth would I be able to secure myself a scholarship? We didn't have the money for me to go to a school in the USA. I attended a perfectly good university already. Was this even where I wanted to go? Was this what I was meant to be doing? It wasn't one of the big schools I dreamed about going to. While Australian universities are amazing, an athletics program in the USA at a good school offers a prospective athlete much more than anything available here in Australia, unless they are attached to the QAS (Queensland Academy of Sport) or the AIS (Australian Institute of Sport). This is the hardest part about being an athlete in this country. We still lose so much talent overseas or to the 'too hard basket' because the personal investment is just too difficult. In the USA, boosters sponsor most sports; well, that's how I understood it. They are people that have an interest in the college or university and will fund scholarships and programs, like investors.

I needn't have worried about the finances, as it happened, as the package also had a letter of offer, which included a half scholarship. It was split in thirds between Academics, Soccer, and Track and Field. It was more than I could have hoped for. I hadn't even sent them any video footage as it was all too old now and I hadn't had a chance to get any other footage. So, it was a risk for them and a risk for me.

So, what do you think I did?

Well, of course I had to go! Who wouldn't? It was an opportunity to start again; it was the opportunity to change my life. I was caught in a whirl of excitement and craziness over the next couple of months after I accepted their offer and got myself prepared. I was playing good Football. It had taken me nearly 18 months to get back on my feet. I was still competing well in athletics, and I was settling into things in a way that I previously couldn't. The difference now was, I was focussed. I had my mind set on one thing, and I wanted to do it well at any cost.

To raise funds, we sent out a whole bunch of sponsorship requests to businesses all over my local area and Gladstone, with the help of some dear family friends. The result was that we were successful in obtaining enough funds for me to make the journey and to stay for one year! After all I had been through, this was a relief to say the least. It was done. I was going, finally. Surely, nothing could go wrong now, right?

• • •

About six weeks before I was due to fly out of the country, I was playing on the left wing in a Brisbane game. There was a long ball and I went for it. I was fast and got it just before it got to the end line, having beaten the defender. I smashed a cross in over the 18-yard box. As I did so, one of the opposing defenders came flying in, cleats up and did a big slide tackle that took out my left ankle. I screamed like a banshee then cried as I heard it pop. I was scared for a moment and started to panic and hyperventilate.

She got a yellow card, and I got carted off the field. I was angry. I was so, so angry with her, but it's what happens, and I just had to deal with it! Here we go again! I was in a better mental space this time, and after my initial panic, I could rationalise. I didn't worry so much because I didn't know anything yet. Not like when I got hit by a car and my whole life turned into a panic... I could still put a tiny bit of weight on it, but I needed rehab and quick. Two days later, instead of 12 months, I was all over it emotionally.

I notified Coach Gibbs, the USA coach. He was OK, but I still had to get ready for the pre-season over there. It was going to be a hard slog to do pre-season training with the Jamestown College Women's Team right after I had finished with my team in Australia. I had to fly in two weeks before 'school' (that is, 'university' in America) started, to commence the pre-season training. I focussed on what I could do rather than what I could not...

I went to see a physio about my ankle and was told my anterior ligament was damaged and that I was out for six weeks. I would arrive in the USA being able to just get my feet in the game. Well, that was poor timing! Other things were coming together; I was going to have a host family look after me while I was in the USA. They were an older couple, Meg and Jim, who had a small fluffy dog. I saw some pictures of their house via email. It was a lovely quaint house with plenty of space. At least I had somewhere to live, with nice people.

It was only a week until I flew out, and two weeks until pre-season training started. I wasn't ready for that. From what I knew, it would probably the hardest training I would ever do. It made me anxious to say the least. Essentially it was two to three sessions a day, morning and afternoon, and then a gym session. I also had to acclimatise, of which I really had no previous concept. So overall, I was extremely nervous.

Gosh, this packing business was getting hard. I had to fit in all my stuff that I needed for a whole year and keep the suitcase under 23 kilograms! We had everything laid out on the pool table and were listening to music when two songs came on that Mum decided to sing to me - *Wind Beneath my Wings* by Bette Midler and Rod Stewart's *Have I Told You Lately?* I sobbed, crying my heart out for all that we had been through and all that had been done. She told me how much she loved me and how much I would be missed. But Mum was also very matter of fact with things and was ready to send me on my way.

We had a going-away party with heaps of people - our 'extended family' - including all our neighbours and close friends. We all cried saying goodbye! Many of my friends gave me money as a going-away present. Their unconditional support was unexpected and so beautiful. You see, I had been feeling so alone in my battle and very few people knew what had happened with my uncle. I knew Mum understood even though we didn't choose to talk about it. We had a silent solidarity. I guess Mum must have felt alone like I did back then, and I knew without her saying that she had my back.

I was humbled to say the least, and ever so grateful, which solidified my desire to succeed in the USA. My friends alone provided me with just under $2,000 - a lot of money back then. I went down to my aunt and uncle's in Brisbane to stay for the night and have a barbecue. My last meal the night before I flew out was a whole kilogram of cooked tiger prawns. I sat down and ate every single one, along with a cold beer. Yep, I was going to miss prawns, barbecues and beers. I was still underage to drink in the USA, as I was 20.

The whirlwind that was my life had completely exhausted me, and I felt like it would stay that way for the rest of the year! It was the kind of exhaustion you feel when you know you have given your all. I took a deep breath that night and envisioned cheerleaders and orange and black streamers. I cried as I realised what I was about to do. I had no idea how this chapter would unfold, but I thanked God for giving me a hope, a chance.

We got to the airport and I was ready to go, embarking on the journey of a lifetime with a whole plethora of unknowns. As I said goodbye, Dad's face made me cry like a little girl. There was a lot that I wanted to tell him but had run out of time. I could tell he was both proud of me and scared for me. Mum I could handle; she understood me. She knew. It was painful to say goodbye, but I wanted to make sure Dad was OK. I think I needed to know he could hold it all together; watch the kids and take care of everyone. As you know, I had felt like the protector, and I was leaving them all. At least I knew that Uncle Bob was gone. He was locked away, so he couldn't hurt them any more than he already had. We were OK, and we would *be* OK. I could not know what was going to happen and how the family would deal with things when I was gone. I would not know for many years. I flew out of the country on my birthday, the fifth of August 2001. I cried all the way to Tokyo. Everything was still fresh and raw.

• • •

The adventures that would unfold while I was in the USA were to be nothing short of incredible and such a blessing. I found healing in my adopted American families, and the joy of my friendships I still hold dear today. I don't recall a Sunday church session or worship time where I had dry eyes. I lived in America for just under four years, and for three of those I went through a healing process, getting my strength back.

I did incredible things with my athletics in the USA and maintained my strengths in hurdles and hammer throw. I made a personal best time of 8.4 seconds in the 60 metre indoor hurdles, but I was a thrower. (Sally Pearson in 2012 won the world indoor champs for the 60 metre hurdles in 7.8 seconds.) I made every national championship team while I was competing in the USA, in both indoor and outdoor track and field, and placed in the top ten for most events, even at national level. A conference is like a cluster of Universities in a Region. I managed to win awards for being the most outstanding field athlete in the entire conference (over 81 colleges), and I placed in the top five for almost every event I went in. I even managed to wriggle my 800 metres time down to 2.22.00s for the heptathlon and jump well over 5.50 metres in long jump. I trained my ass off, and I paid for it. I usually had to take around five ibuprofens before I competed to numb the pain in my shins. I was always afraid that if I didn't perform, I would lose my scholarship. It would have been fine, but basically, when you start talking about money, scholarships and US sport, it's like a scene from Jerry Maguire and about them getting 'bang for their buck.'

After my first year in the USA, I burnt out after training for some five hours a day, every day. My broken body, while it was strong, couldn't cope with training for both athletics and soccer, so I reverted to my love for track and field. The heptathlete dream had to stop, thanks to my shin splints. I scaled my events down, so that instead of training for thirteen events, I only trained for five. That was still a huge feat for a college athlete. I shared all this with some amazing friends who stood by me through this often difficult but incredible journey.

I had flown to the biggest country in the world on a one-way ticket, having no idea what would happen or whether I would stay or could afford another year of college. Our family had little in terms of money, but I was loved and supported and there was always enough, even though my faith would be tested time and again. I did come home after my first year, only for another university, North Dakota State, to offer me a scholarship for my second year of college. So, after a short time at home, I flew back to the USA with a bigger scholarship to a bigger university.

It was incredible, and it was there I got fully involved in life in the USA. I look back now at what I did, and I can appreciate what it took to get those kinds of distances and times across so many events. Many there supported me, those I affectionately group into my 'American family'. I love my American family, my friends, coaches and college professors who helped me to achieve my dreams, to give me a college experience I will never forget.

I saw everything on this journey; from the biggest trucks and houses I have ever seen to supersized food straight out of the movies. I travelled from one end of the USA to the other. I experienced life and connected with people on all levels. I shared homes, people's dreams, faith and love. This I believe was the greatest experience I could have had. To be embraced, openly accepted and loved is more than I could have asked for.

I had it in my heart to graduate after four years from university and come home to train for the upcoming Commonwealth Games. I did come home. That was extremely difficult because I loved my life in the USA. I had found friends and family who I am still connected with today. I found a fulfilment and happiness I only remembered having as a little girl.

I secretly arrived home on Christmas Eve 2004, but only Mum knew about it. I dressed in a Santa suit and gave out lollies from my Santa sack to all the kids and my family (nearly dying in the December heat - I had left the USA in -10°F (-23°C) degree temperatures (it can get to -51°F during blizzards; that's -41°Celcius!). I gave myself away by telling everyone I had a sack full of 'candy' in an American accent. Oops. It was a tearful reunion and so beautiful to be home with my family.

• • •

In the USA, my amazing healing journey gave me strength to stand strong. I went to Church and became a more committed Christian, meaning I moved from an idea of faith to a real understanding of who God was to me, and I to Him. It was just so beautiful to know I was loved by a God who saw my awful shame and the darkness inside me, and loved me still.

Many of us have been broken by our faith or by what other people have said or demonstrated in the name of God or faith. I know this because I was one of them. I fought with my understanding of who God is or was, and His heart for me, because of how Uncle Bob manipulated my thinking. However, I can say my ability to be introspective in seeking my own answers has helped. I understand that no matter how people embellish or destroy what God is supposed to look like, the truth about who He is, and His love, is written on the tabernacle of our hearts. And when you remove false and awful people from your life, or stop listening to their lies, the voice inside you is clear if you listen.

In all of this, I knew God was with me. It just took so long for me to understand how God saw me - that I am precious and beautiful in His eyes. Not the kind of precious and beautiful that my uncle saw and tried to rob me of.

• • •

From the paddocks of my home in Australia to the fields of North Dakota, God answered my prayer. I only realised this recently as I wrote out these pages. I had prayed to Him; in fact, I had screamed out to Him. I recall standing in the middle of the paddock, raising my hands up and yelling, 'Make it stop!' I asked Him to make me a bird, so I could fly far away. America is far away, and I flew to the USA on the biggest bird He could find, to chase a dream I never thought I could have.

When you think that your prayers are echoing around and He doesn't hear, know that He will answer your prayer, but in His own time.

As a child desperately wanting to be rescued, sometimes I wasn't able to find Him anywhere, not when I felt like I needed Him. But now I know that He heard every cry. In fact, maybe God placed in my heart my drive and passion to be an athlete in the US as part of His plan to indeed help me fly away!

I found Him, or rather God found me, and I have never turned from Him again. I have wavered. Faith always wavers. I have been angry, but nothing compares to knowing that I was rescued, with a real love. I found a purpose and a passion that was hidden in layers of hurt and pride.

Over the four years following after hopping on that first plane to the USA, I was stripped bare and then raised high with the healing love of God's people and a revelation of who God really is. While I cried and healed, I grew stronger and found a happiness I never knew possible. It is the same happiness that I find when I am with people I truly love. The same happiness that I find when I am doing what I know is my true passion, and the same happiness I find when I am spending time with God. I'm not here to preach to you. I am telling you that for me, there is no greater love and it is the only way I can now confidently lift my head. For that love, and knowing I don't have to carry around that shame, that hurt or the pain any more, I will forever be grateful. Thank you, Jesus.

1. Me with Coach Lemm, Jamestown College North Dakota **2.** Champions, North Dakota State University. Me, with now famous US Athlete Amanda Smock **3.** St Paul, Minnesota full of Charlie Brown Icons - my very special nickname **4.** Graduating North Dakota State University BA Sc/Psychology. I made it!

Farm girl chasing an Olympic dream

By ROY COOK

BOROREN farm girl Kelly Humphries returns to the United States this week to continue her sporting education in pursuit of an Olympic dream.

Humphries, buoyed by Australia's record Commonwealth Games medal haul in Manchester, is primed to build on an eye-catching debut track and field season in the US.

The strongly-built youngster, who celebrated her 21st birthday with family and friends on Monday, finished eighth in the pentathlon when representing Jamestown College (North Da...) the National As... Atl...

She has secured a new scholarship with the North Dakota State University and is looking forward to resuming a tough training program after two months at home, a far cry from the snow she experienced for the first time in the US.

"I was training or competing six days a week in the US so it was a good chance to rest a bit ... although I did play seven matches for the Yaralla Soccer Club."

Humphries is a talented soccer player, scoring the most goals for the gold medal-winning Queensland Northern Conference soccer team when studying in Toowoomba and being named in the Australian University Games squad.

Her strength is complemented...

1. News Travels back home. An update for the locals after a season in the USA 2. One of the very few images I have playing Soccer in the USA. This was in South Dakota 3. Getting ready for a big throw. North Dakota State University.

Final Reflections

Thank you for reading and thank you for spending the time to share part of my journey with me. This project has not been easy by any means and daily I learn something new about who I am, what I am capable of and my capacity to grow. I don't know everything… I am but one person on a journey. We all have a story, one that is unique to us. To compare stories is difficult, as I don't feel for one second we should rate someone's experience as better or worse. Every person is unique and each person has the capacity to either survive his or her experience, to grow, to learn, to love and ultimately choose how they will continue to live their life, in spite of their past. Everyone has a different understanding of coping, healing and a different capacity to understand what has happened to him or her.

There are many stories about rape and sexual abuse that never see the light of day. There are other experiences of trauma that continue to occur, which at times make me question humanity and our capacity to love and respect one another. Part of my mission is to share love and bring healing through my own vulnerabilities.

This is my journey, and it is still not over. Your journey may have only just begun. The voyage, however, as a victim of childhood trauma of any kind is never forgotten. What does happen when you choose to take the lessons and apply them is you simply get better at life. You get better at living despite your past. Soon 'the thing that happened to you' is but a moment in time that seems like it didn't really happen. The scars fade. You won, you survived and you learn to put that experience in a space where you can (hopefully) safely keep it.

This book is about how one sexual predator acted, with very typical methods. It certainly does not predict or assume how all predators will behave in terms of sexual abuse and violence. You may not have the same coping strategies I had, or the ability to detach emotionally. You may not have filled the many gaps the same way I did. I was able to focus on sport and my dreams, which fuelled a determination in me to achieve as a means of survival. You may have done many things in the name of 'proving your worth,' but I am telling you, you're already worthy! You may not have faith, or even know where to begin to find it. That's OK; it's all going to be OK. I did what I could, as I am sure you have, too... sometimes you must just keep trying.

My story is to provide hope in despair, bring light where it's dark; certainly not to condemn or make it seem like it's 'all better' now, because it's not - we all have our struggles and stories, and this is just one. One story too many in a sea of stories where people have made it. I encourage you to find a way to make the struggle a little easier. Reach out. You are not alone, and you will certainly find no judgment here. I implore you: become a voice for yourself. Stand up, and if you can't, find someone who will or who knows your pain. Ask them to hold your hand for a while, until you can stand on your own. Choose to live with conviction and integrity, and in doing so you can let go of guilt, knowing there is nothing that you could have done better.

Not everyone will have the chance to close certain chapters and break their silence like I have. Yes, my sexual predator was charged. Yes, my family supported me when I finally allowed them to. Maybe you had this, too; maybe you haven't. Either way, don't let the perceived embarrassment of speaking, the shame, guilt and 'what ifs' get in the way or silence you.

Unfortunately, we are living in a world where understanding trauma, and the impacts of trauma are still overlooked and are not where it needs to be. Sadly, we also exist in a blaming culture. People, organisations and governments will find a way to point the blame and make someone else responsible. Women, it's your fault - look at the clothes you wear. Men, it's your fault because you think with your penis, not your head. Mothers, it's your fault because you raise weak girls. Fathers, it's your fault for not raising stronger boys. Media, it's your fault for sensationalising gender abuse of females by males. God, it's your fault for allowing these sexual abusers to walk the earth. Internet, it's your fault for making it all so easy for abusers!

We could list pages and pages of fault, blame, excuses and reasons why abuse happens, which only serves to *perpetuate* myths that harm, rather than bring about any kind of solutions. Sexual abuse and child abuse of any form is *never OK*, and together we have a responsibility to stand up for what is right. This is why I am more focused on developing a safe space for people to speak: to find healing, and present hope for a better future.

Sexual abuse does not have a single image. Sexual predators do not have a stereotype to easily identify; and every victim is different. Even offender sentencing can vary. There are reasons to hope, and there are reasons to be sceptical. But it is about working together, taking a stand and targeting this epidemic. Regardless of how long ago that abuse occurred, or if it is even still occurring, take a stand. No matter how much it hurts to think of doing this, it will not be nearly as painful as the suffocating chains that will weigh you down by maintaining your silence; this I know to be true.

There are so many lessons I have had to learn and unlearn on this journey. I could play the bitter resentment card and be angry for the rest of my life with what has happened, but I must accept and take responsibility for who I am and the life that has been dealt for me, whether I like it or not. In this acceptance I find freedom. I can choose how it will now play out, and I choose life. I choose to walk free from those chains that have held me down. I choose to step out of my mental prison and into the light. Sometimes while you cannot physically escape, the places and the freedom you can find in the power of your thinking can be overlooked.

I have struggled immensely with my faith, but what I believe is that by having faith, I now have the strength and fortitude to stand up under the weight of this commanding assignment. This assignment is so powerfully written on my heart that I cannot now turn left or right without bumping into this divine purpose for my life. What is this assignment and purpose, you ask?

To break cycles, to make change, to educate, empower, bridge gaps, shape lives, and help people find freedom and purpose - and become who I was meant to be.

I cannot say whether I truly forgive my uncle or not. Have I spoken to him since? No, and I don't know what I would say if I saw him again. There is freedom in forgiveness, and what I can say is that I have forgiven myself. This is truly one of the hardest things that I have had to do.

I have learned through my job to be calm, to look at all sides and carefully pick my words. I still get defensive, but it is generally for good reason. I still feel like I am being attacked and need reassurance at times, but I have learned to stand on my feet and have moral courage that is not determined by a need to protect other people but in essence proclaim what is right and just. I know I can be the peacekeeper and the peacemaker. I can play all cards and play them well. I have turned this aspect of my pain into a cornerstone of problem solving. However, I believe that before I finish writing this book I will conquer the greatest battle I still face, which is two-fold.

Firstly, I am learning to deal with personal confrontation by saying no and confronting those closest to me with problems that I may have, without fear. I am at times still afraid to stand up for myself. After all, I am so used to keeping quiet and not wanting to upset anyone, that this kind of confrontation comes with an insurmountable level of emotion that is difficult for me to deal with (I am getting better at this).

The second part of this is undoing my fear, conquering the part of me that is afraid to bare my soul. Luckily, I feel I have God on my side (just as you do). This is the understanding that I don't need to seek reassurance that what I have done is OK, or that I am wanted or needed or even in fact loveable. I am getting there, and I do believe this is the last card I need to deal in order to free myself completely of my past.

I have packed a lot into this life, and I can say that I have, more than anything, learned to overcome. What I have shared with you through the pages of this book have been some of the hardest battles I have had to deal with - yet I could share so much more with you. I wonder what it would have been like if this was not my story but someone else's. Would I have already reached the Olympics? Would I have already achieved my greatest victory? To be honest, I believe I have, and I am more than a conqueror. I don't need an Olympic medal to feel worthy. I have a bag in my study that has over 250 medallions in it, depicting an athletic and sporting history that I am not sure is over. It's always been about the journey.

Perhaps you, like me, have fought to protect yourself. I built my very own Great Wall of Kel around my heart. We do this to protect who we are, that is, protecting all that we know that is left inside of us. Sometimes people come into our lives and shake us up, from the most intimate parts of who we are to the very world around us. Sometimes this is a good thing and sometimes not. You know it's good when it brings out the best in you. When it's a hurtful dark situation, sometimes all we have left is our soul. All we can do is reach out, cry out to God and pray.

Do I still struggle? Yes, but I would be kidding myself if I said that the world was an easy place to live in. Do I blame my uncle for things that happen now? No, I don't, but sometimes I do find myself drifting back and wondering whether it would have been different if...and then I have to cut that thought off, because it serves no purpose. You must take hold of the emotion or situation and ask yourself, 'What is important *right now?* Is this going to help me move forward?'

Do I struggle with relationships? Yes, always, but that journey has come with understanding my sexual identity and affirming that sex is not love and love is not sex. Finding a person who can match my determinism and fierce outlook on life has been hard, but I have had amazing people around me. I have been in and out of relationships for most of my life, and I have hurt people and been hurt because I simply did not know who I was. I struggled to communicate with them, which is a pattern of behaviour stemming from my childhood. I now have a lovely partner who challenges me with this communication daily, and loves me in spite of all that has happened in this life.

Am I happy? Well, I have a house, a job, a partner, and money in the bank, a car, food, two dogs, two cats, chickens and a dream in my pocket. I guess I could say to a degree I am happy. But this may not be what makes you happy. I want you to sit for a minute and ask yourself, 'Can I be happy? Can I be happy if I hold this in? Can I be happy if I speak it out?' Only you can answer that…but I ask you: If you spoke your story as I have done mine, would you regret it? If you knew you were taking a stand, taking the first steps away from the pain…taking the first steps to freedom…I think you would already know the answer.

They say that some people didn't even know they were sexually abused until they found out what it was. Others know exactly what it is and don't even know how to respond. I know some are scared to speak because they fear they won't be believed anyway, and some speak because they are scared they will die from the abuse if they don't. Don't judge yourself by what others have done. Be the judge of where you want to go next.

You only get one life, and if it hasn't worked out so far, you need to make some empowering decisions for yourself. Yes, I have had 'things' happen. But I know without those 'things' I would not hold the depth of compassion and understanding that I do today, nor would I be so grateful or privileged in what I have achieved so far. It never makes it OK, any of what happened. It just makes me qualified in the journey of life. Don't be afraid; you are not alone. Hold on to the parts of you that are you and hold them tight. No one can ever take that away from you. That is your *Unscathed Beauty*.

• • •

Next in this book is a BONUS CHAPTER:
Working with the Police and Courts.
There you will find some extra guidelines and clarification
on the Court Process and working with police including an
in-depth look at 'Making a Police Report.'

Please keep in touch and make sure you subscribe to my
website for great deals on new books, courses, blogs and
much more!

Visit www.kellyhumphries.com.

Working with the Police and Courts

Making a Police Report

How do you make a report of sexual assault or abuse, and what happens at the start? My aim here is to simply try to make the process of reporting what has happened much easier for you and eliminate some of those fears that may be rearing their ugly heads.

Firstly, let me say that any police officer can take a report, but not all police officers who take reports are those who end up being the investigators. If your first experience with a police officer is not helpful, if it is not comfortable, or for some unfortunate reason you are turned away, please be persistent. I would think that this would be a very rare occurrence, and I would hope that this would not be your first experience when reporting a matter to police. I know that some people's experience with police has been unpleasant, and I cannot comment on that. What I can say is that police are people too, and like anyone else they can make mistakes. This is why I say please be persistent, and when you disclose what has happened to you, make sure the person you disclose to will listen, understand and validate you, whether they be law enforcement officers, or people in your family.

You may wish to simply notify the police of something that happened. In which case you can inform them that you do not want to proceed with a formal complaint but believe the police should know about a certain offender or person's behaviour.

I recommend you make a report straight away. You can always withdraw your complaint later if you think you need to (but I hope you won't). The longer you wait to report the matter to the police, the more likely it is that valuable evidence is lost. Time is crucial in police investigations, however, police can still pick up the pieces if needed and if there is a delay in reporting for some reason. That is what investigators are good at. It will take longer to put it all together if not reported straight away, and it does make the job much harder.

I know there is often a fear of talking to the police, but you are stronger than you know. So, hold on, OK! Making a report simply starts with making a decision - the decision to report. For some, it is the decision that the offending behaviour needs to stop, not only for themselves but also for the safety of others. Sometimes it takes courage to believe you are worth it and to accept yourself in spite of what has happened to you. It definitely takes courage to make that complaint and break your silence.

On the other side of darkness is light. One only needs to be brave for a moment to have freedom for a lifetime. Don't make a prison for yourself and hide from the world. The shame that is felt doesn't belong to the victim; it is something that is imposed upon them.

Following this is a generic and brief overview of how to make an initial report to the police. An initial report is the same as making a complaint to the police, in most cases. Remember, you make the complaint, the police make the charges, and the courts make decisions.

Initial police report process

This chart could relate to any matter.
For this purpose, consider a sexually motivated offence has occurred.

An offence is committed against you. You are a victim of crime. It may have happened in the past, or currently happening to you. It is possible that you know it's going to happen in the future.

Make a decision to report the matter to the police. **In an emergency, call 000**. If you would like an investigation to occur, it's not enough to tell a police officer what happened. You need to tell them, 'I would like to make a complaint.'
Ways you can do this; (In Australia) Phone: 131 444 (Non urgent)
In person (Attend a police station or speak to an officer)
'000' (If urgent)

If **the offence has just happened**, police *may* take details from you and do one or any of the following:
- Declare a crime scene to investigate the offence.
- Take you to a hospital to ensure that any DNA or forensic evidence is obtained. This is known as a SAK (Sexual Assault Kit). They may also conduct Forensic testing where the incident happened.
- Seize evidence, which may include clothing, any weapons or bedding (to name a few).
- Police will take evidentiary photos.

If **the offence happened in the past**, the method of the investigation will depend on how long ago it occurred.

Police may consider the same strategies as if it had just happened. However, if not reported immediately, the same evidence may no longer exist.

STATEMENT OBTAINED

If a sexual offence happens to a child under the age of 16, a digital recording of what happened is taken. This may vary depending on where you live. If you are an adult, chances are you will provide a statement, which is typed by an officer. Others involved, that is witnesses, may also be spoken to and statements taken.
The investigation has already started. This collecting of information is necessary, so police can get everything in order before making an arrest. How fast an arrest happens will depend on the safety requirements of the victim and others who may be at risk.. Further investigation may also happen after an offender is arrested. Everything is assessed on a case-by-case basis.

The Arrest and Court Process

As you know now, I am considered one of the statistics. Depending on where you look, those statistics can vary. According to CASA (Centres Against Sexual Assault) Forum, one in five girls will experience childhood sexual abuse by the age of sixteen. After many jobs and career paths, I chose to become a member of the Police service. There are many reasons I chose this job, which I have highlighted in my book. It was the work of dedicated and wonderful police officers who planted those seeds early on. I have over 10 years' experience in policing now, and I can safely say I know what reporting looks like, the victim's journey and the process generally, from a number of different angles. I have also looked at the side of the offender whilst dealing with countless 'clients' during my time in the police service. There are certain questions police officers must ask, in order to have enough information and evidence to prove your case. They also have a requirement to meet certain criteria for their reporting. Sometimes finding that solid and crucial evidence can be difficult, and putting forward that case and providing the right evidence and information to a court can be extremely difficult.

The police are not trying to be insensitive when asking you deep and confronting questions. These questions are asked because if the matter (should it proceed to court) is challenged, or if the person in question decides to plead 'not guilty', the evidence is already available to be produced to the court. The police, by gathering this information early, have already got the evidence they need from the beginning. The police try their best to make the case as tight as it can be and compile as much evidence and credibility as possible to convict the person at fault. Why? Because police officers do care.

People who investigate sexual crimes are considered specialist investigators. Police who choose to do general duties policing can specialise in general policing. Whatever the case may be, it takes dedication and commitment to be a police officer. Those in particular who investigate sexual offences, have had to go through a great deal of training to do their role. They believe in their cause and nothing makes an investigator happier when doing their job than getting a solid conviction and justice for a victim.

Not only this, but the police service and officers who work in the service thrive on a good reputation. In policing, your name will precede you wherever you go in whichever area you choose to work. So, regardless, it is *always* in an individual officer's best interest to do a good job, and more importantly, to be successful in any conviction or trial. Whether the police get a conviction or not, it means that the investigator has done all they can to create a strong, solid case. If the case isn't as good as it can be, officers are heavily judged, and their performance is critiqued and measured.

Officers are trained and given feedback to ensure that what is presented in court is the best it can be. So, if you are the victim providing a statement, the more information provided at the beginning, the easier it will be on you as the victim as the process of reporting unfolds. What I will also emphasise is don't leave things out because you are afraid of being judged or not believed.

Many times, victims feel a fear once they start to report and disclose what happened to them. They become anxious, and like when I wanted to tell my mum at the kitchen sink what was happening to me, I shut down and I denied what happened. Some people go as far as changing their story. This happens when people want to protect their vulnerabilities, but it can have damaging repercussions to your case and your credibility. Being completely honest is the best, safest, and most convincing argument there is.

Why do I tell you all this? Because I have heard hundreds of reasons people do not report matters to police. I understand fear, and I have lived the journey myself. Statements I hear too often might sound like, *the police don't care, or they won't believe me; they will think it's a joke … and It's just too hard*. So, to make the process easier, I will try to tell you all I can to help you move forward on the journey as painlessly as possible. I hope to remind you that police officers do care and will always try to do

> *Please don't give up on yourself. You are worth it, and while the process can take some time, the freedom on the other side of that courage is incredible.*

their best.

Please don't give up on yourself. You are worth it, and while the process can take some time, the freedom on the other side of that courage is incredible.

There are many reasons people can be afraid to report to the police. It could be the emotional journey, physically they may feel like it is too hard, or don't want to deal with the stress, they have legitimate fears that there will be a follow-on effect in their family and sometimes for safety reasons. I can't tell you whether you should make a complaint or not. I hope that all people who are ever victims of crimes make a report. There are times when a person may have legitimate fears for their safety if they disclose, and that is why it's good to seek advice from your local police about the protective measures available to you if you make the decision to report. There are certainly things that most policing jurisdictions can put in place for the purpose of protecting victims.

Sometimes the complexity of the court process can really influence whether someone decides to go through with a complaint. Court processes are changing and are now much more accommodating to those who have been victims of crimes. Being informed and understanding the process is one of the best ways to reduce your stress when it comes to these processes. Clarity is a good thing!

It is hard to know the exact process each matter will undertake as each case has its own complexities. While police have investigative strategies, the process can take a short amount of time or can sometimes carry on for years depending on the individual case. That is why it is important to communicate with the officer you speak with, so you understand what is happening with your case. Be patient with them; policing is a dynamic and sometimes very busy occupation. It is also hard to advise of an exact process because the justice system is always changing, and while some things remain the same, other areas are dynamic. It is even hard for the police to keep up.

So, what I have attempted to do is come up with a flow chart that I hope will make it easier for you to see how an offender is dealt with and how the court process unfolds. I have done this from my own understanding and have not taken this from a police handbook or textbook. The reason I have done this is, firstly, because every police jurisdiction across the world will be different. Secondly, I believe this is the best way to understand the process that I can share with you in this way. Either way, remember you can always ask. Another reason I have created these models is to take some of the fear away from making a report. I know how overwhelming it can feel. It is important to know that if a trial is run, and then lost - police cannot recharge the offender, even upon full admissions after a trial has been completed. This is known as double jeopardy. There are some exceptions to the rule and it is somewhat complicated. The only way the offender can be charged after prosecution and trial is when new information arising indicates a separate offence has occurred.

I hope that the below chart gives you some idea how it all works so it's less overwhelming for you. You should also know in most places there are court workers and agencies to assist you with court proceedings - it is always good to have someone support you in this process. There is always someone around who can help you. Don't be afraid to ask.

The Arrest and Court Process

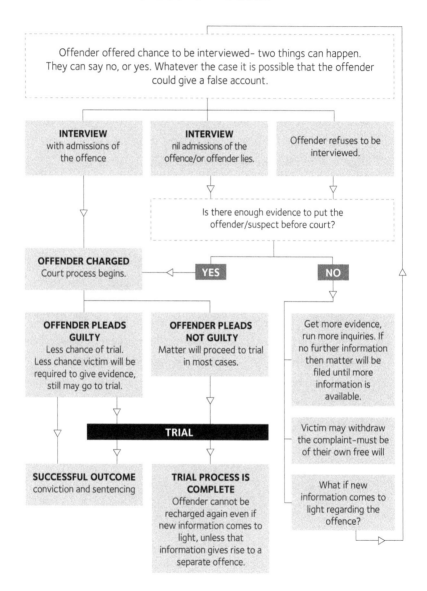

Offender offered chance to be interviewed- two things can happen. They can say no, or yes. Whatever the case it is possible that the offender could give a false account.

INTERVIEW with admissions of the offence

INTERVIEW nil admissions of the offence/or offender lies.

Offender refuses to be interviewed.

Is there enough evidence to put the offender/suspect before court?

OFFENDER CHARGED Court process begins.

YES

NO

OFFENDER PLEADS GUILTY Less chance of trial. Less chance victim will be required to give evidence, still may go to trial.

OFFENDER PLEADS NOT GUILTY Matter will proceed to trial in most cases.

Get more evidence, run more inquiries. If no further information then matter will be filed until more information is available.

Victim may withdraw the complaint-must be of their own free will

TRIAL

SUCCESSFUL OUTCOME conviction and sentencing

TRIAL PROCESS IS COMPLETE Offender cannot be recharged again even if new information comes to light, unless that information gives rise to a separate offence.

What if new information comes to light regarding the offence?

Resources

There are a number of services for sexual abuse and childhood trauma available for you to access support and assistance, whether it is for a short time, or a long time. My hope is that you will be able to stand on your own again. You may just need a word of advice or words of support, or perhaps you need a whole makeover, and that's totally OK. I think in my lifetime I have utilised all of these. If you have read this book, you will know I have had several makeovers already in my life. Just remember that wherever you are at, you are never alone and there is always someone willing to take your hand and walk with you. If you struggle to believe this for yourself, please know that I believe you are strong enough and you can make it. You can do it. You are made beautiful, unique, and fully capable of the mission and purpose for your life.

Don't ever be ashamed to reach out and ask for support. Remember, people who work in service agencies are there because they are passionate about helping people. Why else would they do it if they didn't like seeing people break through their fears, get strong and achieve their potential?

If you are in immediate danger, please call 000 in Australia. To report sexual abuse to police, please attend a police station or call 131 444 for Police Link (Australia) or contact your local police in your country.

For the most up-to-date information on support services, visit my website where I have listed organisations who support survivors of sexual abuse and trauma in their healing journey.

To seek support or assistance regarding personal trauma, coaching, reaching your full potential or stepping into your success - please head to my website listed below. I also conduct workshops for organisations and groups.

To provide feedback on my publication - or if you have burning questions you would like me to answer, I would love to hear from you.

I am a firm believer in transformation. So please keep an eye on what I am up to, so you know when new events are coming up!

Visit my website and Subscribe for great offers.
www.kellyhumphries.com

Note: I am a very approachable and friendly person, I promise. However, I am only a single entity who can really only offer advice, coaching and workshops. I am not a psychologist and cannot provide crisis counselling support. Please see above for crisis support and contact '000' or head to my website for links and phone numbers in case of emergencies.

Acknowledgements

If I think of all the people that have poured their time, love and energy into me and stood by me throughout my journey, I am overwhelmed. I am incredibly blessed, and I thank you all.

I firstly want to thank *you*, the reader of this book. If you are reading these pages, it is because you have found something in my writing that resonates with you. Perhaps you desire change, seek understanding or are simply looking to be inspired. Without you, there is no purpose for this book and there is no impact. Thank you for taking the time to invest in you, and to support my family and I with purchasing and reading this publication, not to mention standing with me as we move forward together to break these cycles of abuse.

I would like to express sincerest of thanks to my beta readers. My goodness, without your valuable time and feedback, I would not have the book I do now, not to mention the feedback which has equipped me to ensure I provide adequate support services, gone deeper, explained more and ultimately reassured me that *Unscathed Beauty* was not only a good story, but as a reader it held *value*. I needed that reassurance and I am grateful for it. Thank you.

Thank you those friends who were able to support me with a fresh set of eyes, and help bring this book to life - *finally*. All the punctuation, grammar checks and advice, and the reassurance provided as I tried to make this labour of love perfect. In particular Emma Jenks, I cannot thank you enough… and Vikki your hugs and final checks; you have both blessed me immensely.

I would like to thank Sonya Ryan, the CEO and Founder of the Carly Ryan Foundation, who shared her thoughts in the Foreword. Sonya, I am honoured that you would call me a friend, and I am privileged and grateful for the support and love you so willingly share. You are a testament to all that is good, and I am inspired by your advocacy and courage to make this a better world. Thank you for sharing even a small part of that journey with me.

I want to thank my mother, June Allyson Humphries. Mum, your story inspired me to write mine. You sang a song to me once - *You are the Wind Beneath My Wings* by Bette Midler. But Mum, you are the wind beneath mine. Thank you for helping me to be strong enough, brave enough and courageous enough to stand as a voice of hope. Thank you for being brave and sharing your story together with mine. It is the most beautiful and honest way to stand beside me on this journey, and I am so humbled and grateful that I am your daughter. There really are not enough words.

To my dad Kevin, I know that you sometimes feel that we kids don't see you. But I would not be standing here if I did not know that your belief in me was stronger than the belief I had in myself. Your heart is strong, and your courage and vulnerability as a man is more beautiful than you will ever know. You were my best mate growing up, and while time bears its scars and we all grow up, I'm still your little girl and I still need you. Thank you for all that you do and for your unconditional love and support.

To my brother Brandon, without the fun, laughter and joy of our childhood - the poo, water fights, bike rides, yabby hunts and wrestling on the front yard to name a few - I would not have had a childhood. I would not have been strong enough to know what I was fighting for. Thanks for being my bro, my mate and most of all someone I could talk to.

To my little sis, Laura, you taught me innocence. Without you, I would never have known what innocence was. I still struggled to find it, but your beautiful spirit, like Brandon's, made me strong enough to stand and brave enough to fight. Certainly, when it came time to make a report, I could do that because of you. That courage was found in the depths of the love I had for you, my sister.

Thank you both, Brandon and Laura, for standing with me and for your support now as I bare our family skeleton, and for your understanding and unconditional love. Thanks to my nieces and nephews who also remind me of the innocence and joy of childhood.

To my dad Gary, for loving me as I am, and reminding me that there are some things that don't need to be said. For your down-to-earth nature, understanding and unbridled support and love, I am grateful. Time heals all scars and I know that I can find you whenever I need. I am blessed that you are my dad, who loves me for me.

My friends and extended family, the 'Daisy Dell Clan' (there are so many of you); you have *always* been an army of love and support. I love you!

To my American family…you know who you are. Thank you for your investment in me, your love and welcoming arms. Thank you for your prayers and sharing your homes and hearts with me.

To the Queensland Police Service, thank you for your support and encouragement. I cannot tell you what it means to have you stand with me. With honour we serve and with courage I will continue to stand bravely.

To Sarah 'Sculley Design,' you have brought my pages and imagination to life. You have incredible skill and insight and for that I cannot thank you enough. What a talent and incredible artist you are. I am so happy with the final product! Thank you!

To my editor Wendy Millgate of Wendy & Words, I have sworn at you so many times! You just didn't hear me while I ranted at my screen through this editing process. 'Go deeper,' you say… Ugh! Thank you for pushing me and helping through this healing journey. Thank you for your hard work, your incredible words, and guidance and friendship. Thanks for your patience and prayers and, more than any of those things, your incredible insight.

To Amanda Gearing, (investigative journalist) Thank you for your friendship, your courage and willingness to stand for victims of child abuse, for your time and the support to do what I couldn't.

To Karen Crombie at Exact Editing, you did exactly what you said you would and buffed the edges and polished my dust-covered diamond. Thank you for your precision and professionalism.

Sarah, my Lamb Chop. You drive me crazy! You have pushed me, you enable me, you inspire me, and you have reminded me what love is. It has hurt, and it has healed. Thank you for putting up with the pain and the tears of going through this journey with me, and your patience, as I have indeed had to find my way all over again. You have taught me to hold on and push past my default patterns which at times are destructive - but through them all you have seen me for me. Love is love.

To you, my Heavenly Father. Well, you already knew I could do this. Thank you for your healing, your grace and your unfailing love. When I thought you weren't there, you reminded me through this journey that you never left my side.

About the Author

Just read the book and you will know all you need to know about Kelly Humphries. But there is more than this story, of course - and there will be more to come.

Kelly Humphries lives in Brisbane, Queensland with her family. Her parents and family home are still on the top of the hill overlooking Mount Coulston, Bororen, Central Queensland. The spear-grass heads still dance along with the wind and home will always be on Humphries Hill in the beautiful Australian bushland.

A passionate and transformational public speaker, internationally certified results coach, author and member of the John Maxwell Team (to name a few), Kelly set out to start sharing her message in 2015 after spending a whole lifetime learning what it means to speak up and speak out. Kelly is passionate about breaking cycles of silence that cultivate closets of fear.

She believes that each person has a unique gift, purpose and path. Her heart is to help people find that despite any trauma. Not only this, she also helps survivors of sexual abuse, trauma, domestic violence and those feeling broken to shine their authentic and powerful light in the world through her speaking, coaching and workshops.

Kelly is an avid writer, and while *Unscathed Beauty* is her first book, there are at least two more books to come in this particular series, including *Finding Your Unscathed Beauty* and *Unleashing Your Unscathed Beauty*. Kelly draws her wisdom and insight from her experiences. From her long and successful international athletic and sporting career, to her in-depth policing experience, dealing with the absolute best and worst that humanity produces. She shares her personal story with courage and conviction to encourage, inspire, bring hope and break cycles, reminding us that we all have Unscathed Beauty.

If you would like to contact Kelly Humphries to: arrange an author talk or speaking appearance; seek advice or assistance; provide feedback or testimony regarding this publication; or for any other matter, you can connect through any of the following ways:

Website: www.kellyhumphries.com
Facebook: https://m.facebook.com/KellyHumphriesSpeaker
LinkedIn: Kelly Humphries.
Linkedin.com/in/kelly-humphries-764b638b
Twitter: Kelly Humphries@KellyAHumphries
Email: Humphries.Kel@gmail.com

In fact, Kelly would love to hear from you! Your encouragement and support keep her pushing forward and bringing this Unscathed Beauty message!

Coming Soon!

10 Steps to Finding Your Unscathed Beauty

Do you want to know how to find your own Unscathed Beauty? Well you can in these 10 incredibly defining ways, which will allow you to peel off those layers after trauma, and find your own unique *Unscathed Beauty*. I get it. I realised very quickly when I started to write this book, *Unscathed Beauty*, that there were many things I was still carrying around in my backpack. How was I ever going to fully rid myself of all of the 'stuff' that was holding me back, if I continued to hide away and give in to my fears? I felt I deserved to be successful and find my ultimate joy, but I didn't fully understand why I felt the way I did. This is my journey to find me, my journey to understanding what happened and why. I am going to take you with me on that journey and explain the reality of what beliefs and strongholds are created through child abuse and child trauma as best as I can. If you walk it with me… it will be a journey of discovery, through understanding your anger, guilt, and shame, on to forgiveness, hope and healing. You deserve to have the best in this life. Don't let the pain of whatever has happened to you hold you back from being the best person you can be! This really is about breaking the cycle and standing up for all you are. #YouMatter.

10 Steps to Unleashing Your Unscathed Beauty

Stepping your way into success after trauma. In a world of opportunity, how is it that so many who have experiences with trauma seem to end up trapped in poor thinking patterns and self-sabotaging thoughts? How do you unlearn that which you have been told and taught? How do you change your thinking so that you can achieve your purpose and live with intentionality? Perhaps you just need a new way of thinking?

You are so worth it! It is time to break free of those chains! Trauma should not define you or confine you, but give you the strength and courage to unleash all that you are, and all that you dream of being, in spite of any past or experiences you may have had. This book is about stepping into your success and finding your sweet spot. Trauma can rob you of your zest and joy for life. In these 10 steps, you can find the tools to equip you for the life you deserve and were born for. Redefine and rediscover all you were meant to be and join me on a journey to step into your Unscathed Beauty and unleash it with clarity and purpose. Your Unscathed Beauty is waiting for you and I want to share with you just how you can set it free!

www.kellyhumphries.com

Author's Bonus Offer

You can receive special offers and discounts when you subscribe to www.kellyhumphries.com

Lightning Source UK Ltd.
Milton Keynes UK
UKHW010636270422
402137UK00002B/446

9 780648 243403